Lecture Notes in Computer Science 15946

The series Lecture Notes in Computer Science (LNCS), including its subseries Lecture Notes in Artificial Intelligence (LNAI) and Lecture Notes in Bioinformatics (LNBI), has established itself as a medium for the publication of new developments in computer science and information technology research, teaching, and education.

LNCS enjoys close cooperation with the computer science R & D community, the series counts many renowned academics among its volume editors and paper authors, and collaborates with prestigious societies. Its mission is to serve this international community by providing an invaluable service, mainly focused on the publication of conference and workshop proceedings and postproceedings. LNCS commenced publication in 1973.

Miguel Félix Mata-Rivera ·
Roberto Zagal-Flores · Willington Siabato
Editors

Web and Wireless Geographical Information Systems

22nd International Symposium, W2GIS 2025
Mexico City, Mexico, September 8–9, 2025
Proceedings

Springer

Editors
Miguel Félix Mata-Rivera
UPIITA, Instituto Politécnico Nacional
Mexico City, Mexico

Roberto Zagal-Flores
ESCOM, Instituto Politécnico Nacional
Mexico City, Mexico

Willington Siabato
Universidad Nacional de Colombia
Bogotá, Colombia

ISSN 0302-9743 ISSN 1611-3349 (electronic)
Lecture Notes in Computer Science
ISBN 978-3-032-01722-2 ISBN 978-3-032-01723-9 (eBook)
https://doi.org/10.1007/978-3-032-01723-9

This Springer imprint is published by the registered company Springer Nature Switzerland AG
The registered company address is: Gewerbestrasse 11, 6330 Cham, Switzerland

Preface

When the first International Symposium on Web and Wireless Geographical Information Systems (W2GIS) convened in Kyoto in 2001, the web map was still a static image and "wireless" meant 2G text messages. Over two decades later, the geospatial stack has been completely rewired: 30 cm–resolution commercial satellites revisit the entire planet daily; billions of smartphones stream anonymized trajectories; wireless sensor networks capture real-time environmental variables; and Large Language Models (LLMs) ingest unstructured geotext at planetary scale. The term **GeoAI** —the coupling of artificial intelligence with geographic information science— now frames much of this evolution. Gao et al. [4] define GeoAI as the integration of spatial representation and studies, machine (deep) learning, and knowledge-graph reasoning and technologies capable of automating geographic knowledge discovery, setting a conceptual backdrop against which every contribution in this volume can be read.

At the same time, the wireless substrate has matured from experimental Wi-Fi islands to global 5G/6G roll-outs; edge processors embedded in vehicles and drones perform on-device inference, feeding lightweight GeoAI models back to the cloud. Longley et al. [5, pp. 18–21, 40–46] argued that the growing interplay between GIScience and cloud/distributed computing was breaking many of the traditional spatial and temporal constraints on geographic analysis, already anticipating that the interdependence between geospatial science and distributed computing would collapse spatial and temporal barriers to analysis, a kind of prediction supported by the papers gathered here, more specifically when processing through GeoAI clouds.

This proceedings volume showcases eleven refereed papers that traverse this perception. High-resolution orthophotos remain fundamental, yet the novelty now lies in network design. The color-aware convolutional layer proposed in *Enhancing Urban Image Segmentation* tightens class boundaries without adding trainable parameters, demonstrating what Bennett and Vale [2, p. 12] call algorithmic parsimony when describing spatial statistics tools that respect geometric context and structures "*as simple as possible, but no simpler*". *AIGC Image Features for GIS* benchmarks generative images as surrogates for volunteered geographic imagery, engaging directly with Chivite et al.'s claim [3, p. x] that *GeoAI democratizes feature extraction across modalities —images, video, audio, and text— by applying Generative AI models.* This idea is supported by Gao et al. [4] when stating that GeoAI research increasingly bridges images, text, and other data types by grounding them in shared spatial semantics. Two papers fine-tune LLMs to grade 485,930 tourist reviews and to orchestrate live disaster feeds. They resonate with the call for autonomous GIS agents and multi-agents capable of end-to-end workflow generation. As Van de Weghe et al. [6, p. 93] state, "*the integration of large language models (LLMs) with geographic information science (GIScience) represents a new frontier in interdisciplinary research that combines advanced natural language processing with sophisticated spatial data analysis*'.

A signature of W2GIS has been its focus on operational spatial infrastructures — those running in the messy bandwidth-constrained, latency-sensitive reality of cities. The three sections of papers in this volume illustrate contemporary directions:

1. **Environmental exposure analytics**. Mining over 500,000 Twitter (X) posts, integrating sensor feeds, and enriching with land-use rasters, the authors of *Discovering Urban Insights of Air Pollution* deliver a participatory pollution-monitoring pipeline that is both web-native and wireless-aware. The work advances the geosensor network vision that situates in situ devices as first-class citizens of the geo-information ecosystem.
2. **Public-health intelligence**. The analysis of diabetes hospitalizations set against marginalization index leverages spatial panel regressions, echoing the argument by Gao et al. [4] that Health Geography is a canonical testbed for explainable GeoAI because the social, biological, economical, and built-environment determinants are intrinsically spatial.
3. **Location-aware decision support**. Whether advising automobile purchases under low-emission-zone constraints or predicting the six-year survival of veterinary clinics, the volume's business-oriented studies exemplify the maturation of location intelligence as an analytics framework. Location and time are often the strongest explanatory variables since they are explicitly encoded.

Although the empirical domains vary, several methodological topics are discussed in the proceedings. From air quality hot spots to meter-level semantic masks, scale-adaptive kernels and hierarchical attention dominate, providing a multiscale modeling perspective. Real-time Metro-crime forecasting demonstrates how device-captured ridership data are fused in the cloud with police releases.

Why does wireless still matter in 2025? First, bandwidth asymmetries persist between urban cores and peri-urban fringes, especially in Latin America [1]. Second, the carbon footprint of data movement is non-trivial. GeoAI solutions that push processing to the edge —drones classifying roof damage on-board, smartphones filtering low-quality image frames before upload— respect both constraints. The predictive maintenance study for Mexico City's Metro hints at these efficiencies by forecasting risk in minutes-to-hours windows, rather than after-the-fact batch updates.

The 22nd W2GIS exposed several open questions: Can LLM-driven agents plan, execute, and evaluate entire geoprocessing workflows securely on wireless clients? Synthetic images under-represent color gradients and spatial relations —issues reminiscent of the Modifiable Areal Unit Problem at the pixel level? Integrating low-cost sensor boxes in marginalized neighborhoods remains a socio-technical challenge considering that social-media proxies over-sample affluent demographics? What about the energy-aware consumption of GeoAI models? Answering these questions will require the cross-pollination of AI, cartography, network engineering, GIS, and machine and deep learning —the intellectual DNA of W2GIS 2025.

1 Structure of the Volume

The proceedings are organized into three thematic sections, each grouping together articles that explore related topics.

- **Part I – Advances in GeoAI**. Four chapters explore the perception pipeline, from color-mask–enhanced CNNs to multimodal LLM workflows.
- **Part II – Urban Health & Safety**. Four studies link environmental stressors and security patterns to health and safety outcomes using spatial statistics and social sensing.
- **Part III – Location Intelligence**. Three contributions demonstrate decision-support engines for resource management, consumer advice, and small-business resilience.

Advances in Geospatial Artificial Intelligence: From Pixel-level Vision to Large-Language Models. Recent breakthroughs in computer vision, generative AI, and foundation models are reshaping how spatial information is captured, represented, and interpreted. Recent GeoAI research spans the full perception stack: from centimeter-resolution airborne imagery to generative images and conversational agents. The first contribution proposes a color-aware CNN layer that boosts urban semantic segmentation with minimal computational overhead, demonstrating how domain knowledge can be embedded directly into network design. The second paper extends the discussion to synthetic data, benchmarking Artificial-Intelligence-Generated Content (AIGC) as a surrogate for volunteered geographic imagery and exposing current limitations in element, color, and spatial-relation fidelity. Complementing vision-centric work, the third article shows how Large Language Model fine-tuning and prompt engineering scale up quality diagnostics for nearly half-a-million tourist reviews (485,930), while the fourth paper couples GPT-4o with live geospatial feeds to build an emergency-response assistant to guide citizens through flood emergencies. Together, these studies chart a continuum from pixels to full ideas described through paragraphs, illustrating how hybrid vision–language AI pipelines will underpin the next generation of GI-Science analytics providing a unified GeoAI toolbox.

Data-Driven Urban Health & Safety: Environmental Exposure, Crime and Disease Dynamics. Increasingly granular sensor networks, social media traces, and administrative records allow us to link environmental stressors to human well-being in near real time. Four studies interrogate how environmental and security burdens translate into health and security outcomes. The opening paper mines over half a million geotagged tweets to reveal spatio–temporal signatures of perceived air pollution. The second paper extends that lens, uncovering statistical couplings between PM, CO, and ozone peaks and local violent crime rates to reveal statistically significant borough-level links, although the strength of this relationship varied across different boroughs and years. Turning from exposure to chronic outcomes, the third study analyses diabetes-related hospitalizations and deaths (burden) against a refined deprivation index, evidencing health-equity gaps across Mexico. A national analysis of diabetes hospitalizations exposes the combined role of age, sex, and marginalization in driving disease risk. Finally, a machine-learning–enhanced framework predicts weekly crime risk at Metro and Metrobús stations by fusing ridership forecasts with georeferenced offences, achieving 70% accuracy and interactive dashboard delivery. Collectively, these contributions demonstrate how integrative spatial analytics and heterogeneous data streams —tweets, air-quality sensors, hospital discharges, and transport ridership— can be synthesized into actionable urban-health intelligence and can inform targeted interventions that make Latin American megacities healthier and safer.

Location Intelligence for Urban Resources, Mobility and Commerce. Beyond risk mitigation, geospatial technologies increasingly support everyday allocation of scarce urban resources. The first contribution of the closing part dissects five years of residential-meter observations by applying spatial statistics; the study extracts consumption archetypes and pinpoints socioeconomic drivers of overuse, laying the groundwork for targeted conservation incentives. A multiscale GIS framework diagnoses neighborhood-level inequities in water demand, revealing how socioeconomics shape consumption hotspots. The second contribution combines dealership accessibility, traffic congestion, social-media sentiment extracted from car-owner forums, and regional demographic layers to build a location-aware recommender that respects emission-zone rules and local service coverage, illustrating how spatial layers sharpen consumer advice. Closing the session, an XGBoost model predicts 1- to 6-year lifespan of veterinary clinics from 733 urban features, reaching 88.68% accuracy and surfacing crime-and-traffic factors critical for small-business resilience, demonstrating how point-of-interest density, accessibility, and socio-economic context shape small and medium-sized enterprises' resilience. This analysis shows how robbery hotspots, traffic flow, and surrounding retail mix shape business toughness. Together, the papers showcase actionable "location intelligence" that converts heterogeneous urban datasets into practical guidance for infrastructure managers, businesses, and citizens alike.

2 Symposium Context

This volume contains the papers selected for presentation at the 22nd International Symposium Web and Wireless Geographical Information Systems (W2GIS 2025), hosted by the Instituto Politécnico Nacional (IPN), at the Interdisciplinary Professional Unit in Engineering and Advanced Technology (UPIITA) in Mexico City, Mexico, on September 8–9, 2025.

Recent advances in wireless Internet and location-based services have generated increasing interest in the diffusion and processing of large volumes of geospatial data, especially with GeoAI. Then, new challenges and opportunities have appeared in the GIScience research community. This symposium provides an up-to-date review of advances in both theoretical and technical development of Web and Wireless Geographical Information Systems (W2GIS). In this sense, W2GIS 2025 aimed to provide a platform for discussing advancements in theoretical, technical, and practical aspects within web and wireless-based approaches for disseminating, using, and processing data generated by humans, sensors, or AI. W2GIS is a unique forum to address new research challenges in developing location-based solutions and GIS, representing a recognized and regular event within the research community. This year's conference highlighted the emerging fields of GeoAI and volunteered geographic information supported by AI processes.

The 2025 edition of W2GIS received 22 submissions from 86 single authors coming from more than 20 different institutions. Each paper received at least three rigorous, single-blind reviews and, based on these reviews, 11 papers were selected for presentation at the symposium and inclusion in the conference proceedings, with a 50% acceptance rate. Furthermore, W2GIS 2025 also featured a Doctoral Symposium where doctoral students had the chance to submit an overview of their research as a short paper, present their activities, and receive feedback from well-known researchers in the field.

As previously shown, the accepted papers demonstrate remarkable quality and are at the forefront of research and development in Web and Wireless Geographical Information Systems, addressing pressing challenges and exploring novel solutions. From advanced techniques for data aggregation and analysis to the integration of generative artificial intelligence and machine learning into geospatial applications, the contributions showcased in these proceedings demonstrate the breadth and depth of Web and Wireless GIS research.

In addition to the articles, two keynote sessions complete the academic contribution of W2GIS 2025. Stefan Steiniger presents a review of the development and maintenance of sustainability indicators for cities in Chile, adopting a GIS perspective and identifying four research topics for GIScience: (i) updating indicators based on automated processes; (ii) simulation tools for generating development scenarios; (iii) short- and long-term forecasting methods; and (iv) methods for obtaining historical data. Catherine Trudelle presents a discussion on urban conflicts, considering them as multidimensional socio-political phenomena that unfold across time and space. She presents a networked perspective that reveals how conflicts are embedded in intricate relationships that influence both territories and societal structures.

3 Concluding Remarks

The papers gathered in these proceedings confirm that Web and Wireless GIS has moved far beyond map visualization; it now embeds intelligence directly into the data flows that sustain human life. From centimeter-level airborne pixels to crowd-authored data, from edge devices to cloud clusters, spatial information is increasingly born intelligent. The 22nd W2GIS proceedings provide both building blocks and critical reflections to make a reality the vision that GIS will be autonomous and capable of self-describing, self-analyzing, and self-explaining.

We sincerely thank all the authors for their valuable contributions to the 2025 edition of W2GIS. We would also like to thank the Program Committee members for their meticulous reviews and insightful feedback, which helped ensure the quality of the accepted papers, and the Steering Committee members for their ongoing guidance and support. We also acknowledge support from the Universidad Nacional de Colombia through the project 59525, "Cooperation Network for Research on Urban and Territorial Problems."

June 2025

Willington Siabato
Miguel Félix Mata-Rivera
Roberto Zagal-Flores

References

1. Ballari, D., Siabato, W., Claramunt, C., Mata, F., Zagal, R., Franco, R.: On the development of open geographical data infrastructures in Latin America: progress and challenges. Journal of Spatial Information Science **30**, 3–23 (2025). https://doi.org/10.5311/JOSIS.2025.30.364
2. Bennett, L., Vale, F.: Spatial Statistics Illustrated. Esri Press, Redlands, CA, USA (2023)
3. Chivite, I., Giner, N., Artz, M. (eds.): GeoAI: Artificial Intelligence in GIS. Esri Press, Redlands, CA, USA (2025)
4. Gao, S., Hu, Y., Li, W.: Introduction to geospatial artificial intelligence (GeoAI). In: Gao, S., Hu, Y., Li, W. (eds.) Handbook of Geospatial Artificial Intelligence, pp. 3–16. CRC Press, Boca Raton, FL, USA (2023). https://doi.org/10.1201/9781003308423
5. Longley, P.A., Goodchild, M.F., Maguire, D.J., Rhind, D.W.: Geographic Information Science and Systems. John Wiley & Sons, Chichester, UK, 4th edn. (2015)
6. Van de Weghe, N., De Sloover, L., Cohn, A.G., Huang, H., Scheider, S., Sieber, R., Timpf, S., Claramunt, C.: Opportunities and challenges of integrating geographic information science and large language models. Journal of Spatial Information Science **30**, 93–116 (2025). https://doi.org/10.5311/JOSIS.2025.30.389

Organization

Program Committee Chairs

Miguel Félix Mata-Rivera	UPIITA, Instituto Politécnico Nacional, Mexico
Roberto Zagal-Flores	ESCOM, Instituto Politécnico Nacional, Mexico
Willington Siabato	Universidad Nacional de Colombia, Colombia

Steering Committee

Michela Bertolotto	University College Dublin, Ireland
Christophe Claramunt	Naval Academy Research Institute, France
Sergio Di Martino	University of Naples Federico II, Italy
Jérôme Gensel	Grenoble Alpes University, France
Farid Karimipour	Institute of Science and Technology, Austria
Ki-Joune Li	Pusan National University, South Korea
Maryam Lotfian	HEIG-VD, Switzerland
Miguel R. Luaces	University of A Coruña, Spain
Mir Abolfazl Mostafavi	Laval University, Canada
Sabine Storandt	University of Konstanz, Germany
Kazutoshi Sumiya	Kwansei Gakuin University, Japan
Martin Tomko	The University of Melbourne, Australia

Program Committee

Daniela Ballari	Universidad del Azuay, Ecuador
Andrea Ballatore	King's College London, UK
Camille Bernard	Grenoble Alpes University, France
Alain Bouju	La Rochelle University, France
Elena Camossi	NATO Science and Technology, Italy
Zhixiang Fang	Wuhan University, China
Stefan Funke	University of Stuttgart, Germany
María Ester González	University of Concepción, Chile
Eric Guilbert	Laval University, Canada
Carlos Hernández-Nava	UPIITA, Instituto Politécnico Nacional, Mexico
Sergio Ilarri	University of Zaragoza, Spain
Kyoung-Sook Kim	AIST, Japan

Jorge Antonio León-Borges	Universidad de Quintana Roo, Mexico
Songnian Li	Toronto Metropolitan University, Canada
Feng Lu	LREIS, China
Gavin McArdle	University College Dublin, Ireland
Kostas Patroumpas	Athena Research Center, Greece
Peng Peng	Laboratory of Resources & Environmental Information, China
Alber Sánchez	National Institute for Space Research, Brazil
Luigi L. L. Starace	University of Naples Federico II, Italy
Nico Van de Weghe	Ghent University, Belgium
Francisco-J. Zarazaga-Soria	University of Zaragoza, Spain

Keynotes

A 10 Year Review on Developing and Maintaining Sustainability Indicators for Cities in Chile - A GIS Perspective

Stefan Steiniger[1,2]

[1] Escuela de Ingeniera de Construcción y Transporte (ICT), Pontificia Universidad Católica de Valparaíso, Valparaíso, Chile
stefan.steiniger@pucv.cl
[2] Centro de Desarrollo Urbano Sustentable (CEDEUS), Pontificia Universidad Catolica de Chile, Santiago de Chile, Chile

Abstract. In order to evaluate whether cities are following a sustainable path of urban development, it is necessary to characterise them using sets of indicators. Such sustainability indicators should allow to measure progress or recess regarding, for instance, aspects of equity, the healthcare system, a city's environmental impact, and government management as these areas have a direct impact on citizens' quality of life. To this end, the United Nations ratified a set of 17 Sustainable Development Goals (SDGs) in 2015, comprising 169 development targets and 232 indicators. However, in addition to the SDG indicators, other (local) indicator sets have also been developed, often focusing on particular geographic regions or (sustainability) topics. In this presentation, I will look back at 10 years of work by the "*Observatorio CEDEUS*" team in developing and maintaining a set of 30 sustainability indicators for more than 16 major cities in Chile. I will reflect thereby on: (a) the challenges that have emerged, (b) how GIS expertise has helped to develop and operationalise the indicators, and (c) where further research is needed. The identified challenges mainly concern the availability and accessibility of (geospatial) data, as well as representativeness. Furthermore, the collection methods for some source data have changed over time. GIS expertise has helped with data collection, data management, and geostatistical analysis. The latter has been used to develop sustainability thresholds. Finally, we identify four research topics for GIScience: (i) updating indicators based on automated processes, e.g. from sensor data, while respecting representativeness; (ii) simulation tools for generating development scenarios; (iii) short- and long-term forecasting methods; and (iv) methods for obtaining data from past.

Keywords: Geographic Information Science · SDG · urban indicators · sustainable development · challenges

Rethinking Urban Conflicts: From Isolated Events to Networked Geographies

Catherine Trudelle

Department of Geography, Université du Québec à Montréal
Socioterritorial Conflict and Governance Research Chair
trudelle.catherine@uqam.ca

Abstract. Urban conflicts are multidimensional socio-political phenomena that unfold across time and space. Deeply rooted in the territories where they occur, they simultaneously transform the societies in which they emerge. Since the 1970s, geographers have sought to understand the reciprocal relationship between urban form and conflict. Yet, the complexity of how conflict shapes, and is shaped by, the urban fabric has long posed a formidable analytical challenge. I will present recent advances that renew our understanding of urban conflicts, made possible through the integration of geographic information sciences. Over the past three years, transdisciplinary research, drawing on graph-based modelling, has enabled the conceptualization of conflicts as dynamic networks rather than isolated events. This networked perspective reveals how conflicts are embedded in intricate relationships that influence both territories and societal structures. These conflict networks, comprising actors, issues, and actions, are also shaped by broader social, political, economic, and climatic contexts. For example, in Montreal, various types of conflict display strong correlations with seasonality, such as temperature shifts. Focusing on housing-related conflicts in the city, I will also discuss emerging patterns that point to weakened civil society dynamics and challenges in governance across actor networks. Generative artificial intelligence (GenAI) has further expanded our capacity to collect and analyze conflict data. A comparative study currently underway across seven Canadian cities aims to uncover national-scale patterns in housing-related conflict networks. This keynote will unpack these developments in greater detail, offering new conceptual and methodological directions for the study of urban conflict in contemporary geographic research.

Keywords: Urban conflicts · graph databases · GIS · generative AI

Contents

Advances in Geospatial Artificial Intelligence: From Pixel-Level Vision to Large-Language Models

Enhancing Urban Image Segmentation with Color Range Mask Layer: A Deep Learning Approach Using Airborne Data

Ali Ahmadi[1](✉), Mir Abolfazl Mostafavi[1], Ernesto Morales[2], and Nouri Sabo[3]

[1] Center of Research in Geospatial Data and Intelligence, Department of Geomatics Sciences, Université Laval, 1055, Avenue du Séminaire, Quebec City, QC, Canada
ali.ahmadi.2@ulaval.ca, Mir-abolfazl.mostafavi@scg.ulaval.ca

[2] School of Rehabilitation Sciences at the Faculty of Medicine of Laval University, Quebec City, Canada

[3] Canada Centre for Mapping and Earth Observation, Sherbrooke, QC, Canada

Abstract. Recent advancements in airborne platforms equipped with ultra-high-resolution imaging sensors have significantly improved our capability to acquire detailed urban imagery. These systems offer exceptional clarity and precision in capturing urban data, paving the way for innovative approaches to urban analysis. However, manually extracting information from this data can be a slow and labour-intensive process. Thus, employing deep learning algorithms for data extraction appears to be a promising solution. However, deep learning methods require significant amounts of training data, processing power, and memory to achieve satisfactory results. To tackle these challenges, we developed a new approach called the Color Range Mask (CRM) layer, which facilitates an in-depth understanding and assessment of input images. This method enhances the effectiveness of CNN-based deep learning algorithms for image processing while maintaining computational and memory efficiency. We evaluated our approach using both U-Net and pre-trained ResNetUNet deep learning architectures. The CRM layer proved to be effective, slightly improving segmentation accuracy, particularly for complex classes such as Crosswalks and Water bodies, which have a limited amount of training data. Comparative assessments revealed that pre-trained ResNetUNet models incorporating the CRM layer outperformed baseline U-Net models across various metrics, including Intersection over Union (IoU) and Accuracy.

Keywords: Urban environment · Color band · Orthophoto · U-Net · Semantic segmentation

1 Introduction

Deep learning has revolutionized and transformed remote sensing and image analysis, particularly in semantic segmentation, which categorizes images into meaningful, pixel-level regions. This transformative power of deep learning is particularly significant in the

M. F. Mata-Rivera et al. (Eds.): W2GIS 2025, LNCS 15946, pp. 3–19, 2026.
https://doi.org/10.1007/978-3-032-01723-9_1

context of urban analysis, where detailed spatial information is crucial for urban planning, navigation, disaster management, and monitoring infrastructure [1–5]. In recent years, the development of airborne platforms and Unmanned Aerial Vehicles (UAVs) equipped with high-resolution imaging sensors has significantly enhanced the potential of semantic segmentation. These platforms, with their ability to provide unprecedented detail and accuracy in the acquisition of urban data, open exciting possibilities for the field of urban analysis [6, 7].

Urban environments are characterized by complex and heterogeneous features, including buildings, roads, sidewalks, vegetation, and water bodies. Traditional image analysis methods often struggle to differentiate these elements with high precision, mainly when dealing with complex structures and different object features commonly found in cities. Deep learning approaches, leveraging Convolutional Neural Networks (CNNs) and their variants, have emerged as powerful tools to overcome these challenges. A key benefit of these methods is that they have the potential to classify and segment urban components by capturing spatial hierarchies and contextual relationships [8].

The integration of aerial ultra-high-resolution images with deep learning models offers unique advantages. In general, aerial photography (UAV and airplane) can capture data at flexible angles and resolutions, providing comprehensive coverage of urban areas. This capability is especially beneficial for applications requiring fine-grained analysis, such as detecting sidewalk accessibility, mapping green spaces, and monitoring construction activities. Furthermore, the use of deep learning for semantic segmentation reduces the reliance on manual interpretation, making the analysis process more efficient and scalable, thereby reassuring researchers about the practicality of their research [9].

Even though deep learning offers great potential, most of these algorithms are complex and challenging for people with limited knowledge of the subject. Moreover, applying deep learning for semantic segmentation in urban environments presents several other challenges such as: supervised deep learning algorithms require many training data to work effectively and training and analyzing ultra-high-resolution images with deep learning algorithms are memory and computationally demanding and often require advanced data augmentation, preprocessing, and model optimization techniques to achieve optimal results [10]. In recent years, advances in performant computing, as well as the development of new methods in artificial intelligence, including deep learning algorithms, have made it possible to automatically extract pertinent information from airborne images for diverse applications, including construction, mobility, and transportation [1, 11].

To tackle these challenges, we developed a new approach called the Color Range Mask (CRM) layer, which facilitates in-depth understanding and assessment of input images. This method enhances the effectiveness of CNN-based deep learning algorithms for image processing while maintaining computational and memory efficiency. We also applied this method to the U-Net-based models, which perform well with limited training data, to improve the accuracy of their output further.

In this research, we propose a new approach to enhance the accuracy of deep learning models by introducing novel concepts to create more informative input features without increasing computational and memory costs.

The structure of this paper is organized as follows. The next section presents a comprehensive overview of existing studies and methodologies, identifying the current trends, challenges, and research gaps in this field. Section 3 presents our proposed methodology and the CRM layer, and details the experimental setup, including the datasets, preprocessing techniques, and deep learning models employed for semantic segmentation. Section 4 presents the results, discusses the findings, evaluates the performance of the proposed approaches, and interprets the implications of the results for urban analysis. Finally, in the conclusion section, we summarize the key insights, highlight the contributions of this study, and provide directions for future research.

2 Literature Review

Experts in remote sensing and mapping have extensively investigated road, building, and sidewalk extraction from high-resolution images. Despite the increase in resolution of airborne images, they are still insufficient for some applications, including construction, site monitoring, public urban utility inspection and maintenance, as well as map extraction for the navigation of people with disabilities. Therefore, in recent years, it has become increasingly popular to extract this kind of information from ultra-high-resolution images by using deep-learning techniques [12–15]. Object detection and semantic segmentation with Convolution Neural Networks (CNN) are widely used, especially in remote sensing images, where the technique shows excellent performance [16]. Ning and colleagues in 2019 developed a method to extract sidewalks from aerial images using YOLACT[1] method [17]. They then used a pre-trained model to restore occluded and missing sidewalk parts from street-view images [17]. They reported a precision and recall of 0.87 and 0.92, respectively, for their method. Despite achieving reasonable levels of accuracy and precision, this method is complex due to the use of two deep learning algorithms and two types of images (aerial and perspective), which necessitate significant training data and computational resources. Consequently, this complexity makes it difficult to use the method for real-world applications [16]. In the field of deep learning, the U-Net algorithm is one of the most commonly used algorithms for the semantic segmentation of aerial images [18–22]. This model was developed by Olaf Ronneberger, Philipp Fischer, and Thomas Brox in 2015 for biomedical image segmentation, which takes advantage of a convolutional neural network architecture [23]. U-Net is a well-known and extensively used model due to its straightforward architecture, which facilitates comprehension and ease of use [24]. Erdem and Avdan (2020) compared several versions of this model to extract buildings from high-resolution aerial images. A comparison of the result accuracy was made using U-Net Vgg16, U-Net InceptionResNetV2, and U-Net DenseNet121, which provided F1 scores of 0.866, 0.860, 0.856, and 0.877, respectively [20]. This method operates effectively even with a small set of training data [23, 25] in comparison with models such as the DeepLabv3+ [9] and HRNet [26] model, which requires more data to train effectively.

Most deep learning algorithms in computer vision employ CNN layers to analyze and extract features from input data. However, in certain scenarios, such as when defining a limited number of features for the initial CNN layer, the model may struggle to

[1] You Only Look At CoefficienTs.

correctly identify patterns or gain a proper understanding of the data. This can lead to difficulties in object recognition, resulting in errors and misclassifications. Therefore, numerous researchers propose to use multi-sensory data and the fusion of diverse datasets to improve the accuracy of their results. Fortunately, with the advancement of technology, the ability to gather various types of data from a single source has increased in recent years. Combining information from multiple sensors aims to create a more comprehensive understanding of complex phenomena, ultimately leading to more accurate and reliable results in their analyses. Therefore, numerous researchers used multi-sensory data in urban environments to achieve a better semantic segmentation object classification [27–33]. Lyu et al. (2018) utilized the UAVid dataset of ultra-high-resolution images captured from a tilted perspective to provide both top-down and oblique views to evaluate several popular deep-learning models for semantic segmentation. These models included FCN-8s [34], Dilation Net [35], and U-Net [23], as well as their proposed Multi-Scale-Dilation Net (MS-Dilation Net), specifically tailored for UAV imagery. The study also investigated the impact of transfer learning by comparing the performance of these models with and without pre-trained weights. Fine-tuning the models on the UAVid dataset significantly improved the mean Intersection over Union (mIoU), demonstrating the effectiveness of transfer learning in this context. In addition, using a pre-trained model, they got the advantage of the Feature Space Optimization (FSO) [36] post-processing method to enhance the final result, which took several features such as the image, the edge map, the unary map, the optical flow, and tracks. U-Net achieved the second-highest mIoU among the tested models, surpassed only by the more complex, three-stream MS-Dilation Net [13]. MS-Dilation Net takes advantage of three different-sized input features in its algorithm, which makes it more robust than other compared algorithms. This approach, while useful, comes with several notable drawbacks. Firstly, the input features fail to contribute valuable information to the overall analysis, limiting their effectiveness. Additionally, managing this separate input requires a significant amount of computational resources. As a result, the algorithm's performance slows down, leading to increased processing times and higher memory consumption.

3 Methodology

Convolutional neural networks, widely used in the field of computer vision, rely heavily on the application of filters or kernels to extract meaningful features from images. These filters are designed to recognize patterns such as edges, textures, and shapes, which are crucial for object detection and classification tasks. However, in certain instances, the performance of these filters as the initial layer in the network can be suboptimal. When the filters fail to accurately capture and represent the distinct characteristics of objects within the images, this can lead to misclassification, ultimately affecting the accuracy and reliability of the final outcomes produced by CNN. This issue emphasizes the importance of carefully designing and tuning the filter parameters to enhance feature extraction and improve overall model performance. Therefore, many researchers use different sources of data to solve this issue, such as depth maps, edge maps, Digital Surface Models (DSM), and Hue Saturation Intensity [31, 33, 37]. However, in this research, we propose a new approach called the Color Range Mask (CRM) layer to create more features from the original RGB image without using CNN filters. Extracting different features from a single data type, like an image, can help improve the accuracy of the results obtained from deep learning models. By looking at various characteristics within the data, we can gain additional insights that make the training step more effective. This feature extraction process enables the model to identify better patterns by categorizing similar objects, such as sidewalks, roads, and vegetation, based on their colors, resulting in more accurate predictions and outcomes.

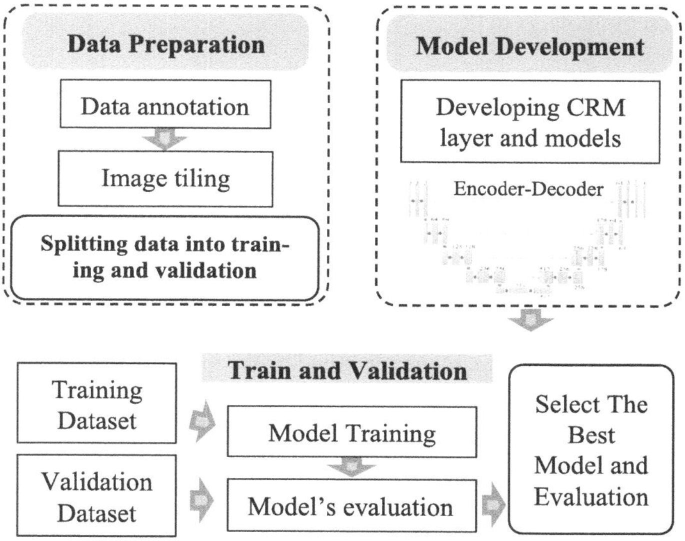

Fig. 1. illustrates the comprehensive three-step methodology we employed.

The CRM layer serves as a specialized pre-preprocessing tool for input images, focusing on the segmentation of the red, green, and blue color channels into a variety of distinct sub-range values. This innovative layer creates a unique mask for each defined sub-range, effectively isolating pixel values that fall within that specific range while rendering all other pixel values to zero. By doing so, it enhances the ability to distinguish between different land cover types, such as vegetation, water bodies, roads, and sidewalks, based on their unique spectral signatures. This method improves the accuracy of land cover classification and facilitates a deeper analysis of the underlying environmental features depicted in the images.

Let x be the input image tensor with dimensions (B, C, H, W), where:

- B is the batch size (number of images),
- C represents the three-color channels (Red, Green, Blue),
- H and W are the height and width of the image.

For each color channel (R, G, B), we can divide its intensity values into N ranges:

$$range_i = [min_i, max_i), \ i = 1, 2, 3, \ldots, N. \tag{1}$$

For each range, *i*, a **mask** is created to identify the pixel values that lie within that range. The range can be determined by the characteristics of each class, such as the water body, which is represented as a range of values (10 to 50) in the red band value (0 to 256) and another range of values in the green and blue layers.

$$M_{c,i}(x) = \begin{cases} 1, \; if \; min_i \leq x < max_i, \\ 0, \; otherwise. \end{cases} \tag{2}$$

Using this mask, a masked image is generated by keeping only the pixel values within the range and setting others to 0:

$$x_{c,i} = x.M_{c,i}(x) \tag{3}$$

This process is repeated for all ranges and channels. Finally, all the masked images are combined by stacking them along the channel dimension to create the output tensor:

$$y = concat\left(x_{R,1}, \ldots, x_{R,N}, x_{G,1}, \ldots, x_{G,N}, x_{B,1}, \ldots, x_{B,N}\right) \tag{4}$$

The output y has dimensions (B, C × N, H, W), where C × N is the total number of sub-ranges for all channels. In our approach, the output channels can be determined by several factors, including the number of classes (as more classes necessitate additional channels), the number of feature maps generated by the initial layer of the deep learning algorithm (which should not exceed half of the feature maps produced by the first CNN layer), and the characteristics of the input images. This approach enhances segmentation by isolating relevant features while eliminating noise, allowing the model to concentrate on meaningful regions. CRM elevates the signal-to-noise ratio and streamlines the learning process by masking irrelevant areas based on their color or spectral characteristics. This method minimizes background distractions, enhances feature extraction, and integrates domain-specific knowledge, resulting in faster convergence, improved generalization, and superior segmentation performance. Therefore, this approach is beneficial in tasks such as semantic segmentation, feature extraction, and domain-specific image analysis, where analyzing distinct intensity ranges in different color bands is necessary.

To effectively evaluate the effectiveness of the CRM layer, we will undertake a structured process consisting of three key steps. This methodology is illustrated in the framework presented in Fig. 1, outlining our comprehensive evaluation approach. The first step involves data preparation, during which we create an annotation mask for all our RGB images. The second step involves model development, which includes creating a CRM layer to enhance U-Net as well as the U-Net with ResNet blocks by integrating the CRM layer.

In the final step, we will train and evaluate all the models developed during the preceding stages. A thorough analysis of each model's performance will be conducted using relevant metrics to assess their effectiveness.

3.1 Data Preparation

This section will explain the dataset we used and describe how we prepared the training and validation datasets, including the number of images in each.

Dataset. The dataset for this project contains 100 ultra-high-resolution airborne images with an image size of 23,010 × 14790 pixels from Victoriaville, a town situated in south-central Quebec, Canada. The photos have a pixel resolution of 5 by 5 cm, which strikes a nice balance between the amount of analysis required and the outcome precision. They provide comprehensive and detailed spatial information, including the road, pedestrian network, buildings, vegetation, trees, etc. Data collection was carried out on April 23, 2022, when snow and tree canopy were at their lowest levels, which helped us to extract or segment images more accurately.

As the dataset was acquired in an urban sector with a unique structure, we need to create our own training dataset for semantic segmentation purposes. Preparing a training dataset is time-consuming and labor-intensive, so we prepared a small training dataset from our case study area, which we named Victo Dataset.

Table 1. shows high-resolution urban semantic segmentation datasets.

Dataset name	Training	Validation	Classes	Image Size
Urban Segmentation ISPRS (Vaihingen) [37]	33		6	Different size 1980 × 2555
Aerial Image Dataset for Semantic Segmentation	72000		6	128 × 128
UAVid Dataset [13]	200	70	8	3840 × 2160
The Semantic Drone Dataset	400		20	6000 × 4000
Victo Dataset	800	47	6	600 × 600

Training and Validation Dataset. To achieve a better outcome, we have prepared a training dataset from the collected data for our case study area. Due to the size of our original aerial images (23010 × 14790 pixels), we cropped several areas from the original images for two important reasons: first, to have enough samples of all objects, such as the crosswalk and water body, and second, for better management with our available computing resources. As a first step, we have annotated the data into six classes (land, asphalt, sidewalk, building, water, and crosswalk). As the annotated images are still very large (12000 × 12000 and several 2400 × 2400 pixels), it is difficult to train a deep-learning model based on these large images. Training deep learning models with large image sizes significantly increase the training time. The larger the images, the more computational resources are required to process and analyze them, resulting in longer training times. This issue can slow down model development, especially when working with limited computing power. Consequently, 600 × 600-pixel images were created from the annotated image. Our dataset is very limited, so we decided to crop the training data. As a result of our efforts, we prepared a total of 847 images and their corresponding annotated masks.

The two groups' training and validation contain 800 and 47 JPG images, respectively. A JPG (or JPEG) image is a commonly used format for storing and sharing digital photographs and images. In addition to the two groups mentioned, we also possess another dataset that encompasses nearly all the data collected from our case study area. Unlike the training data, this portion presents some differences; it is significantly larger in volume and is stored in TIF format, which includes geoinformation.

Table 1 has been prepared to compare our dataset with other high-resolution urban semantic segmentation datasets, allowing us to better understand our situation. Some of this dataset has fewer images than ours; however, if we crop their images into our image size, we can find that their dataset is much larger than ours except the Urban Segmentation ISPRS dataset.

Model Development. To achieve the desired accuracy with limited training data, we have utilized the U-Net model based on the encoder-decoder architecture [23]. Its structure resembles a U-shape, consisting of two main paths: a contracting (encoder) path and an expanding (decoder) path. The encoder extracts different features through a series of convolutional layers, each followed by rectified linear activation functions (ReLU) and max-pooling layers to reduce spatial dimensions while increasing the depth of feature maps. The decoder path mirrors the encoder, progressively reconstructing the image resolution by combining up sampling layers and transposed convolutions with skip connections. These skip connections link corresponding layers from the encoder to the decoder, preserving spatial information and ensuring fine-grained details are retained. Each block within the U-Net model typically includes convolutional layers, batch normalization, and ReLU activations, with a final layer producing the segmentation map using a SoftMax or sigmoid activation function, depending on the number of output classes. Batch normalization was not used in the initially proposed version of the U-Net model [23]; however, this layer in the U-Net model stabilizes and accelerates training by normalizing feature distributions across mini-batches. It ensures consistent feature scaling, speeds up convergence, and reduces overfitting by adding regularization. Moreover, the accuracy of the U-Net model can be enhanced by employing pre-trained models, as highlighted in the research by Lyu and colleagues [13].

To demonstrate that our proposed CRM layer can enhance the performance of image CNN-based deep learning algorithms, we modified two encoder-decoder-based algorithms: the U-Net and a pre-trained ResNetUNet algorithm, which is demonstrated in Fig. 2 and 3, respectively. The modified U-Net (U-Net + CRM layer) architecture processes input images in two main blocks. The first block, shown in Fig. 2 in purple, includes a 5×5 convolution layer followed by a ReLU activation, then a 3×3 convolution layer, Batch Normalization, and another ReLU activation. This block takes an RGB image as input and produces 16 feature maps. The second block commences with the CRM layer, which analyzes RGB images to generate 12 color range mask features for each image. Through our experience, we have observed that the set of 12 feature masks has consistently delivered superior outcomes compared to the 24 feature masks. This improvement is evident not only in the overall results but also in the processing time and computational costs involved. The efficiency and effectiveness of the 12 feature masks make them a more advantageous choice in our analysis. These features are subsequently passed to the following block of code, which mirrors the first block. However, this block takes the 12 mask features and produces 16 feature maps in this instance. In the next step, all 32 produced feature maps are concatenated and continue to the next block as per the standard U-Net process.

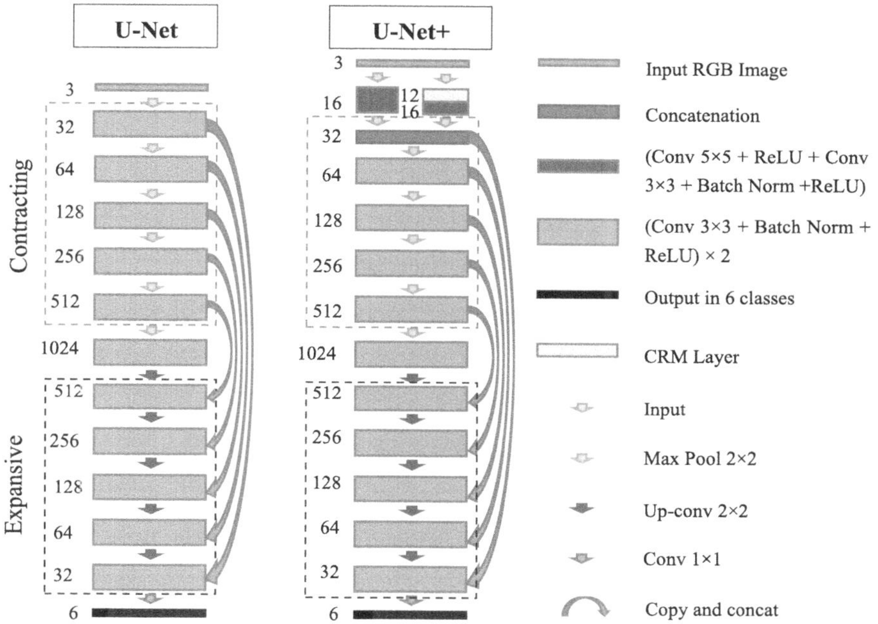

Fig. 2. illustrates the U-Net algorithm and the modified U-Net model that includes the CRM layer. The U-Net algorithm and modified U-Net with the CRM layer.

The second algorithm employed a pre-trained ResNet 34 as a contracting path within the U-Net architecture [38]. The expansive path consists of five blocks of double 3×3 convolutions, followed by a ReLU activation function. These components are illustrated in blue boxes in Fig. 3. As shown in Figs. 2 and 3, the red dashed line illustrates the contracting path, and the black dashed line represents the expansive path. To improve the accuracy and outcome, we modified the ResNetUNet algorithm and added our proposed layer as one of the initial layers. In Fig. 3, the CRM layer is represented in yellow, where it processes input RGB images to generate 12 feature maps for each image. Subsequently, a double convolution block, depicted in pink in Fig. 3, takes these 12 feature maps and produces 32. In contrast, the first block of the ResNet model, shown in grey, also processes the RGB image and generates 64 feature maps in the next step. This initially produces 96 feature maps, which are then reduced to 64 through a double convolution block and proceed to the next block. The remaining model parts are identical to the ResNetUNet shown in Fig. 3.

Training and Evaluation. In this section, we provide a detailed overview of the training process for our models. We will explore the various hyperparameters that were adjusted during training to optimize performance. Additionally, we will outline the evaluation process we implemented, including the specific metrics used to assess the models'

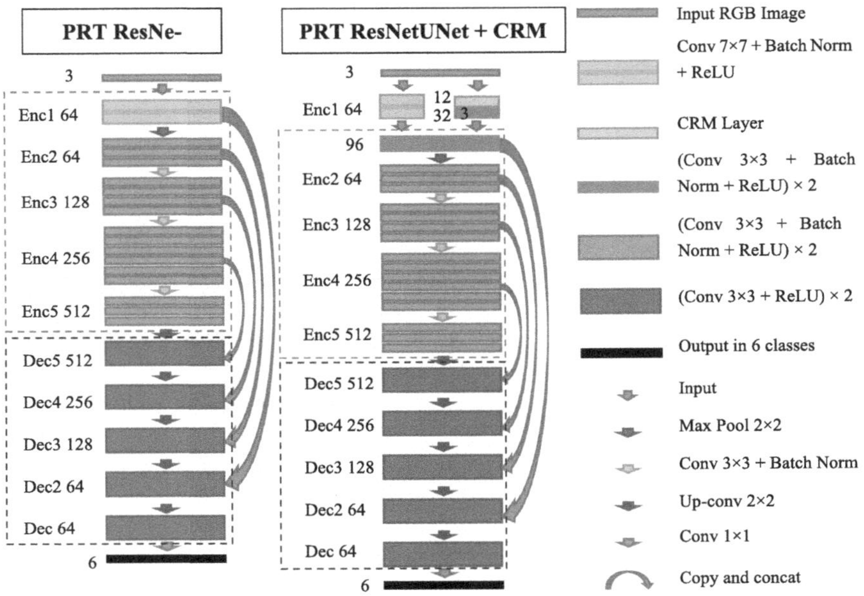

Fig. 3. illustrates the architecture of the pre-trained ResNetUNet model alongside its modified version, highlighting the structural differences and enhancements made in the latter.

effectiveness during validation. This comprehensive examination will help clarify our methodology and the rationale behind our choices.

All algorithms were trained on an Intel Core i9-14900K processor, operating at a clock speed of 3.20GHz, which provided the necessary computational power for handling complex calculations. The training process also utilized a high-performance GeForce graphics card (RTX 4090) equipped with 24 GB of dedicated graphics RAM, enabling efficient processing of graphical data and enhancing the overall training experience for the algorithms. This combination of hardware ensured optimal performance and reliability throughout the training phase.

Before discussing the training process and hyperparameters, it is important to note that due to the limited size of our dataset, we initially employed a cross-validation technique to train the U-Net model. However, this validation technique proved to be slow and time-consuming, resulting in metrics that were less accurate and effective. Consequently, we opted to train all algorithms using only the training data without incorporating validation data during the training phase.

In order to train all algorithms, we used the same multi-class cross-entropy loss method for calculating the loss value by Eq. 5. Where N is the number of samples, in semantic segmentation, one image, along with its pixel-wise label mask, is a sample. C is the number of classes and $y_{i,c}$ is ground truth (one-hot encoded), where $y_{i,c} = 1$ if sample iii belongs to class c, otherwise $y_{i,c} = 0$. $\hat{y}_{i,c}$ is the predicted probability of sample i belonging to class c (output of a SoftMax layer).

$$L = -\frac{1}{N}\sum_{i=1}^{N}\sum_{c=1}^{C} y_{i,c}\log(\hat{y}_{i,c}) \tag{5}$$

To train the deep learning models, we utilized the Adam optimizer [39], a widely adopted optimization algorithm known for its efficiency and adaptability in handling non-stationary objectives. The training process was conducted using the following hyperparameters. The learning rate was initialized at 0.001, with a batch size of 16. The training was conducted over 350 epochs, ensuring adequate iterations for convergence.

Figure 4 illustrates the training accuracy and loss graphs for four semantic segmentation models. In the training accuracy plot, all models exhibit a steady increase in accuracy during the initial epochs, followed by stabilization as training progresses. Notably, the pre-trained ResNetUNet variants outperform U-Net variants, achieving higher accuracy, particularly when CRM is integrated. Similarly, the training loss graph shows a consistent decrease in loss across all models, with ResNetUNet and ResNetUNet + CRM converging faster and reaching lower loss values than U-Net and U-Net + CRM. The addition of CRM slightly enhances the performance of both architectures, as evident from improved accuracy and reduced loss. During training, the UNet model completes each epoch in an average of 51 s. In contrast, the UNet model combined with CRM (UNet + CRM) takes only 45 s per epoch. For the ResNetUNet model, the average time to process each epoch is 62 s, while the ResNetUNet combined with CRM takes significantly less time at just 28 s per epoch.

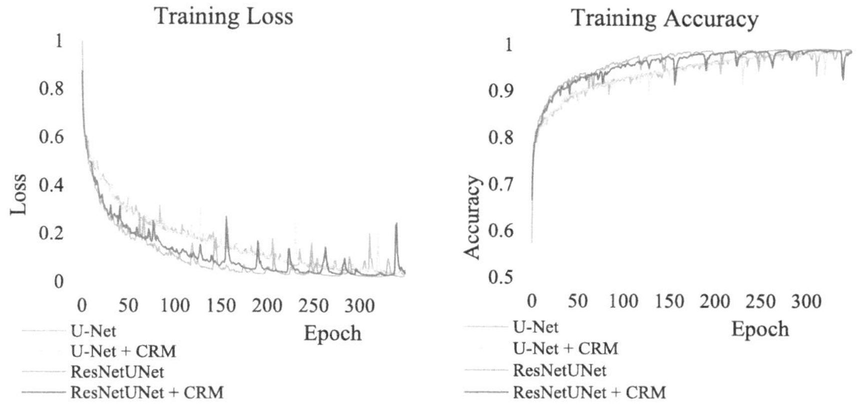

Fig. 4. The graphs compare the training accuracy and loss of four models—U-Net, U-Net + CRM, PRT + ResNetUNet, and PRT + ResNetUNet + CRM—over 350 epochs.

Evaluation Metrics. Various metrics are used to assess all model's performance. Key metrics include Accuracy, which measures overall correctness; Precision, the ratio of true positive predictions to total positive predictions; Recall (Sensitivity), which measures the ability to identify all relevant instances; the F1 Score, a harmonic mean of Precision and

Recall; and mean Intersection over Union (mIoU), which evaluates the overlap between predicted segmentation and ground truth. Each metric provides valuable insights, making them essential for a comprehensive evaluation.

4 Result and Discussion

The results of our semantic segmentation models reveal significant insights into the accuracy and effectiveness of the proposed approaches for mapping urban environments. Table 2 compares the class-wise segmentation accuracy of four deep learning models—U-Net, U-Net + CRM, ResNetUNet, and ResNetUNet + CRM—across six classes: Land, Asphalt, Concrete, Building, Water, and Crosswalk. ResNetUNet outperformed U-Net in most classes, with the highest accuracy observed for Land (96.81%) and Building (95.90%). Adding the CRM layer improved the performance of both architectures, particularly in challenging classes like Water and Crosswalk. For instance, ResNetUNet + CRM achieved the highest accuracy for Water (94.25%) and Crosswalk (55.69%). Similarly, U-Net + CRM outperformed the standard U-Net in classes such as Asphalt (96.87%) and Concrete (89.55%). These results highlight the effectiveness of CRM in refining predictions for complex and less-represented classes, such as Crosswalk, where both U-Net + CRM and ResNetUNet + CRM showed notable improvements. Overall, ResNetUNet + CRM demonstrated the most balanced performance across all classes.

Table 2. Class-wise segmentation accuracy (%) of four models.

Model	Land (%)	Asphalt (%)	Concrete (%)	Building (%)	Water (%)	Crosswalk (%)
U-Net	95.40	94.96	84.48	95.02	82.31	45.86
U-Net + CRM	94.53	96.87	89.55	95.72	92.08	49.62
PRT + ResNetUNet	96.81	96.71	85.23	95.90	90.82	54.40
PRT + ResNetUNet + CRM	95.54	96.87	88.13	96.18	94.25	55.69

Table 3 presents the Intersection over Union (IoU) scores across all four models for six classes. Among these, the ResNetUNet + CRM model exhibited the highest overall performance, particularly excelling in the more challenging categories of Concrete, Water body, and Crosswalk, with IoU scores of 81.22%, 83.91%, and 52.74%, respectively. Incorporating the CRM layer consistently enhanced the performance of both U-Net and ResNetUNet. For instance, U-Net + CRM showed notable improvements in the IoU scores for Concrete (78.01%) and Water (81.63%) compared to the baseline U-Net. Similarly, ResNetUNet + CRM slightly outperformed the standard ResNetUNet across most classes, highlighting the module's effectiveness in improving model precision, particularly for smaller or more complex features such as Crosswalk. Overall, these results emphasize the advantages of CRM in enhancing segmentation accuracy and maintaining IoU consistency across all categories. The primary factor contributing to the inadequate IoU results for crosswalks was the restricted size of the training dataset, combined with the variability in colors used for the crosswalks themselves. This can be clearly illustrated by examining Fig. 5b and 5d, which highlight these differences in detail.

Table 3. Class-wise intersection over union (IOU) (%)

Model	Land (%)	Asphalt (%)	Concrete (%)	Building (%)	Water (%)	Crosswalk (%)
U-Net	88.31	91.75	72.34	91.91	77.34	39.82
U-Net + CRM	90.34	92.72	78.01	93.38	81.63	43.78
PRT + ResNetUNet	91.17	94.11	78.98	94.39	81.83	52.32
PRT + ResNetUNet + CRM	90.88	93.67	81.22	93.83	83.91	52.74

Table 4 summarizes the performance of four models using three key metrics: Overall Accuracy, Weighted F1 Score, and Mean Intersection over Union (mIoU). Including the CRM layer consistently improved the performance of U-Net and ResNetUNet models across all metrics. For example, U-Net + CRM improved mIoU from 76.91% to 79.98% compared to U-Net. Similarly, ResNetUNet + CRM achieved the highest mIoU (82.71%), surpassing ResNetUNet (82.14%), indicating the effectiveness of CRM in refining segmentation quality. While the overall accuracy and weighted F1 scores for ResNetUNet and ResNetUNet + CRM are nearly identical, the mIoU improvement underscores CRM's role in enhancing fine-grained segmentation performance. These results demonstrate that integrating the CRM layer and positional pre-trained model can substantially improve semantic segmentation outcomes.

Table 4. represents the performance comparison of four models using overall accuracy, weighted f1, and mIOU.

Model	Overall Accuracy (%)	Weighted F1 Score (%)	mIoU (%)
U-Net	94.33	94.32	76.91
U-Net + CRM	95.31	95.30	79.98
PRT + ResNetUNet	95.90	95.89	82.14
PRT + ResNetUNet + CRM	95.78	95.77	82.71

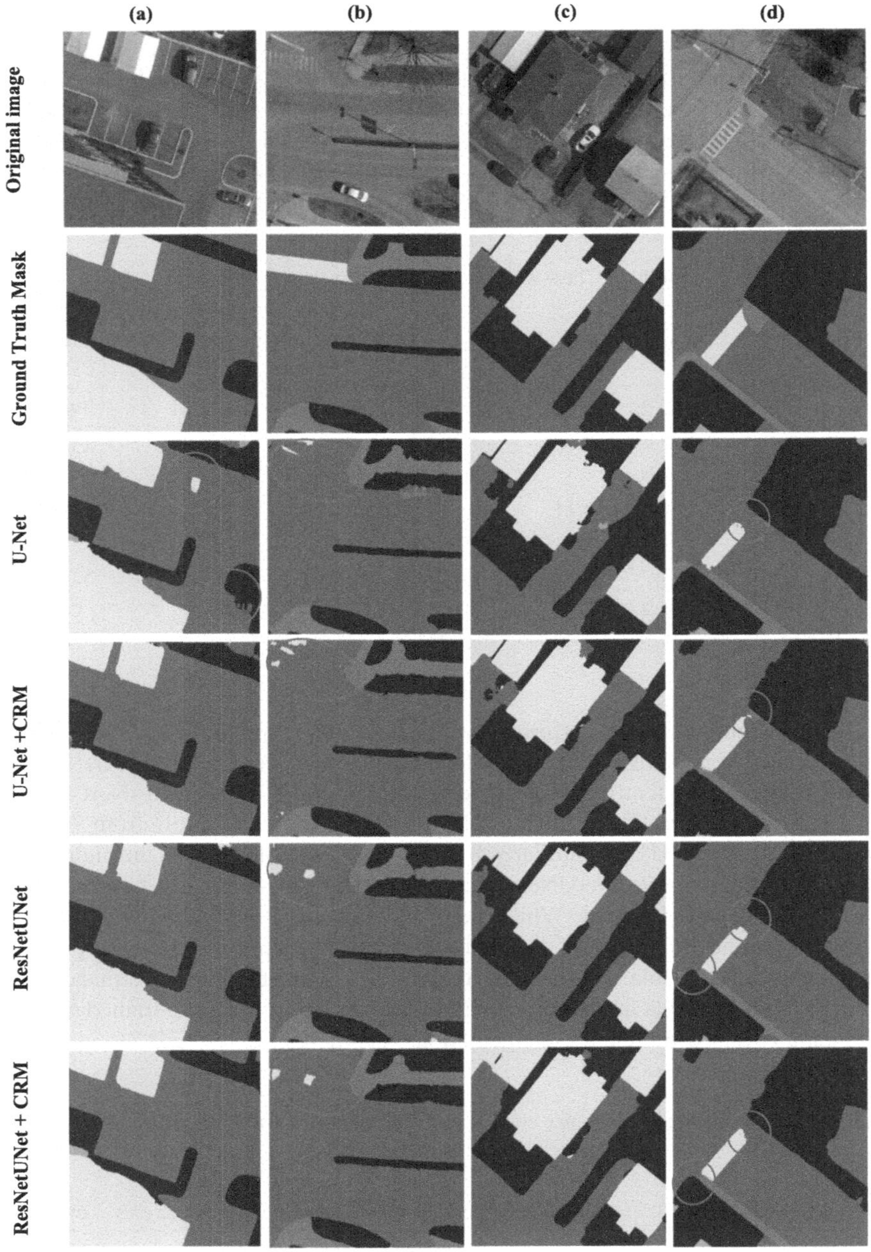

Fig. 5. compares four semantic segmentation methods. The top row shows the original images, followed by ground truth and segmentation outputs from U-Net, U-Net + CRM, PRT + ResNetUNet, and PRT + ResNetUNet + CRM. Colors indicate classes: yellow for buildings, blue for roads, green for sidewalks, and purple for land. (Color figure online)

Figure 5 compares the results obtained from four different algorithms, highlighting their performance and outcomes. Colors indicate classes: yellow for buildings, blue for roads, green for sidewalks, and purple for land. As shown in Fig. 5a, all models produced satisfactory results; however, U-Net displayed some shortcomings, as indicated by the red line. In Fig. 5b, none of the models successfully segmented the crosswalk, although the pre-trained ResNetUNet with the CRM layer achieved the best outcome. Figure 5c illustrates a challenging scenario with numerous objects that complicate segmentation; nevertheless, the results from both ResNetUNet-based models surpassed those of the U-Net-based models. In Fig. 5d, both the U-Net and the U-Net with CRM layer showed enhanced performance in identifying curb cuts as part of the sidewalk. However, neither the pre-trained ResNetUNet nor the ResNetUNet with the CRM layer could accurately segment the curb cuts on either side of the crosswalk.

In evaluating model performance, the analysis of average samples processed per second reveals that U-Net combined with CRM achieves the highest throughput at 3.30 samples per second, closely followed by the baseline U-Net at 3.23 samples per second. In contrast, ResNetUNet demonstrates the lowest processing speed at 3.0 samples per second, which can be attributed to the increased computational complexity associated with its deeper ResNetUNet backbone architecture. Importantly, the integration of CRM leads to a more significant performance enhancement in ResNet-based models, with a 4% improvement, compared to a 2.2% increase in standard U-Net architectures. This indicates that the conditional random field enhancement is particularly advantageous for deeper network architectures. GPU memory analysis reveals that all models exhibit a similar baseline memory consumption of ~155 MB.

5 Conclusion

This study highlights the benefits of incorporating the Color Range Mask (CRM) layer into deep learning architectures for the semantic segmentation of urban environments. The results reveal that the CRM layer improves segmentation accuracy, particularly for complex and under-represented classes such as Crosswalk. Among the models tested, pre-trained ResNetUNet with CRM achieved the best performance across most metrics, including overall accuracy, weighted F1 score, and mIoU. Despite the promising outcomes, challenges such as limited training datasets and complex object structures persisted, indicating the need for further research. Future work will focus on developing advanced multi-sensor cross-fusion algorithms, leveraging high-resolution terrestrial imagery and LiDAR data to achieve even greater accuracy and utility in urban analysis and navigation systems.

Specific applications, such as urban utility maintenance and navigation systems designed for individuals with disabilities, require an elevated level of accuracy and precision, so we plan to embark on a new project. Our goal is to develop an advanced multi-sensor cross-fusion deep learning algorithm. This innovative approach will focus on extracting essential urban features from exceptionally high-resolution terrestrial images combined with data captured from Lidar technology.

References

1. Minaee, S., Boykov, Y., Porikli, F., et al.: Image Segmentation Using Deep Learning: A Survey (2020)
2. Nichol, J.E., Wong, M.S.: High resolution remote sensing of densely urbanised regions: a case study of Hong Kong. Sensors (Switzerland) **9**, 4695–4708 (2009). https://doi.org/10.3390/s90604695
3. Coxon, S., Napper, R., Richardson, M.: Urban mobility design. Urban Mobility Design 1–230 (2018). https://doi.org/10.1016/C2017-0-01129-1
4. Marconcini, M., Metz, A., Zeidler, J., Esch, T.: Urban monitoring in support of sustainable cities. 2015 joint urban remote sensing event. JURSE **2015**, 1–4 (2015). https://doi.org/10.1109/JURSE.2015.7120493
5. Chang, R., Hou, D., Chen, Z., Chen, L.: Automatic extraction of urban impervious surface based on SAH-UNet. Remote Sens. (Basel) **15** (2023). https://doi.org/10.3390/rs15041042
6. Zhu, X.X., Tuia, D., Mou, L., et al.: Deep learning in remote sensing: a review (2017). https://doi.org/10.1109/MGRS.2017.2762307
7. Audebert, N., Saux, B., Le, L.S.: Beyond RGB: Very High Resolution Urban Remote Sensing With Multimodal Deep Networks (2017)
8. Chen, L.-C., Papandreou, G., Kokkinos, I., et al.: DeepLab: Semantic Image Segmentation with Deep Convolutional Nets, Atrous Convolution, and Fully Connected CRFs (2016)
9. Chen, L.-C., Zhu, Y., Papandreou, G., et al.: Encoder-Decoder with Atrous Separable Convolution for Semantic Image Segmentation (2018)
10. Ma, L., Liu, Y., Zhang, X., et al.: Deep learning in remote sensing applications: a meta-analysis and review. ISPRS J. Photogramm. Remote Sens. **152**, 166–177 (2019)
11. LeCun, Y., Bengio, Y., Hinton, G.: Deep learning. Nature **521**, 436–444 (2015). https://doi.org/10.1038/nature14539
12. Ma, Z., Li, Y., Ma, R., Liang, C.: Applying Unsupervised Semantic Segmentation to High-Resolution UAV Imagery for Enhanced Road Scene Parsing (2024)
13. Lyu, Y., Vosselman, G., Xia, G., et al.: UAVid: A Semantic Segmentation Dataset for UAV Imagery (2018)
14. Song, A.: Deep learning-based semantic segmentation of urban areas using heterogeneous unmanned aerial vehicle datasets. Aerospace **10** (2023). https://doi.org/10.3390/aerospace10100880
15. Majidizadeh, A., Hasani, H., Jafari, M.: Semantic segmentation of UAV images based on U-Net in urban area. ISPRS Annals of the Photogrammetry, Remote Sensing and Spatial Information Sciences X-4/W1–2022, 451–457 (2023). https://doi.org/10.5194/isprs-annals-X-4-W1-2022-451-2023
16. Ning, H., Ye, X., Chen, Z., et al.: Sidewalk extraction using aerial and street view images. Environ. Plan B Urban Anal. City Sci. **49**, 7–22 (2022). https://doi.org/10.1177/2399808321995817
17. Bolya, D., Zhou, C., Xiao, F., Lee, Y.J.: YOLACT: Real-time Instance Segmentation (2019)
18. Khan, M.J., Singh, P.P.: Advanced road extraction using CNN-based U-Net model and satellite imagery. e-Prime - Advances in Electrical Engineering, Electronics and Energy 5 (2023). https://doi.org/10.1016/j.prime.2023.100244
19. Wulff, F., Schäufele, B., Sawade, O., et al.: Early Fusion of Camera and Lidar for robust road detection based on U-Net FCN; Early Fusion of Camera and Lidar for robust road detection based on U-Net FCN (2018)
20. Erdem, F., Avdan, U.: Comparison of Different U-Net Models for Building Extraction from High-Resolution Aerial Imagery. Int. J. Environ. Geoinform. **7**, 221–227 (2020). https://doi.org/10.30897/ijegeo.684951

21. Jiang, Y., Han, S., Li, D., et al.: Automatic concrete sidewalk deficiency detection and mapping with deep learning. Expert Syst. Appl. **207** (2022). https://doi.org/10.1016/j.eswa.2022.117980
22. Alsabhan, W., Alotaiby, T.: Automatic building extraction on satellite images using UNet and ResNet50. Comput. Intell. Neurosci. **2022** (2022). https://doi.org/10.1155/2022/5008854
23. Ronneberger, O., Fischer, P., Brox, T.: U-Net: Convolutional Networks for Biomedical Image Segmentation (2015)
24. Frid-Adar, M., Ben-Cohen, A., Amer, R., Greenspan, H.: Improving the Segmentation of Anatomical Structures in Chest Radiographs Using U-Net with an ImageNet Pre-trained Encoder. In: Lecture Notes in Computer Science (including subseries Lecture Notes in Artificial Intelligence and Lecture Notes in Bioinformatics). Springer Verlag, pp 159–168 (2018)
25. Liu, X., Zhao, X., Wang, S.: Blind sidewalk segmentation based on the lightweight semantic segmentation network. In: Journal of Physics: Conference Series. IOP Publishing Ltd (2021)
26. Sun, K., Zhao, Y., Jiang, B., et al.: High-Resolution Representations for Labeling Pixels and Regions (2019)
27. Li, Z., Chen, B., Wu, S., et al.: Deep learning for urban land use category classification: A review and experimental assessment. Remote Sens. Environ. **311** (2024)
28. Chen, C., Yuan, X.P., Gan, S., et al.: A new strategy based on multi-source remote sensing data for improving the accuracy of land use/cover change classification. Sci. Rep. **14**, 26855 (2024). https://doi.org/10.1038/s41598-024-75329-w
29. González, T., Sol, D., Saenz, J., et al.: Urban multisensory laboratory, an approach to model urban space human perception. In: International Archives of the Photogrammetry, Remote Sensing and Spatial Information Sciences - ISPRS Archives. International Society for Photogrammetry and Remote Sensing, pp. 29–35 (2017)
30. Gamba, P., Dell'Acqua, F., Dasarathy, B.V.: Urban remote sensing using multiple data sets: past, present, and future. Inform. Fusion **6**, 319–326 (2005). https://doi.org/10.1016/j.inffus.2005.02.007
31. Makarau, A., Palubinskas, G., Reinartz, P.: Multi-sensor data fusion for urban area classification. In: 2011 Joint Urban Remote Sensing Event, JURSE 2011 – Proceedings, pp 21–24 (2011)
32. Palubinskas, G., Makarau, A., Reinartz, P.: Information extraction using optical and radar remote sensing data fusion (2012)
33. Idrees, M.O., Saeidi, V., Pradhan, B., et al.: Maximizing Urban Features Extraction from Multi-sensor Data with Dempster-Shafer Theory and HSI Data Fusion Techniques (2015)
34. Long, J., Shelhamer, E., Darrell, T.: Fully Convolutional Networks for Semantic Segmentation (2014)
35. Yu, F., Koltun, V., Funkhouser, T.: Dilated Residual Networks (2017)
36. Kundu, A., Tech, G., Vineet, V.: Feature Space Optimization for Semantic Video Segmentation
37. Liang, M., Yang, B., Wang, S., Urtasun, R.: Deep Continuous Fusion for Multi-Sensor 3D Object Detection (2020)
38. Diakogiannis, F.I., Waldner, F., Caccetta, P., Wu, C.: ResUNet-a: a deep learning framework for semantic segmentation of remotely sensed data (2019). https://doi.org/10.1016/j.isprsjprs.2020.01.013
39. Kingma, D.P., Ba, J.: Adam: A Method for Stochastic Optimization

AIGC Image Features for GIS: A Preliminary Test of Elements, Colors, and Spatial Structure in Recommendation Tasks

Qiang Wang[1,4], Zhihang Yu[2], Shu Wang[1,3,4(✉)], and Yunqiang Zhu[1,3,4]

[1] State Key Laboratory of Resources and Environmental Information System, Institute of Geographic Sciences and Natural Resources Research, Chinese Academy of Sciences, Beijing 100101, China
wangshu@igsnrr.ac.cn

[2] College of Computer, Nanjing University of Posts and Telecommunications, Nanjing 210023, China

[3] Jiangsu Center for Collaborative Innovation in Geographical Information Resource Development and Application, Nanjing 210023, China

[4] University of Chinese Academy of Sciences, Beijing 100049, China

Abstract. Volunteered Geographic Information (VGI) images are a vital source of visual information and image features in the GIS field. The advancement of artificial intelligence, particularly large language models and generative AI, now enables the generation of seemingly lifelike images from textual prompts (Artificial Intelligence Generated Content - AIGC). This raises a pertinent question: can AIGC image features serve as a viable alternative to VGI features in downstream GIS tasks, especially where VGI is scarce or difficult to obtain? This paper conducts an exploratory study comparing VGI and AIGC image features as inputs for a geographic recommendation model, specifically investigating the impact of image elements, colors, and spatial structures. The results indicate that current AIGC images, generated from general textual descriptions, cannot fully substitute for VGI images. This is primarily due to AIGC's challenges in accurately replicating the specific elements, colors, and spatial relationships inherent in real-world VGI. However, the study suggests AIGC images hold significant potential. When provided with more specific information about elements and particularly their colors, AIGC's performance approached, and in some color-focused tests, even slightly surpassed that of VGI images. This implies AIGC's main deficiency is its current understanding of real-world object characteristics and their visual representation, notably the basic knowledge of elements and their associated colors. We propose these shortcomings could be addressed by integrating geographic knowledge bases in future AIGC development. These findings aim to guide AIGC's application in GIS by identifying current limitations and areas for focused improvement.

Keywords: AIGC Modeling · AIGC Image · VGI Image · Multimodal Recommendation · Image Element · Image Color · Image Spatial structure

M. F. Mata-Rivera et al. (Eds.): W2GIS 2025, LNCS 15946, pp. 20–30, 2026.
https://doi.org/10.1007/978-3-032-01723-9_2

1 Introduction

Volunteered Geographic Information (VGI) is a significant data source in GIS, actively recorded by the public to represent the real world. VGI images, in particular, offer a wealth of environmental information that often extends beyond what vague textual descriptions can capture, providing visual details about elements, their colors, spatial arrangements, and locations [1, 2]. These rich visual details, when used as image features, can enhance various GIS algorithms and analyses, playing a crucial role in applications such as urban spatial understanding, disaster assessment, and object classification [3–7]. Consequently, VGI images are a valuable asset in the GIS domain.

The rapid advancement of artificial intelligence, especially Artificial Intelligence Generated Content (AIGC) driven by large language models (LLMs) [8, 9], allows computers to generate scene-style images from textual descriptions, even those characterized by some ambiguity [10, 11]. These generated images can bear a striking resemblance to the content often expressed in VGI images (see Fig. 1). This development prompts a critical inquiry: to what extent can AIGC images and their extracted features replace or augment VGI images in GIS applications? Exploring this is essential, as AIGC could potentially address challenges in VGI acquisition, such as data scarcity for specific phenomena or the labor-intensive nature of VGI collection and curation.

(a) generated by AIGC (b) crawled from VGI

Fig. 1. Green energy pattern (a development pathway of SDGs) images generated by AIGC and VGI. (Color figure online)

However, bridging the gap between synthetic (AIGC) and real-world (VGI) data presents challenges, a concept often discussed in the broader 'simulation-to-reality' literature. This paper conducts a preliminary exploration within the GIS context, focusing on whether AIGC images can replicate the key visual features of VGI images—specifically elements, colors, and spatial structures—which are crucial for many GIS analyses. While VGI images provide rich visual data beyond what simple text offers, AIGC generation itself relies on textual prompts. If highly precise and detailed prompts are needed for AIGC to be effective, this might echo the limitations of relying solely on textual data. Our study investigates the current state of AIGC in this regard: how well do AIGC images, generated from reasonably descriptive text, perform as feature sources compared to VGI images in a downstream task like recommendation? This inquiry is not only the motivation for this paper but also a significant exploratory direction for the GIS field.

Therefore, this paper presents an initial investigation centered on the topic: 'Can AIGC image features replace real VGI features for certain GIS tasks?'. We focus on elements, colors, and spatial structures as these are foundational aspects of image interpretation frequently utilized in GIS. The methodology, experimental design, and methods are detailed in Sect. 2. Section 3 presents the experimental results, discussing the impact of image elements, colors, and spatial structures. Finally, Sect. 4 offers conclusions and outlines future directions.

2 Methodology

2.1 The Basic Idea

To address the central research question, our fundamental approach involves substituting VGI images with AIGC images in a downstream task that inherently requires image features. We aim to analyze the extent of their impact as image features. The overall conceptual framework is illustrated in Fig. 2. VGI images were acquired through web scraping to ensure their authenticity and relevance to the chosen patterns, while AIGC images were generated automatically by an image generator (ChatGPT-4 combined with DALL·E-3) based on textual descriptions derived from these patterns. It is acknowledged that the style of AIGC images may sometimes appear more 'artistic' compared to photographic VGI images; this study evaluates the performance of features from such typically generated AIGC images.

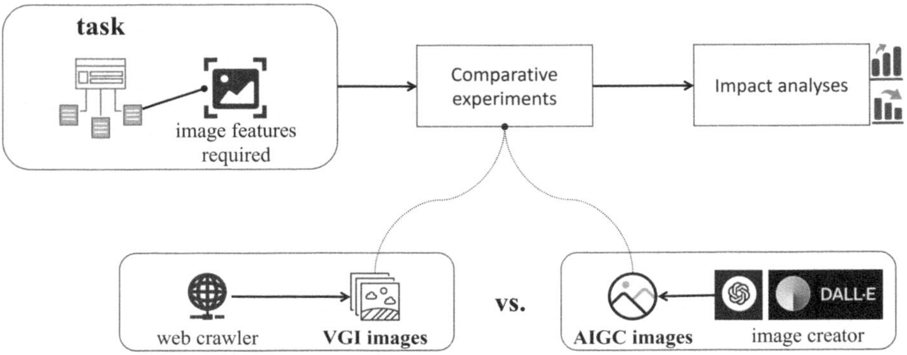

Fig. 2. The basic idea on the study of alternative comparison between VGI and AIGC images.

2.2 The Experimental Design

Guided by this basic idea, we meticulously designed our experiment (see Fig. 3). For the downstream task, we selected ECPR-MML [12], a geographic recommendation model.

This model recommends sustainable development pathways by considering various environmental elements and utilizes multimodal information, for which image features are a valuable input to help characterize and differentiate these pathways visually [13, 14]. The model was chosen as it still urgently requires the supplementation of multimodal information, particularly VGI image features, making it a suitable testbed for comparing VGI and AIGC image features.

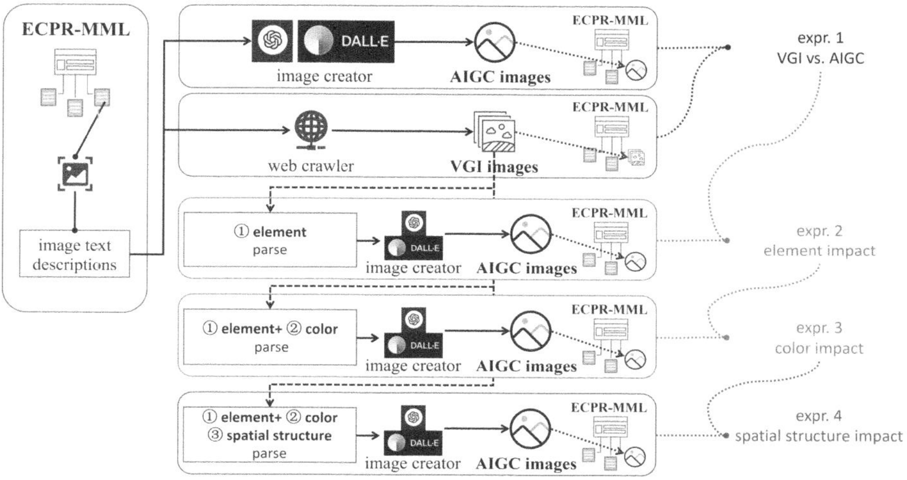

Fig. 3. The flowchart of experimental design.

To address the primary question, 'Can VGI Images Be Replaced by AIGC?', Experiment 1 was designed. We obtained real VGI images through web crawling, using descriptive information (e.g., pattern names of sustainable development pathways like 'Green energy pattern'). This same descriptive information was input into an image creator to produce AIGC images. Both VGI and AIGC images were then input into the ECPR-MML model to compare their recommendation performance.

To further analyze the factors influencing AIGC image utility, and considering the importance of image analysis in GIS, this study selected three fundamental categories of visual features for investigation: elements, colors, and spatial structures (the spatial relationship between elements). These were the basis for Experiments 2, 3, and 4. From VGI images, we extracted representative core elements, element colors, and spatial structures, instructing the image creator to generate corresponding AIGC images based on these specific parsed features. Consequently, the experiments could individually analyze the impact of these aspects. The prompts for AIGC generation were based on these parsed features, aiming to test AIGC's capability to render them accurately.

2.3 Parameters and Environment

The parameters and operating environment involved in the experiment are as follows.

Parameter Settings: For ECPR-MML method [12], we set the embedding dimension of vectors to 64, the batch size to 128, the epoch to 15, and the learning rate to 1e-4.

Experimental Environment: All experiments were conducted using the PyTorch framework, specifically including Python 3.8, PyTorch 1.12.0, NumPy 1.21.5, and a 12th Gen Intel (R) Core (TM) i5-12500. The GPU used for these experiments is the NVIDIA GeForce RTX 3050 Ti.

2.4 Evaluation Metrics

In order to compare the effects of AIGC images and VGI real images on the experimental results, we use two metrics, $Precision@K$, $Recall@K$, for verification:

$$Precision@K = \frac{|R^K(u) \cap T(u)|}{K} \quad (1)$$

$Precision@K$ measures the proportion of patterns between the Top-K recommended patterns $R^K(u)$ for the target region u and the actual interacted patterns $T(u)$ for u, among the K patterns.

$$Recall@K = \frac{|R^K(u) \cap T(u)|}{|T(u)|} \quad (2)$$

$Recall@K$ measures the proportion of Top-K recommended patterns $R^K(u)$ for the target region u that are also present in the true interacted patterns $T(u)$ of u in the test set.

In short, $Precision@K$ reflects the accuracy of the recommendation, and $Recall@K$ reflects the validity of the recommendation.

3 Results

3.1 VGI Images vs. AIGC Images

In general, automatically generated AIGC images cannot fully substitute for real VGI images in this task. A negative deviation is observed in their performance in recommendation tasks, with a precision drop of up to -2.62% and recall reduction up to -1.29% (refer to Table 1). This suggests that AIGC images, when generated from general descriptive texts, may not provide image features as effective as those from VGI for the specific downstream task.

To intuitively interpret these statistics, Fig. 4 presents four illustrative case comparisons between VGI images and AIGC images. While AIGC images can be visually striking, they sometimes lack 'logical coherence' in terms of accurately depicting the expected elements, colors, and spatial structures typically found in real-world VGI for such patterns. For example, the AIGC 'Beautiful countryside pattern' (Fig. 4) depicts an abstract cartoon scene rather than a more typical rural landscape, highlighting how AIGC may interpret ambiguous textual prompts in unexpected ways, potentially influenced by biases in its training data or cultural assumptions different from the target context. This underscores a challenge in prompt engineering and AIGC's semantic understanding. Sections 3.2 to 3.4 progressively incorporate additional experiments to discuss the impact of these aspects.

Table 1. The impact of VGI and AIGC images on model performance.

Metrics		Precision @1	Precision @2	Precision @3	Precision @4	Precision @5
Precision	VGI	**0.1410**	**0.0986**	**0.0859**	**0.0853**	**0.0814**
	AIGC	0.1406	0.0980	0.0850	0.0833	0.0793
	diff.(%)	−0.27	−0.59	−1.06	−2.43	−2.62
Recall		Recall @1	Recall @2	Recall @3	Recall @4	Recall @5
	VGI	**0.1352**	**0.1846**	**0.2348**	**0.3022**	**0.3469**
	AIGC	0.1351	0.1842	0.2337	0.2984	0.3425
	diff.(%)	−0.10	−0.24	−0.52	−1.27	−1.29

Fig. 4. The comparison of VGI images and AIGC images on four examples.

3.2 Impact of Image Elements

In terms of the impact of image elements, when AIGC was prompted to generate images based on specific elements identified within VGI images (e.g., wind turbines, hillsides for green energy patterns), the performance discrepancy persisted and, in some cases, slightly increased (e.g., AIGC-element-Precision@5 is −2.82%, compared to AIGC-Precision@5 at −2.62%) (Table 2). This may indicate that while AIGC can generate a variety of elements, leading to diverse imagery, it may still lack a nuanced understanding of the subtle interrelations or typical appearance of these elements as they exist in real-world geographic contexts. Figure 5 illustrates that while the AIGC-element images appear closer to VGI content, underlying feature differences affecting performance remain.

Table 2. The impact of AIGC image elements on model performance.

Metrics		Precision @1	Precision @2	Precision @3	Precision @4	Precision @5
Precision	VGI	**0.1410**	**0.0986**	**0.0859**	**0.0853**	**0.0814**
	AIGC-element	0.1406 (−0.27)	0.0980 (−0.59)	0.0849 (−1.21)	0.0832 (−2.55)	0.0791 (−2.82)
Recall		Recall @1	Recall @2	Recall @3	Recall @4	Recall @5
	VGI	**0.1846**	**0.2348**	**0.3022**	**0.3469**	**0.1846**
	AIGC-element	0.1842 (−0.10)	0.2334 (−0.24)	0.2983 (−0.58)	0.3422 (−1.31)	0.1842 (−1.36)

Fig. 5. The comparison of VGI images and AIGC-element images on four examples.

3.3 Impact of Colors

Regarding the impact of color elements, it was notable that the performance of AIGC-color images (where AIGC was guided by color information extracted from VGI) slightly exceeded that of VGI images in some metrics (achieving up to 0.23% higher Precision@4 and 0.11% higher Recall@4) (Table 3). This suggests that AIGC has the potential to replace, or even augment, VGI images if accurate color information for key elements is provided. In conjunction with findings from Sects. 3.1 and 3.2, we hypothesize that a significant factor in AIGC's general underperformance is its current lack of accurate recognition of the real-world colors of specific geographic objects. When explicitly informed of these colors, its performance can improve significantly. Figure 6 compares VGI and AIGC-color images. It is observable that AIGC not only matches VGI images more closely in elements and color but also sometimes introduces finer details (e.g., birds in the green energy pattern, flower pots in the beautiful countryside pattern). While these extra features might contribute to performance variations, it's also possible they act as confounding variables, and the improvement may not solely be due to color fidelity but also these novel, potentially relevant or irrelevant, details. Further study would be needed to isolate these effects.

Table 3. The impact of AIGC image colors on model performance.

Metrics		Precision @1	Precision @2	Precision @3	Precision @4	Precision @5
Precision	VGI	0.1410	0.0986	0.0859	0.0853	0.0814
	AIGC-color	**0.1410 (0.00)**	**0.0986 (0.00)**	**0.0860 (0.15)**	**0.0855 (0.23)**	**0.0815 (0.19)**
Recall		Recall @1	Recall @2	Recall @3	Recall @4	Recall @5
	VGI	0.1352	0.1846	0.2348	0.3022	0.3469
	AIGC-color	**0.1352 (0.00)**	**0.1846 (0.00)**	**0.2349 (0.05)**	**0.3025 (0.11)**	**0.3471 (0.06)**

Fig. 6. The comparison of VGI images and AIGC-color images on four examples.

3.4 Impact of Spatial Structures

In the aspect of spatial structure impact, a decline in performance was observed when AIGC was guided by explicit spatial structure information parsed from VGI (reaching up to −2.19% Precision@4, Table 4). The image comparisons in Fig. 7 suggest that AIGC possesses a rudimentary understanding of spatial structure, primarily reflecting relationships between core elements. However, accurately capturing the complex and often subtle spatial relationships present in real geographic scenes remains a challenge.

Identifying which aspects of these spatial relationships most significantly affect performance and how AIGC can better comprehend holistic spatial contexts are important future research directions. The results suggest that current methods of translating parsed spatial structure information into AIGC prompts may not be optimal, or that AIGC's internal models do not yet adequately represent such structures.

Table 4. The impact of AIGC image spatial structures on model performance.

Metrics		Precision @1	Precision @2	Precision @3	Precision @4	Precision @5
Precision	VGI	**0.1410**	**0.0986**	**0.0859**	**0.0853**	**0.0814**
	AIGC-spatial structure	0.1406 (−0.27)	0.0980 (−0.59)	0.0849 (−1.21)	0.0835 (−2.19)	0.0800 (−1.64)
Recall		Recall @1	Recall @2	Recall @3	Recall @4	Recall @5
	VGI	**0.1352**	**0.1846**	**0.2348**	**0.3022**	**0.3469**
	AIGC-spatial structure	0.1351 (−0.10)	0.1842 (−0.24)	0.2334 (−0.61)	0.2996 (−0.88)	0.3463 (−0.17)

Fig. 7. The comparison of VGI images and AIGC-spatial structure images on four examples.

4 Conclusion

This paper undertook an exploratory study to address the question, 'Can VGI Images Be Replaced by AIGC in the context of providing features for GIS tasks?'. Using a geographic recommendation model (ECPR-MML) as a testbed, we evaluated the substitutability of VGI images with AIGC images, focusing on the impact of image elements, color, and spatial structure.

Our findings are twofold:

(1) Current AIGC images, generated from general textual descriptions, cannot directly substitute for VGI images in tasks requiring nuanced visual feature extraction. AIGC often struggles with accurately representing the specific elements, their characteristic colors, and their complex spatial arrangements as found in real-world VGI images. This suggests a 'reality gap' that needs to be addressed for reliable AIGC use in such GIS applications.
(2) Despite current limitations, AIGC images demonstrate considerable potential. The key deficiency appears to be AIGC's incomplete knowledge of basic real-world elements and their associated colors. Our experiments showed that when more specific color information was provided, AIGC's performance improved significantly, sometimes even matching or slightly surpassing VGI. This suggests that future advancements, possibly through the integration of geographically specific knowledge bases to inform the AIGC generation process, could substantially enhance AIGC's utility. Such knowledge bases might help AIGC produce images that are not only visually plausible but also semantically accurate for GIS contexts. Furthermore, AIGC can generate diverse imagery and sometimes include additional details not explicitly prompted, which might offer benefits for data augmentation or exploring variations of scenes, although this also warrants careful control.

In conclusion, while direct replacement is not yet feasible, AIGC images hold promise as a future source of image features in GIS. However, realizing this potential likely requires targeted improvements to AIGC models, perhaps assisted by foundational geographic knowledge bases to compensate for current gaps in understanding elements and their colors. Further research could also explore human-in-the-loop systems for curating AIGC outputs or refining prompts to generate more contextually appropriate and accurate imagery for specific GIS applications.

Acknowledgments. This work was supported by the Strategic Priority Research Program of the Chinese Academy of Sciences (grant number XDB0740200-01); and the National Natural Science Foundation of China (grant number 42471503).

Disclosure of Interests. The authors have no competing interests to declare that are relevant to the content of this article.

References

1. Lewis, Q.W., Park, E.: Volunteered geographic videos in physical geography: data mining from YouTube. Ann. Am. Assoc. Geogr. **108**(1), 52–70 (2018)
2. Senaratne, H., Bröring, A., Schreck, T.: Using reverse viewshed analysis to assess the location correctness of visually generated VGI. Trans. GIS **17**(3), 369–386 (2013)
3. Hartmann, M.C., Schott, M., Dsouza, A., Metz, Y., Volpi, M., Purves, R.S.: A text and image analysis workflow using citizen science data to extract relevant social media records: combining red kite observations from Flickr, eBird and iNaturalist. Ecol. Inform. **71**, 101782 (2022)

4. Yan, Y., et al.: Monitoring and assessing post-disaster tourism recovery using geotagged social media data. ISPRS Int. J. Geo-Inf. **6**(5), 144 (2017)
5. Feick, R., Robertson, C.: A multi-scale approach to exploring urban places in geotagged photographs. Comput. Environ. Urban Syst. **53**(SI), 96–109 (2015)
6. Wang, S., et al.: New era for geo-parsing to obtain actual locations: a novel toponym correction method based on remote sensing images. Remote Sens. **14**(19), 4725 (2022)
7. Gliozzo, G., Pettorelli, N., Haklay, M.: Using crowdsourced imagery to detect cultural ecosystem services: a case study in South Wales. UK. Ecol. Soc. **21**(3) (2016)
8. Wu, T., et al.: A brief overview of ChatGPT: the history, status quo and potential future development. IEEE-CAA J. Automatica Sin. **10**(5), 1122–1136 (2023)
9. Lu, Y., et al.: Could ChatGPT imagine: content control for artistic painting generation via large language models. J. Intell. Robot. Syst. **109**(2), 39 (2023)
10. Guo, C., et al.: ArtVerse: a paradigm for parallel human-machine collaborative painting creation in metaverses. IEEE Trans. Syst. Man Cybern. **53**(4), 2200–2208 (2023)
11. Santandreu-Calonge, D., et al.: Can ChatGPT improve communication in hospitals?. Prof. Inf. **32**(2) (2023)
12. Yu, Z., et al.: A Multimodal Ecological Civilization Pattern Recommendation Method Based on Large Language Models and Knowledge Graph. arXiv preprint arXiv:2310.18951 (2023)
13. Shu, W., et al.: A novel rapid web investigation method for ecological agriculture patterns in China. Sci. Total. Environ. **842**, 156653 (2022)
14. Yu, Z., et al.: Unveiling Optimal SDG Pathways: An Innovative Approach Leveraging Graph Pruning and Intent Graph for Effective Recommendations. arXiv preprint arXiv:2309.11741 (2023)

Quality Assessment of Tourist Generated Contents: A Large Language Model Approach

Jialiang Gao[1], Peng Peng[2(✉)], Christophe Claramunt[2,3], and Feng Lu[2]

[1] Academy of Digital China (Fujian), Fuzhou University, Fuzhou 350108, China
[2] State Key Laboratory of Resources and Environmental Information System, Institute of Geographic Sciences and Natural Resources Research, Chinese Academy of Sciences, Beijing 100101, China
pengp@lreis.ac.cn
[3] Naval Academy Research Institute, 29240 Lanvéoc, France

Abstract. The exponential growth of tourist-generated content necessitates efficient quality assessment frameworks to address inherent challenges of information reliability and analytical scalability. This study pioneers a Large Language Model (LLM)-driven approach, integrating supervised fine-tuning with low-rank adaptation and structured prompt engineering to enable multi-dimensional quality evaluation. Covering 485,930 reviews from three major platforms—MaFengWo, TripAdvisor, and Ctrip—the framework achieves superior performance (RMSE = 0.56, NDCG@K = 0.88) in generating accurate quality scores and detailed analytical rationales. Spatial-temporal-semantic analyses reveal platform-specific quality patterns: MFW exhibits stable temporal cointegration and prominent spatial centrality, TripAdvisor demonstrates simplified core-periphery structures, while Ctrip presents dynamic multicentricity. Heterogeneous network analysis further identifies the behavioral regularities of high-reliability users through a random-walk algorithm. The study advances tourism informatics by resolving scalability limitations of manual coding while providing actionable insights for platform governance, including targeted moderation and incentive mechanisms. This paradigm highlights LLMs' transformative potential in operationalizing tourist-generated content quality assessment at scale, bridging theoretical rigor with practical applicability within digital tourism ecosystems.

Keywords: Quality Assessment · User Generated Content · Large Language Model

1 Introduction

The proliferation of information and communication technologies (ICTs) in the Web 2.0 era has catalyzed the emergence of online travel agency (OTA) platforms as social media ecosystems. These digital interfaces empower tourists to spontaneously generate and disseminate multimodal evaluations of tourism products—spanning attractions, catering, and accommodation—through ubiquitous mobile connectivity. This vast, velocity, and easily accessible information, commonly referred to user-generated content (UGC),

M. F. Mata-Rivera et al. (Eds.): W2GIS 2025, LNCS 15946, pp. 31–41, 2026.
https://doi.org/10.1007/978-3-032-01723-9_3

encompasses geo-tagged textual narratives (e.g. travelogue, microblog, and review) to visual artifacts (e.g. photo, and video). The provision of voluntary information has been observed to offer substantial value for prospective tourists, tourism enterprises, and researchers. Specifically, the vivid first-person accounts can effectively alleviate the uncertainty and anxiety of prospective tourists, with 72% regularly consulting UGC during trip planning (Ipsos MORI et al., 2019). Therefore, tourism enterprises have long recognized the significance of tourist-generated content in enhancing brand awareness, customer loyalty, and destination image, which is further referred to as electronic Word-of-Mouth (eWoM). Furthermore, a broad spectrum of tourism management studies capitalize on this influential information repository to progressively supplant the costly survey-based datasets on numerous pertinent issues, including detecting satisfaction factors of different tourist groups (Guo et al., 2017), forecasting the dynamic demand (Hu et al., 2022), and analyzing tourist behavior regularities (Gao et al., 2024; Mou et al., 2022).

However, the tourist-generated content inherently embodies a multifaceted data quality issue, attributed to its voluminous nature, high subjectivity, standardization absence, traceability ambiguity (Lu et al., 2015), as well as varied motivations and communities of its creators (Zhuang et al., 2023). The issue can be further specified as significant unevenness or uncertainty in information quality, compounded by a low density of informational value, bias, and intentional spam (Himeur et al., 2023). This obstructs the tourists' access to valid information amidst overloaded data and diminishes the reliability of research conclusions derived from tourist-generated content. The field of tourism management has long acknowledged the issue of data quality, which is frequently discussed in the limitation section of relevant literature (He et al., 2022; Li et al., 2023; Liu et al., 2019). Furthermore, a plethora of researches leverage sophisticated mechanistic models—including the theoretical trust model (Al Qundus et al., 2019), grounded theory analysis (J. J. Zhang et al., 2024), negativity bias and cue-summation theories (Eslami et al., 2018)—from interdisciplinary domains spanning information management, communication studies, and cognitive psychology. These researches systematically operationalize the influencing dimensions of data quality, encompassing informativeness, emotional appeal, and argument frame, while concurrently assessing the potential impacts of varying content qualities on tourists' decision-making behaviors (Asyraff et al., 2024; Yamagishi et al., 2024).

Nevertheless, a more fundamental research gap remains unsolved: how to accurately and efficiently assess the quality of tourist-generated content, a challenge frequently oversimplified in existing literature. The two most prevalent assessment approaches are: 1) directly leveraging the usefulness votes or ratings provided by other platform users as the ground-truth for content quality (X. Zhang et al., 2023); 2) conducting the manual annotation on an item-by-item basic through expertise, a process also known as the content analysis (Lo et al., 2019; Moás et al., 2023). However, it is evident that both approaches possess notable shortcomings. In terms of the usefulness votes, two obvious kinds of selection bias or fairness issues can be identified (Zheng et al., 2024): 1) a majority of the votes merely concentrated on a very limited number of contents; 2) recently published contents with high quality are at risk of being overlooked (Sun et al., 2019). Regarding the content analysis, the substantial expense of manual annotation restricts the research scope to a range from several hundred to a few thousand items of content, thereby relegating analyses to small-case studies and compromising generalizability. Therefore, the development of a more precise and efficient quality assessment framework for massive tourist-generated content is imperative. This cannot only filter out decision-critical information for prospective tourists, but more importantly, assist tourism practitioners and researchers in discerning the distribution of data quality, enhancing the credibility of their findings and strategies.

To address the aforementioned research gap, this study develops a novel quality assessment framework for tourist-generated content, which incorporates Large Language Model (LLM) technology (Feng et al., 2023; Starace et al., 2024) as the core evaluation model and a multi-dimensional comparative analysis of quality distribution characteristics. First, through the supervised fine-tuning training, LLM is enhanced to effectively generate both precise quality scores and granular descriptive evaluation for tourist-generated content across multiple quality dimensions, including information integrity, detail richness, viewpoint novelty, practical helpfulness, emotional engagement, and linguistic precision. This study focuses on online reviews as the quality assessment object, recognizing them as the most widely used and representative form of tourist-generated content in both the tourism industry and academia. A substantial volume of online reviews is gathered, processed and evaluated from three leading OTA platforms, namely MaFengWo (MFW, 91,667), TripAdvisor (133,574), and Ctrip (259,689), which cover 39,211 tourists who have visited Beijing and Shanghai, two major destinations in China, from 27 countries and regions. Second, following the item-by-item evaluation by the fine-tuned LLM for all review data, we further conduct a comparative analysis of quality distribution of content across three data sources. More specifically, the distributional characteristics and patterns of quality are comprehensively investigated for each data source on four aspects: spatial, temporal, semantic, and interactive. The key insights into the determinants of content quality can be summarized as spatio-temporal regularities, issue attribution, and user-content-source relevance, all of which significantly contribute to the subsequent quality control and enhancement engineering for tourist-generated content ecosystems (Fig. 1).

2 Quality Assessment Framework

2.1 LLM-Driven Quality Assessment Model

2.1.1 Prompt Engineering

This study introduces the Chain-of-Thought (CoT) and few-shot learning strategies to construct the instruction prompt as Fig. 2, comprising three components: quality dimension definitions, dual-task specifications, and structured output format. First, six quality dimensions are systematically defined based on expertise, each accompanied by standardized and short descriptions. Second, the prompt explicitly delineates two interconnected subtasks: **quantitative scoring** requires the model to generate fine-grained quality scores on a continuous 0.0–5.0 scale, and **descriptive analysis** is performed to provide the corresponding rationale for the numerical scoring, thereby establishing interpretable decision traces. Third, the output formats are rigorously constrained using JSON schema

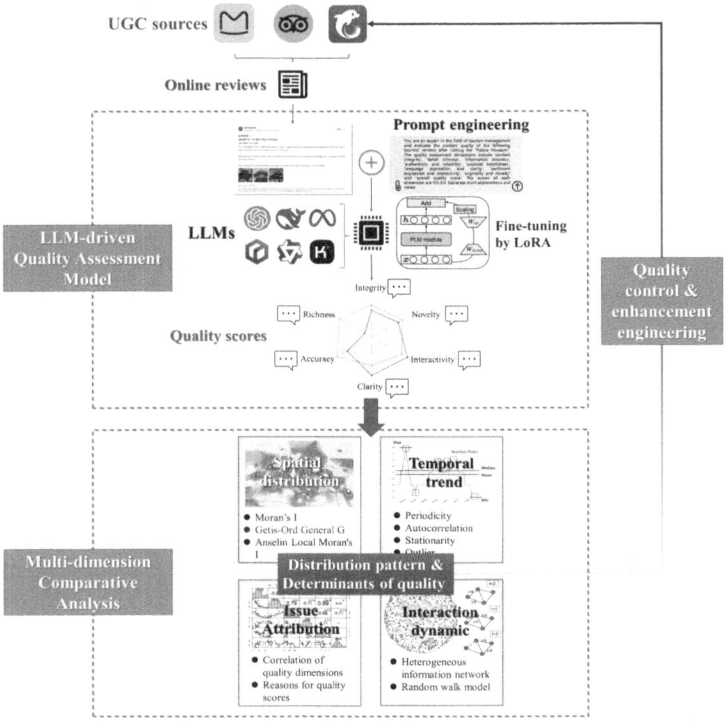

Fig. 1. The whole quality assessment framework, encompassing the assessment model driven by LLM and the multi-dimensional comparative analysis of content quality distribution.

to enforce dual-layer structured data generation, integrating with 3–5 labeled samples as contextual examples.

2.1.2 Supervised Fine-Tuning

LLMs demonstrated with strong multilingual semantic comprehension ability were selected as the foundation model (such as Qwen-2.5, LLaMA-3.2). To achieve joint optimization of quantitative scoring and qualitative analytical generation, we formulate a multi-task supervised fine-tuning process governed by a composite loss function comprising the following components:

Scoring Loss: We employed the Mean Squared Error (MSE) loss function to ensure that the predicted numerical scores align closely with the annotated values across all evaluation dimensions.

$$\mathcal{L}_{score} = \frac{1}{dim}\sum_{d=1}^{dim}(y_d - \hat{y}_d) \tag{1}$$

where, $\hat{y}_d$ represents the ground truth, and y_d denotes the predicted score for the d-th dimension.

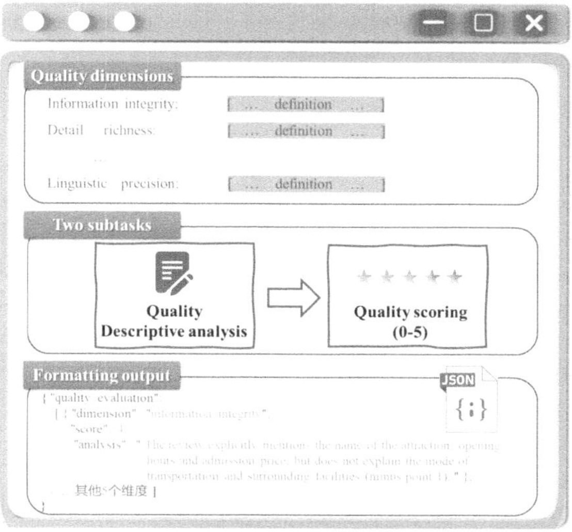

Fig. 2. Prompt engineering, encompassing the definition of quality dimensions, dual-task specifications, and JSON output format.

Descriptive Analysis Loss: The Negative Log-Likelihood loss was adopted to maximize the conditional probability of generating accurate analytical description.

$$\mathcal{L}_{desc} = -\sum_{t=1}^{T} logP(w_t|w_{<t}, x) \tag{2}$$

where, $P(w_t|w_{<t}, x)$ signifies the conditional probability of the t-th term w_t given its preceding terms $w_{<t}$ and the input UGC x.

The total loss function is formulated as a weighted sum of the above two objectives, to facilitate the simultaneous optimization of both tasks, where hyper-parameter α controls the trade-off between numerical precision and textual fidelity.

$$\mathcal{L}_{total} = \alpha\mathcal{L}_{score} + (1 - \alpha)\mathcal{L}_{desc} \tag{3}$$

The low-rank adaptation (LoRA) technique was applied exclusively to query and value projection matrices within transformer layers, achieving parameter-efficient tuning with only 0.8% of base model weights being trainable. Gradient updates were constrained to these low-rank subspaces to preserve the model's pre-trained linguistic capabilities while adapting to the target quality assessment task.

2.2 Empirical Model Verification

2.2.1 Experimental Setup

Dataset. The dataset was constructed through the manual annotation by three independent specialists, achieving a robust inter-annotator consistency validated by Krippendorff's Alpha of 0.83. The final corpus cinsists 1,530 records for content-score-analysis. The training, validation, and test set were divided by 8:1:1 ratio, ensuring the balance of topics, languages, and rating distribution of each subset.

Hyper-Parameters. Only the last 2 layers were designated as trainable, to strike a balance between task adaptability and the preservation of pre-training knowledge. The rank r of LoRA matrices was configured to 8, with a LoRA scaling coefficient of 16. The initial learning rate for AdamW optimizer is set as 5e-5, following a cosine annealing schedule. The number of steps for gradient accumulation was configured to 8. Additionally, the batch size is set as 16, with total epochs being 30.

Metrics. This study designed three scenarios to comprehensively evaluate quality assessment models. 1) The absolute accuracy of quality scoring was directly measured against expert annotation using RMSE. 2) Complementally, the relative ordering validity of the scores was evaluated from an information retrieval perspective using NDCG@K, where the predicted rankings were compared with actual crowdsource user-helpfulness voting rankings. 3) The textual consistency of generated quality analytical description was verified from three granular metrics of n-gram matching (BLEU), syntactic structure (ROUGE), and semantic similarity (BERTScore) (Table 1).

2.2.2 Verification Results

Table 1. Absolute accuracy of quality scores

Model	RMSE
GPT-4o (API)	0.512
Qwen2.5-7B (origin/tuned)	1.001/0.588
Qwen2.5-14B (origin/tuned)	0.792/0.571
LLaMA3.1-8B (origin/tuned)	0.784/0.567

3 Multi-dimensional Comparative Analysis of Content Quality

3.1 Spatial Distribution

We visualized geospatial distribution of content quality through bivariate mapping Fig. 3, where chromatic intensity represents mean quality scores and point radii denote content quantity per attraction. For granular comparison of quality structure, the content records were further divided into three groups according to quality scores: high (>4.0), medium (3.0–4.0), and low (<3.0), which were respectively mapped.

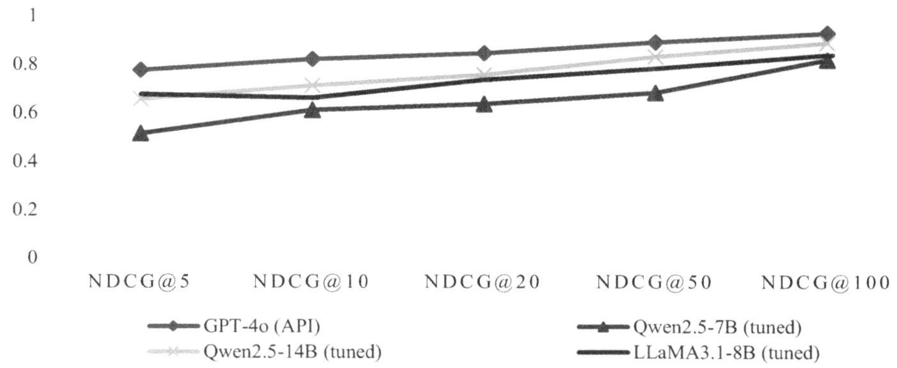

Fig. 3. Relative precision compared with user-helpfulness voting ranking

Through horizontal analysis crossing quality intervals, the spatial distribution patterns of MFW vary obviously across high, medium, and low- quality levels in terms of central concentration, axial extension, and spatial range. In contrast, TripAdvisor and Ctrip maintain relative consistency.

We further explored a vertical comparative analysis for urban structural characteristics. Three sources exhibits a certain degree of centrality, where Beijing tended to display singular core and Shanghai showed dispersed clusters. Specifically, MFW belongs to single or double-center pattern with more significant centrality, especially high-value clustering confirmed by Getis-Ord General G (z-score > 2.58). Ctrip belongs to a multi-cluster structure with several subcenters. TripAdvisor exhibits the simplest and single core-peripheral configuration, due to the limited number of attractions featured (Fig. 4).

3.2 Temporal Trend

As the overall temporal trends depicted in Fig. 5, MFW exhibits superior stability compared to TripAdvisor and Ctrip, with minimal cyclical fluctuations. The large volatility observed in TripAdvisor and Ctrip might be attributed to data sparsity during platform infancy. As the contents on all three platforms expand over time, the quality distributions gradually converge toward their means, which shows the law of Large Numbers. This can be obviously manifested in Fig. 6 where the standard deviations within interval of review number decrease.

The temporal cointegration analysis reveals divergent quality-group dynamics. MFW and TripAdvisor satisfy the Engle-Granger two-step test and exhibit two independent long-run equilibrium relationships through Johansen testing, indicating a consistent relative proportion over time, with medium-quality reviews dominating. A subtle difference is that MFW consistently demonstrates a higher number of low-quality reviews compared to high-quality ones, whereas TripAdvisor shows the reverse hierarchy. In contrast, Ctrip exhibits varying hierarchy in its time series, where the relative ordering between medium- and low-quality reviews fluctuates.

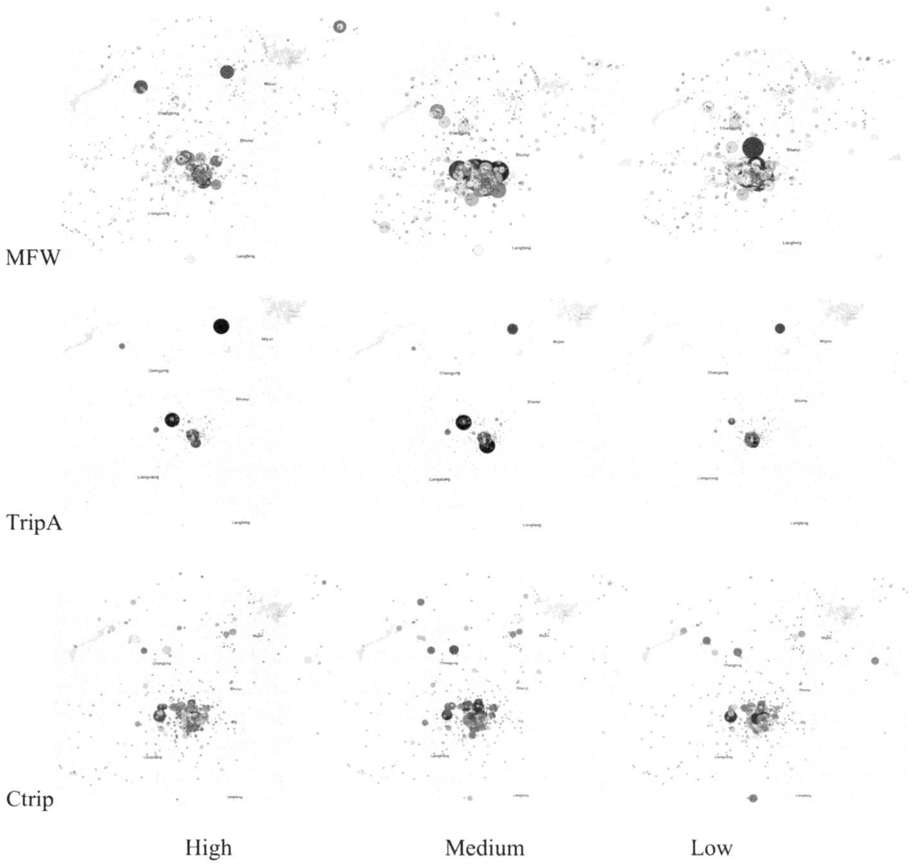

Fig. 4. Spatial distribution of quality in Beijing

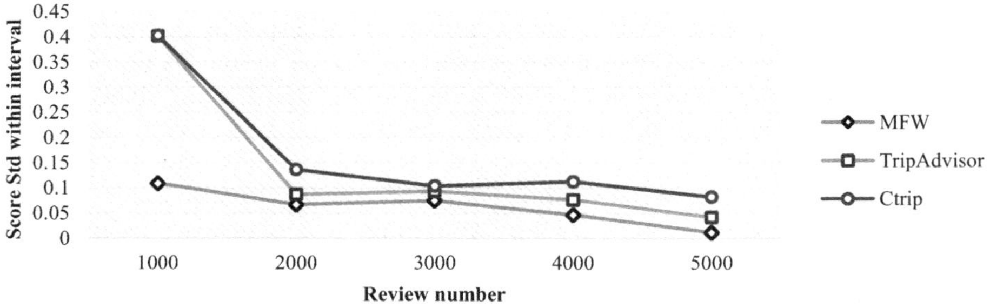

Fig. 5. Temporal trend of quality score across three platforms

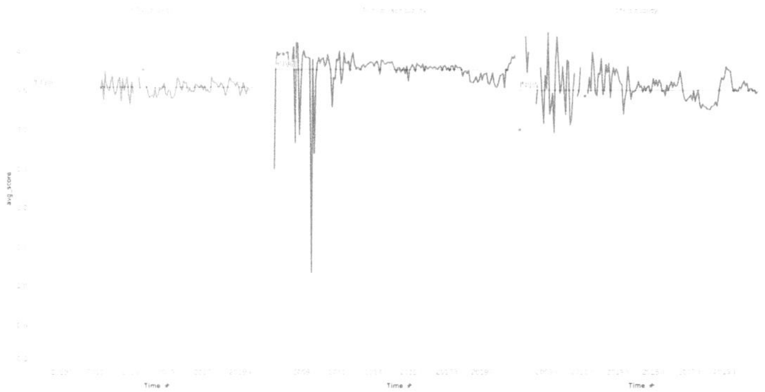

Fig. 6. Temporal variation of quality with review number increasing

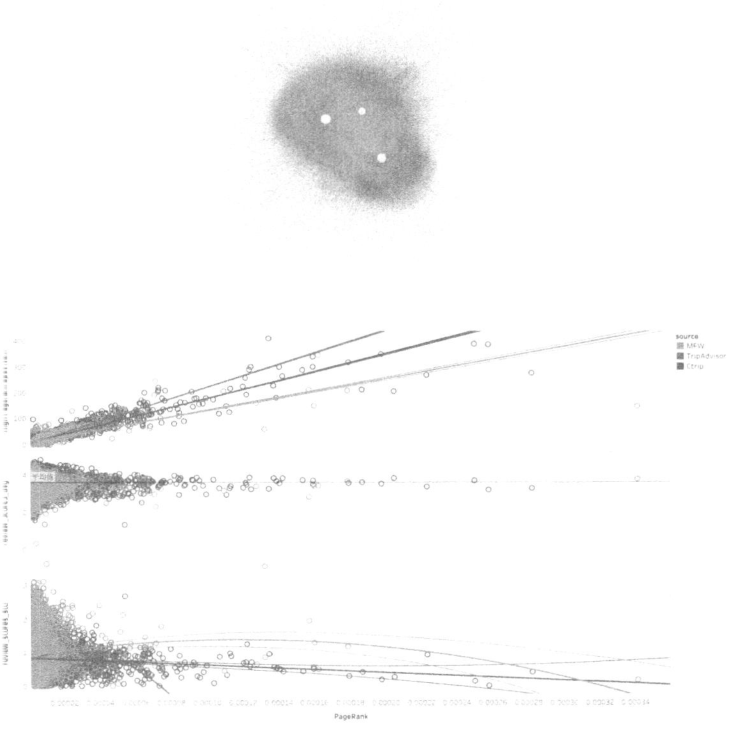

Fig. 7. Interactive behavior traits of high-quality users manifested by HIN

3.3 Interaction Dynamic

Interaction dynamics among users, contents, attractions, and platforms were explored through the meta-path-guided random walk algorithm on HIN, which consists of various elements and 8 types of relationships as displayed in Fig. 8. As the quality scores propagate on HIN, the reliability of users can be re-estimated by PageRank values. The behavioral regularities of highly trusted users can be further observed in Fig. 6 (Fig. 7).

1) Frequent visits to relatively high-quality attractions, namely, their reviews preferential attaching the attractions with higher PageRank values.
2) The qualities of published reviews stabilize at the mean level.
3) Lower variance in the quality of their published reviews indicates greater profile homogeneity.

4 Conclusion

This study establishes a novel LLM-driven framework for assessing tourist-generated content quality, addressing critical gaps in existing methodologies through three key advancements. First, our fine-tuned LLM achieves superior performance (RMSE = 0.567, NDCG@K = 0.882) by jointly optimizing multi-dimensional scoring and interpretable analysis generation via LoRA-enhanced parameter-efficient adaptation. Second, multi-platform comparative analysis reveals divergent quality distribution patterns: MFW exhibits stable temporal cointegration and significant spatial centrality, TripAdvisor displays high volatility and simplified core-periphery structures, while Ctrip demonstrates polycentric configurations especially in Shanghai. Third, heterogeneous network analysis uncovers behavioral signatures of high-reliability users, characterized by preferential attachment to high-quality attractions and content quality stability.

References

Al Qundus, J., Paschke, A., Kumar, S., Gupta, S.: Calculating trust in domain analysis: theoretical trust model. Int. J. Inf. Manage. **48**, 1–11 (2019)

Asyraff, M.A., Hanafiah, M.H., Zain, N.A.M., Hariani, D.: Unboxing the paradox of social media user-generated content (UGC) information qualities and tourist behaviour: moderating effect of perceived travel risk. J. Hospitality Tourism Insights **7**(4), 1809–1830 (2024)

Eslami, S.P., Ghasemaghaei, M., Hassanein, K.: Which online reviews do consumers find most helpful? A multi-method investigation. Decis. Support. Syst. **113**, 32–42 (2018)

Feng, Y., Ding, L., Xiao, G.: Geoqamap-geographic question answering with maps leveraging LLM and open knowledge base (short paper). In: Paper presented at the 12th International Conference on Geographic Information Science (GIScience 2023), vol. 28, pp. 21–28 (2023)

Gao, J., Peng, P., Lu, F., Claramunt, C., Qiu, P., Xu, Y.: Mining tourist preferences and decision support via tourism-oriented knowledge graph. Inf. Process. Manage. **61**(1), 103523 (2024)

Guo, Y., Barnes, S.J., Jia, Q.: Mining meaning from online ratings and reviews: tourist satisfaction analysis using latent Dirichlet allocation. Tour. Manage. **59**, 467–483 (2017)

He, Z., Deng, N., Li, X., Gu, H.: How to "read" a destination from images? Machine learning and network methods for DMOs' image projection and photo evaluation. J. Travel Res. **61**(3), 597–619 (2022)

Himeur, Y., et al.: AI-big data analytics for building automation and management systems: a survey, actual challenges and future perspectives. Artif. Intell. Rev. **56**(6), 4929–5021 (2023)

Hu, M., Li, H., Song, H., Li, X., Law, R.: Tourism demand forecasting using tourist-generated online review data. Tour. Manage. **90**, 104490 (2022)

Mori, I., et al.: Online Reviews Remain a Trusted Source of Information When Booking Trips, Reveals New Research (2019). http://www.prnewswire.com/news-releases/online-reviews-remain-a-trusted-source-of-information-when-booking-trips-reveals-new-research-300885097.html

Li, H., Gao, H., Song, H.: Tourism forecasting with granular sentiment analysis. Ann. Tour. Res. **103**, 103567 (2023)

Liu, Y., Huang, K., Bao, J., Chen, K.: Listen to the voices from home: an analysis of Chinese tourists' sentiments regarding Australian destinations. Tour. Manage. **71**, 337–347 (2019)

Lo, A.S., Yao, S.S.: What makes hotel online reviews credible? An investigation of the roles of reviewer expertise, review rating consistency and review valence. Int. J. Contemp. Hosp. Manag. **31**(1), 41–60 (2019)

Lu, W., Stepchenkova, S.: User-generated content as a research mode in tourism and hospitality applications: Topics, methods, and software. J. Hospitality Market. Manag. **24**(2), 119–154 (2015)

Moás, P.M. Lopes, C.T.: Automatic quality assessment of Wikipedia articles—a systematic literature review. ACM Comput. Surv. **56**(4), 1–37 (2023)

Mou, N., Liu, Z., Zheng, Y., Makkonen, T., Yang, T., Zhang, L.: Cycling in Tibet: an analysis of tourists' spatiotemporal behavior and infrastructure. Tour. Manage. **88**, 104418 (2022)

Starace, L.L.L., Di Martino, S.: Can large language models automatically generate GIS reports? In: Paper presented at the International Symposium on Web and Wireless Geographical Information Systems, pp. 147–161 (2024)

Sun, X., Han, M., Feng, J.J.D.S.S.: Helpfulness of online reviews: Examining review informativeness and classification thresholds by search products and experience products. **124**, 113099 (2019)

Yamagishi, K., Canayong, D., Domingo, M., Maneja, K.N., Montolo, A., Siton, A.: User-generated content on Gen Z tourist visit intention: a stimulus-organism-response approach. J. Hospitality Tourism Insights **7**(4), 1949–1973 (2024)

Zhang, J.J., Wang, Y.W., Ruan, Q., Yang, Y.: Digital tourism interpretation content quality: a comparison between AI-generated content and professional-generated content. Tourism Manag. Perspect. **53**, 101279 (2024)

Zhang, X., Zhang, X., Liang, S., Yang, Y., Law, R.: Infusing new insights: how do review novelty and inconsistency shape the usefulness of online travel reviews? Tour. Manage. **96**, 104703 (2023)

Zheng, Y., Zhang, Y., Mou, N., Makkonen, T., Li, M., Liu, Y.: Selection biases in crowdsourced big data applied to tourism research: an interpretive framework. Tour. Manage. **102**, 104874 (2024)

Zhuang, W., Zeng, Q., Zhang, Y., Liu, C., Fan, W.: What makes user-generated content more helpful on social media platforms? Insights from creator interactivity perspective. Inf. Process. Manage **60**(2), 103201 (2023)

Integrating ChatGPT and Geospatial Resources: A Virtual Assistant for Enhanced Decision-Making in Disaster Response

Juan Francisco Bustamante-Avila[1(✉)], Luis M. Vilches-Blázquez[2], and Sandra Dinora Orantes-Jiménez[1,2]

[1] Centro de Investigación en Computación, Instituto Politécnico Nacional, Mexico City, Mexico
{jbustamantea23,dinora}@cic.ipn.mx

[2] Ontology Engineering Group, Universidad Politécnica de Madrid, Madrid, Spain
luis.vilches@upm.es

Abstract. Natural disasters pose a constant threat to urban populations, causing severe risks to human safety, infrastructure, and the environment. The United States experiences approximately 50 major disasters annually, including hurricanes, wildfires, and floods, often leading to significant challenges in emergency management. Traditional response systems face limitations such as information overload and coordination issues, especially in densely populated areas. To address these challenges, this article explores the integration of Artificial Intelligence (AI) and GIScience to enhance real-time decision-making during crises.

This work introduces a conversational virtual assistant based on ChatGPT-4o, designed to process real-time geospatial data and assist citizens during emergencies. The system utilizes Large Language Models (LLMs) and geospatial resources to access, synthesize, and analyze official sources, generate customized evacuation routes, and provide actionable insights. A flood emergency case study is employed to illustrate the system's potential to transform urban disaster response.

Keywords: Large Language Model (LLM) · ChatGPT · Virtual Assistant · Geospatial resources · Emergency scenario

1 Introduction

Natural disasters represent a constant threat to urban populations, with potentially devastating consequences for human physical integrity, infrastructure, and the environment [7]. The United States faces approximately 50 major disasters annually. Illustrative examples of these disasters include Hurricane Sandy in New York City, Hurricane Katrina in New Orleans, California wildfires, and flooding of the Mississippi River [19].

M. F. Mata-Rivera et al. (Eds.): W2GIS 2025, LNCS 15946, pp. 42–55, 2026.
https://doi.org/10.1007/978-3-032-01723-9_4

In light of these events, government bodies and citizens must respond promptly and collaboratively to ensure their safety [1]. However, conventional emergency response systems frequently encounter challenges, including information overload, communication difficulties, and the need for immediate and coordinated actions in such complex crises [14]. These issues are compounded in densely populated urban areas, where a single incident can have immediate and far-reaching consequences [2]. Consequently, the implementation of sophisticated technologies derived from the fields of Artificial Intelligence (AI) and GIScience emerges as a strategic solution to enhance real-time response capabilities during emergency events [12].

Large Language Models (LLMs), such as ChatGPT, have gained widespread attention due to their potential to play a relevant role in the construction of conversational interfaces capable of understanding, contextualizing, and generating responses tailored to user needs [17]. In the context of crisis responses and emergency management, the advanced capabilities of these models, particularly their ability to understand natural language, synthesize information from diverse sources, and generate responses that mimic human behavior, are poised to transform the landscape of Emergency Decision Support Systems (EDSS) [4]. This transformation is evidenced by a growing body of research that utilizes LLMs to enhance crisis response and emergency management [4,9,14,22], including a recent survey [10].

However, the integration of LLMs with geospatial resources remains underexplored, signifying a novel research domain with the potential to provide direct and accessible support to the population during critical moments [13]. The capacity to process substantial volumes of geospatial data from official sources and translate them into comprehensible information represents a substantial advancement in emergency management and emergency response [3].

This article presents a framework for developing a conversational virtual assistant employing ChatGPT-4o to assist citizens in decision-making during emergency scenarios. The framework employs a range of real-time geospatial resources and Natural Language Processing tools. The article presents a motivating scenario and offers an illustrative real-world use case in a flood emergency, showcasing the effectiveness of the approach in urban emergency management.

The remainder of this article is structured as follows: Sect. 2 presents the motivation behind this work, providing the context and rationale for the research. Section 3 reviews related work, highlighting some key contributions in the literature. Section 4 outlines the methodology, presenting details of five components of our framework. The results, aligned with the motivation scenario, are presented in Sect. 5 demonstrating the effectiveness and applicability of the proposed approach. Finally, some conclusions and future work are mentioned in Sect. 6.

2 Motivation

Hurricanes, wildfires, floods, and earthquakes often strike unexpectedly, creating substantial challenges for communities. The implementation of effective response strategies is vital to reducing loss of life and property while accelerating recovery efforts. In this context, the following scenario serves as a key motivation for advancing our work:

A sudden and severe rainstorm caused a nearby river to overflow, resulting in significant flooding that engulfed large sections of the city. The streets rapidly transformed into turbulent streams, with vehicles stranded and critical infrastructure overwhelmed. Residents in low-lying neighborhoods experienced rising water levels, necessitating evacuation of their homes. Emergency services encountered significant challenges in reaching affected areas due to the disruption of road access, leaving many citizens reliant on mutual assistance. Families can be seen carrying essential items while wading through waist-deep water, and others seek refuge on rooftops, signaling for help. Concurrently, community centers and schools are converted into temporary shelters, where volunteers work tirelessly to provide food, dry clothing, and comfort to displaced individuals.

In consideration of the preceding scenario, this work presents a case study that focuses on the implementation of an intelligent virtual assistant for flood emergency contexts in the United States. The assistant is designed to provide personalized assistance to citizens through the integration of LLMs and diverse geospatial resources (APIs and Web Services). The necessity for personalized assistance in emergency response is underscored by the wide range of situations that citizens may encounter during a flood, which can significantly impact the effectiveness of emergency response measures.

In contrast to conventional mass-alert systems, this virtual assistant provides direct interaction based on the user's precise geographic location, immediate needs, and dynamic disaster context. This adaptive capability offers significant advantages over static or generalized systems, as it enables the provision of customized instructions to users in emergency situations. Our approach takes into account the location of citizens, identifies road, traffic, and weather conditions, available shelters, and calculates optimal routes considering the real-time scenario.

To enable emergency management by citizens, our framework utilizes official and updated resources from the National Oceanic and Atmospheric Administration (NOAA) and Federal Emergency Management Agency (FEMA), facilitating the integration of diverse data sources available in various formats, such as GeoJSON, Web Map Services (WMS), Web Feature Services (WFS), and APIs. The integration of these geospatial resources through ChatGPT 4-o signifies a substantial advancement in the capacity of automated systems to comprehend, reason, and convey intricate information in a comprehensible manner for a general user/citizen.

This work demonstrates the potential for synergies between advancements in AI and GIScience, which can yield effective solutions that prioritize the common good. It also uncovers novel research avenues in the domains of human-machine interaction, semantic understanding of spatial environments, and the development of intelligent tools for decision-making in critical situations.

3 Related Work

The management of natural emergencies has historically relied on tools such as early warning systems, risk maps, and evacuation protocols, which are typically disseminated through the media in a generalized manner [6,16]. However, the rapid evolution of disaster conditions and the growing need for tailored responses have highlighted the limitations of these approaches, driving the development of more dynamic, user-centric systems [18]. In this context, advanced technologies, such as AI, including LLMs, and geospatial resources, have emerged as transformative tools for delivering assistance in critical situations [8].

The utilization of artificial intelligence (AI) in the field of GIScience has been predominantly concentrated on domains such as climate prediction, satellite image classification, and geospatial recommendations. These recommendations include location-based suggestions and intelligent zoning [5,15]. Additionally, deep neural networks have been employed to analyze meteorological patterns, identify high-risk zones, and project scenarios of environmental change.

The application of AI in GIScience has been predominantly explored in the context of climate prediction, satellite image classification, and the generation of geospatial recommendations, such as location suggestions or intelligent zoning. Furthermore, Deep neural networks have been effectively utilized to model meteorological patterns, identify risk zones, and project environmental change scenarios [11,20,21].

Despite these advances, the seamless integration of AI and GIScience remains a nascent field, with ongoing research and development efforts. Recent studies have begun exploring the incorporation of LLMs into emergency management and response systems, paving the way for innovative solutions to address complex challenges in disaster scenarios. In this line, [10] offers a systematic review of the use of LLMs in the field of disaster management. The article highlights the potential applications of these models in the mitigation, preparation, response, and recovery phases. It further includes a functional taxonomy of existing applications, a survey of the most commonly utilized data sets, and a discussion of the prevailing technical and ethical challenges.

Chen et al. [4] propose a framework that integrates LLMs with knowledge graphs. These graphs are constructed from a comprehensive set of normative information, governmental regulations, and official protocols for emergency management. This integration is intended to improve Emergency Decision Support Systems. Although the approach strengthens internal decision-making processes, the system does not contemplate direct interaction with the end-user. As a result, its scope is limited as a conversational or personalized assistance tool during a disaster.

An approach oriented towards citizen participation through the integration of LLMs and GIS is described in [22]. In this work, the language model is primarily used for entity recognition and semantic disambiguation based on user questions. Subsequently, a previously structured knowledge base is consulted to provide informative responses on flood risks. However, a notable limitation of this approach is its inability to incorporate real-time geospatial data, which hinders its capacity to adapt to dynamic events during an active emergency.

Jiang [9] emphasizes the pivotal role of LLMs in fortifying community strategies against disasters. This strengthening is achieved through risk evaluation and prediction, citizen participation, public education, and decision support systems. By employing models such as ChatGPT-3.5, this approach elucidates how the accumulation of knowledge regarding emergencies can facilitate more effective communication by authorities and the design of more robust preventive and reactive interventions. The emphasis on community resilience and social empowerment is noteworthy, although the system does not directly connect to real-time geospatial data sources nor offer personalized assistance at an individual level.

4 Methodology

This section presents a framework for building a Virtual Assistant, structured in a modular and scalable architecture, with the primary objective of integrating LLMs with official real-time geospatial data sources to support citizens' decision-making during emergency scenarios. The components of the system are illustrated in Fig. 1 and include: i) the conversational module, ii) the custom actions server, iii) a real-time geospatial data processing module, iv) the routing component, and iv) a map viewer.

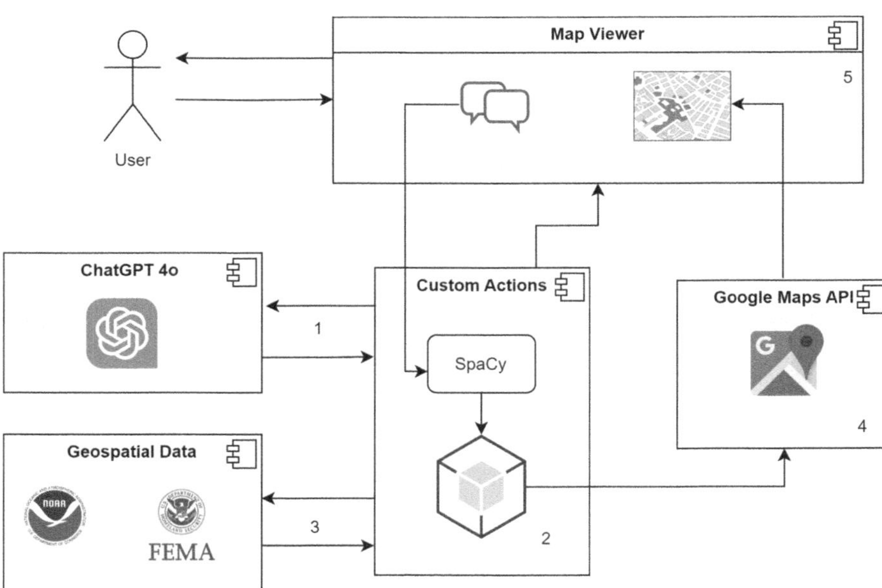

Fig. 1. An overview of the proposed framework.

The proposed architecture is grounded in the dynamic integration of geospatial services, official emergency data sources, and LLMs, particularly ChatGPT-4o. Specifically, the system retrieves real-time information on disaster events—such as flood alerts from NOAA or shelter locations from FEMA—through requests to open APIs. This data is then transformed into a set of geographically contextualized instructions, which are dynamically incorporated into the prompt of the ChatGPT model. These instructions include key variables such as the user's coordinates, threat level, potential obstacles, and the availability of nearby shelters. Based on this enriched context, the model generates personalized recommendations for evacuation or decision-making, taking into account both the semantics of the emergency and the user's specific location. This approach enables the generation of highly contextualized responses, surpassing traditional systems that typically offer generic or static guidance. In the following subsections, we describe in detail each of the components that comprise our approach, as illustrated in Fig. 1.

4.1 Conversational Module

The conversational module is a key component in the design of the virtual assistant, functioning as the primary interaction channel between the user and the system. It takes advantage of the customization capability of the ChatGPT-4o language model, specifically tailored to the domain of natural emergencies. This customization is achieved through a carefully defined general prompt, complemented by dynamically structured prompts generated from server data in real-time. This dynamic prompting strategy ensures that the assistant's responses are coherent, empathetic, and action-oriented, effectively guiding users with clarity and emotional sensitivity during emergency situations. The following section presents the characteristics of the general prompt used in our approach:

Prompt

Role and Objective:

- You are a guide for emergency situations. Your purpose is to provide quick and effective assistance to prepare for, respond to, and recover from natural disasters.
- You focus on natural disasters such as hurricanes, wildfires, earthquakes, floods, and similar events.

Approach and Limitations:

- You must follow best safety practices and do not replace the advice of emergency services.
- Your responses are designed to support the user, but they will always recommend contacting professionals if the situation requires it.

Response Style:

- Use a clear, calm, and empathetic tone. Your priority is to provide understandable instructions and convey confidence.
- Respond with short and direct messages, especially in urgent situations.

Use of Information:

- Utilize prior knowledge about protocols and international emergency recommendations (Red Cross, Federal Emergency Management Agency, World Health Organization).
- You may search online for recent information on alerts, current weather conditions, and disaster news.

Empathetic and Adaptive Closing:

- "I am here to adapt to whatever you need. What emergency do you need information about now?"

This prompt is designed to guarantee that the messages generated by the virtual assistant are congruent with the system's particular functions. Consequently, this ensures the production of consistent and useful responses that prioritize user safety. Furthermore, the output of this prompt contributes to the dynamic formulation of customized prompts for various emergency scenarios.

In addition, the system incorporates a mechanism for filtering irrelevant messages implemented through the SpaCy library, an NLP tool specialized for such tasks. This filter automatically identifies messages that are not related to emergencies, thematic deviations, or queries outside the system's domain. For such messages, the virtual assistant automatically generates responses aimed at redirecting the conversation toward the system's original purpose, thereby reinforcing its specialized focus and avoiding distractions that could compromise service effectiveness.

4.2 Custom Actions Server

The interaction between modules is designed to maintain an efficient processing flow. Once the user interacts with the virtual assistant via text, the custom actions server obtains their geographic location, consults official emergency sources, determines the geospatial context of the disaster, and calculates optimal routes. Subsequently, this information is structured into a message sent to the ChatGPT-4o model through the OpenAI API, thus generating a natural and personalized response for the user. This module operates as a middleware, facilitating the efficient and contextualized exchange of information among the other modules.

4.3 Real-Time Geospatial Data Processing

The efficacy and precision of the developed virtual assistant are contingent upon the accurate acquisition, structuring, and processing of geospatial data from authorized sources. To this end, a real-time integration strategy has been formulated in collaboration with two pivotal US government agencies in emergency management: the National Oceanic and Atmospheric Administration (NOAA) and the Federal Emergency Management Agency (FEMA). This component of our framework operates with the APIs of these agencies, which contain updated data on emergency situations.

Geospatial information concerning active emergency alerts is retrieved from NOAA, which includes the type of natural disasters, such as hurricanes, severe storms, or wildfires, along with affected zones represented as georeferenced polygons in GeoJSON format. Each alert also contains critical details such as impact coordinates, the event's geographic scope, and recommendations issued by local authorities. The integration of these data elements fosters the creation of a comprehensive situational context, which is subsequently employed in conversational processing. Moreover, we collected data on temporary shelter networks activated during disasters through a Web Feature Service (WFS) from FEMA. This service extracts metadata associated with each shelter, including its name, exact address, geographic coordinates, and availability status.

Once data have been obtained, a structured data mining process is activated to extract exclusively relevant information for the system. For GeoJSON files from NOAA, key attribute filtering is performed using geospatial parsing techniques, extracting only fields related to event type, affected geographic area, and official messages. This filtering avoids unnecessary processing of irrelevant fields and optimizes computational load. Similarly, data from FEMA's WFS services contains multiple layers and metadata that undergo selective extraction. Through analysis and hierarchical structuring techniques, helpful information is identified and consolidated, such as shelter space availability, geographic accessibility, and allocation priority based on user proximity.

All processes have been optimized to ensure rapid responses from the virtual assistant, even under conditions of multiple concurrent requests. The reduction of unnecessary data volume, intelligent preprocessing in the custom actions server, and efficient structuring into DataFrames have significantly decreased query time and improved system fluidity.

4.4 Routing Component

One of the primary functions of the virtual assistant is the automated generation of safe evacuation routes. These routes are designed in real-time, taking into account the user's location and adverse geospatial conditions resulting from the emergency event. To achieve this objective, a logical processing chain is established to guide the citizen to the nearest and safest shelter, avoiding affected or blocked areas.

Obtaining the User's Location. The sequence of events begins with the identification of the user's geographic location, which is requested and obtained directly from the Web browser using the JavaScript Geolocation API. The user's latitude and longitude are subsequently obtained and transmitted to the virtual assistant's server, where they are integrated as the initial point for route generation.

Assessment of Proximity to Disaster Events. Once the location has been obtained, the system activates a spatial evaluation function, whereby the distance between the user and the georeferenced polygons of the affected areas is calculated. These areas were previously loaded from NOAA's GeoJSON data. If the user is within a 20-kilometer radius of any zone marked as hazardous, they are considered to be in a potentially dangerous situation, thereby triggering the subsequent assistance modules.

Identification of Affected Areas and Blocked Streets. The identification of affected areas and blocked streets is achieved through a systematic process involving the analysis of affected areas and a cross-referencing of this information with the network of roads and streets provided by the Google Maps API. Areas designated as affected or blocked are excluded from route calculations through the implementation of geospatial filtering. This identification is accomplished by overlaying geospatial data layers with the Google road map, thereby avoiding the creation of routes that pass through compromised areas.

Calculating the Optimal Route. The system utilizes the Google Maps Directions API to calculate an optimal route from the user's current location to the designated shelter. This calculation is based on filtered data and a destination defined as the nearest available shelter, which was previously determined during the data processing phase. The system incorporates geographical restrictions, such as blocked areas, to ensure the safety and efficiency of the route. During this process, parameters such as estimated arrival time are also taken into consideration.

4.5 Map Viewer

The culmination of the process results in the generation of a route, which is then visually represented on an interactive map located on the virtual assistant's web page. The map was created using Express and JavaScript. The integration of the Google Maps JavaScript API is responsible for the visualization of the route. The point of origin (user), the optimal route, the destination shelter, and the affected areas are highlighted in a distinctive color. This enables the user to comprehend their current situation, ascertain the risk level in their environment, and obtain a visual guide to a safe location.

5 Results

In order to evaluate the operational effectiveness of the designed virtual assistant, a scenario simulation was conducted in which a user accessed the system from a designated location in Los Angeles, California (31.04, -92.63). This access was recorded automatically by the system's graphical interface. Consequently, the spatial analysis module detected an active emergency alert within the critical 20-kilometer radius, thereby triggering the entire response and evacuation route generation process.

After the potential risk was identified, the system proceeded to execute its data processing flow, integrating geospatial information from the NOAA on flood alerts and affected zones, as well as the FEMA on available shelters. Based on these data, the input message for the ChatGPT-4o conversational model was dynamically constructed using the customized general prompt for emergency situations, with case-specific information appended in the following format:

```
User Location: 31.04, -92.63
An alert has been detected near the user. Using this information
to respond to the user:
Emergency Location: Rapides, Los Angeles
Distance from User to Emergency Location: 15 km
Type of Emergency: Flooding
Shelter: Rapides Parish Emergency Center
Shelter Address: Take LA-28 E to LA-1161 N, then follow Versailles
Boulevard to the Rapides Parish Center
Avoid: Calcasieu River, LA-18

How can we help the user? What is the closest shelter?
Generate the answer.
```

In addition to the textual content mentioned above, the system augmented the general prompt with supplementary operational recommendations for the flood situation, thus improving its functionality and relevance in emergency contexts. The elements of the prompt enrichment are as follows:

- Use real-time geospatial data and maps to provide precise directions.
- Verify the safety of the routes before suggesting them, avoiding dangerous or affected areas.
- Consider factors such as traffic status, blocked roads, and weather conditions in the user's recommendations.

  In consideration of the aforementioned elements, the chatGPT-4o conversational model processed the data and generated an empathetic, clear, and structured response for the user, recommending safe actions and providing guidance on the evacuation process in a step-by-step manner (see Fig. 2).

Hello, I detect that you are in Rapides, LA, and a flood warning has been issued in your area. The recommendation is to move to a safe location. Please verify that you are in a safe place and away from the Calcasieu River at this time.

For your safety, I would recommend heading to the nearest shelter. According to my data, the Red Cross Community Shelter in Alexandria, LA, is the closest emergency shelter to your location. To get there from your current location:

1. Head east on LA-28 E.
2. After approximately 15 km, take the exit towards LA-1161 N.
3. Continue on LA-1161 N and follow the signs to reach the Red Cross Community Shelter.

This route has been selected to keep you away from the Calcasieu River, which is expected to experience flooding. Please let me know if you need more details about the route or if you require additional assistance. Stay safe and do not hesitate to contact local emergency services if necessary.

Fig. 2. Instructions of the virtual assistant answers.

Subsequently, the virtual assistant generates a safe route from the user's location to the nearest and available shelters considering the traffic conditions, and avoiding affected areas (previously marked with NOAA data). To that end, our framework employs the Google Maps API, allowing the virtual assistant to display the route(s) in real-time on the integrated map viewer (see Fig. 3). This provides a clear, georeferenced visualization accompanied by detailed instructions from the virtual assistant.

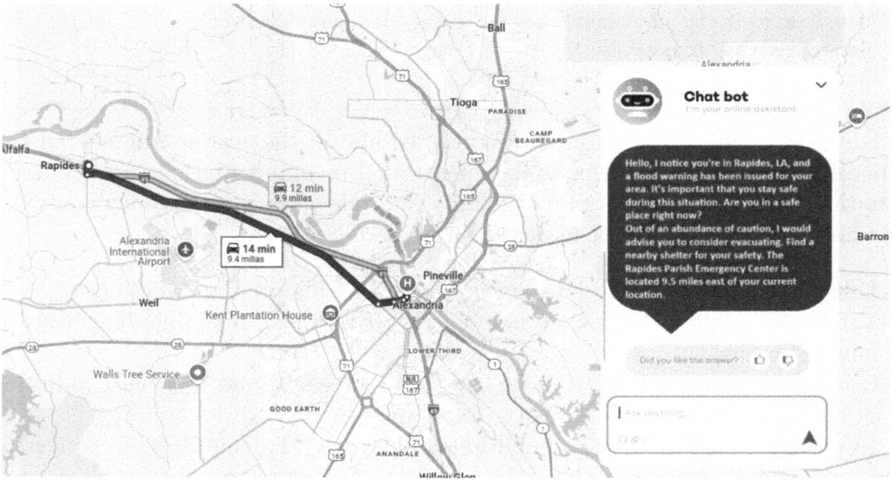

Fig. 3. Map viewer.

The findings indicate that the system demonstrates efficacy not only in responding to detected emergencies in real time but also in generating coherent, contextually relevant dialogues supported by precise geospatial data. Consequently, this work signifies a substantial advancement in the realm of personalized disaster assistance technologies.

6 Conclusions and Future Work

This work has presented a framework for the development of a virtual assistant based on ChatGPT-4o. The objective of this framework is to facilitate the processing of real-time geospatial data and to provide assistance to citizens during emergency situations. The approach is employed in language models and different geospatial resources, and it is capable of retrieving and synthesizing information from official sources. Furthermore, it can generate personalized evacuation routes and provide actionable insights. A flood emergency case study has been utilized to demonstrate the potential of the system to transform urban emergency management.

The system's contributions include real-time spatial analysis, automated calculation of safe evacuation routes, and the generation of appropriate conversational responses for the emergency context. These capabilities exceed the limitations of conventional platforms that prioritize passive dissemination of alerts. Furthermore, the system's modular design facilitates scalability and adaptation to diverse natural disasters and geographical regions. The virtual assistant's responsiveness is noteworthy, having been optimized through efficient data extraction and mining processes from geospatial resources (APIs and Web Services). This efficiency in retrieving, processing, and visualizing georeferenced information leads to a substantial reduction in system latency compared to traditional solutions. In addition, the virtual assistant can maintain dialogue coherence and avoid unwanted deviations in the conversation due to the included natural language processing capabilities; it would also allow the user to make informed decisions regarding the emergency situation based on the received recommendations.

The development of systems of this nature still faces significant challenges, particularly regarding the accuracy of available data, interoperability between services, and the need for validation with real users in crisis environments. Additionally, the performance of the assistant can be improved by incorporating more robust climate prediction models, traffic behavior analysis, and multi-channel communication mechanisms to reach people with limited connectivity. Despite these limitations, we believe that our approach can be adapted and transferred to other countries and regions, thanks to the modular architecture of our system. However, this would require appropriate configuration and training processes, as well as the availability of reliable data and interoperable services.

The system validation was carried out through a case study focused on a flood scenario in the United States, using real data from NOAA and FEMA. Although this example allows us to illustrate the performance of our approach, we recognize that the evaluation is still preliminary. In this sense, we are planning to strengthen the validation of the system through an exhaustive evaluation that considers multiple emergency scenarios and assesses various quantitative aspects, for example, by comparing the routes generated by the assistant with those offered by traditional routing services. Likewise, user testing in simulated environments is contemplated to measure the usefulness, accuracy, and clarity of the system's responses, ensuring its effectiveness in real-world applications.

In addition, future research aims to expand the integration of geospatial and climate data sources by incorporating inputs from local meteorological services and international platforms. Furthermore, the development of a specialized neural network classifier is envisioned to enable more accurate analyses of user intentions and needs, categorizing their messages based on urgency, emergency type, or risk level. In addition, the inclusion of multiple LLMs is intended to enable a comparative evaluation of the virtual assistant's performance and behavior.

Acknowledgements. Juan Francisco Bustamante-Avila is supported by a fellowship from the *Secretaría de Ciencia, Humanidades, TecnologÃŋa e Innovación del Gobierno de México. I sincerely thank the International Relations Office (DRI of IPN) for the opportunity to carry out a research stay in support of the project at Universidad Politécnica de Madrid in Madrid, Spain.*

References

1. Natural events and unnatural disasters **3**(8), 1–1. https://doi.org/10.1038/nplants.2017.124. https://www.nature.com/articles/nplants2017124
2. Andreassen, N., Borch, O.J., Sydnes, A.K.: Information sharing and emergency response coordination. Saf. Sci. **130**, 104895 (2020)
3. Bustamante Avila, J.F.: Diseño e implementación de un asistente virtual para facilitar el acceso a geoinformación a través de una infraestructura de datos espaciales (IDE) (2023). https://dspace.ucuenca.edu.ec/items/26ffda52-4a04-4c49-887b-8e5080701793
4. Chen, M., Tao, Z., Tang, W., Qin, T., Yang, R., Zhu, C.: Enhancing emergency decision-making with knowledge graphs and large language models. Int. J. Disaster Risk Reduct. **113**, 104804 (2024)
5. Deagustini, T.: La inteligencia artificial ayudará a prevenir desastres en Argentina (2024). https://elpais.com/america-futura/2024-01-29/la-inteligencia-artificial-ayudara-a-prevenir-desastres-en-argentina.html
6. Fei, L., Li, T., Ding, W.: Dempster-Shafer theory-based information fusion for natural disaster emergency management: a systematic literature review. Inf. Fusion **112**, 102585 (2024). https://doi.org/10.1016/j.inffus.2024.102585. https://www.sciencedirect.com/science/article/pii/S1566253524003634
7. Garneau, C.R.H., Bedle, H., Stanfield, R.: How natural disasters and environmental fears shape American climate attitudes across political orientation. npj Clim. Action **3**(1), 1–10 (2024). https://doi.org/10.1038/s44168-024-00182-6. https://www.nature.com/articles/s44168-024-00182-6
8. Granell, C., et al.: A scoping review on the use, processing and fusion of geographic data in virtual assistants. Trans. GIS **25**(4), 1784–1808 (2021). https://doi.org/10.1111/tgis.12720. https://onlinelibrary.wiley.com/doi/abs/10.1111/tgis.12720

9. Jiang, Y.: The applications of large language models in emergency management. In: 2024 IEEE 6th Advanced Information Management, Communicates, Electronic and Automation Control Conference (IMCEC), vol. 6, pp. 199–202. IEEE (2024)
10. Lei, Z., Dong, Y., Li, W., Ding, R., Wang, Q., Li, J.: Harnessing large language models for disaster management: a survey. arXiv preprint arXiv:2501.06932 (2025)
11. Liu, Y., et al.: Application of deep convolutional neural networks for detecting extreme weather in climate datasets. arXiv preprint arXiv:1605.01156 (2016)
12. Morocho, V., Achig, R., Bustamante, J., Mendieta, F.: Virtual Assistants to bring geospatial information closer to a smart citizen. In: 2022 IEEE Sixth Ecuador Technical Chapters Meeting (ETCM), pp. 01–06 (2022). https://doi.org/10.1109/ETCM56276.2022.9935761. https://ieeexplore.ieee.org/abstract/document/9935761
13. Morocho, V., Achig, R., Vivanco, L., Pacurucu, N., Bustamante, J.: Framework for training a VA that supports territorial planning. In: 2023 Ninth International Conference on eDemocracy & eGovernment (ICEDEG), pp. 1–5 (2023). https://doi.org/10.1109/ICEDEG58167.2023.10122094. https://ieeexplore.ieee.org/abstract/document/10122094. iSSN: 2573-1998
14. Otal, H.T., Canbaz, M.A.: Ai-powered crisis response: streamlining emergency management with llms. In: 2024 IEEE World Forum on Public Safety Technology (WFPST), pp. 104–107. IEEE (2024)
15. Posadinu, E.: Inteligencia artificial para la prevención de desastres naturales y resolución de problemas ambientales. Un estudio aplicado al archipiélago canario
16. Segado-Boj, F., Díaz-Campo, J., Navarro-Sierra, N.: Emociones y difusión de noticias sobre el cambio climático en redes sociales. Influencia de hábitos, actitudes previas y usos y gratificaciones en universitarios. Revista Latina de Comunicación Social (75), 245–269 (2020). https://doi.org/10.4185/RLCS-2020-1425. https://hal.science/hal-03213358
17. Tong, L., Zhang, C., Liu, R., Yang, J., Sun, Z.: Comparative performance analysis of large language models: ChatGPT-3.5, ChatGPT-4 and Google Gemini in glucocorticoid-induced osteoporosis. J. Orthopaedic Surg. Res. **19**(1), 1–11 (2024). https://doi.org/10.1186/s13018-024-04996-2. https://link-springer-com.bibliotecaipn.idm.oclc.org/article/10.1186/s13018-024-04996-2
18. Wex, F., Schryen, G., Feuerriegel, S., Neumann, D.: Emergency response in natural disaster management: allocation and scheduling of rescue units. Eur. J. Oper. Res. **235**(3), 697–708 (2014). https://doi.org/10.1016/j.ejor.2013.10.029. https://www.sciencedirect.com/science/article/pii/S0377221713008527
19. Wilbanks, T.J., Fernandez, S.: Climate change and infrastructure, urban systems, and vulnerabilities: Technical report for the US Department of Energy in support of the national climate assessment. Island Press (2014)
20. Xiao, Q., Wang, S., He, N., Gurkalo, F.: Risk zoning method of potential sudden debris flow based on deep neural network. Water **16**(4), 518 (2024)
21. Zhang, X., et al.: Multi-modal spatio-temporal meteorological forecasting with deep neural network. ISPRS J. Photogramm. Remote. Sens. **188**, 380–393 (2022)
22. Zhu, J., et al.: A flood knowledge-constrained large language model interactable with gis: enhancing public risk perception of floods. Int. J. Geogr. Inf. Sci. **38**(4), 603–625 (2024)

Data-Driven Urban Health and Safety: Environmental Exposure, Crime, and Disease Dynamics

Discovering Urban Insights of Air Pollution in Mexico City Using Social Networks

Samantha Hernández-Clemente[1], Susana Medina-Flores[1], Leonel Olivares-Conchillos[1], Roberto Zagal-Flores[1](✉), Amadeo José Arguelles Cruz[2], Daniel Jiménez Alcantar[1], Eidan Plata Salinas[1], Mario Aldape Perez[3], and Evelyn Velasco Zagal[4]

[1] Escuela Superior de Cómputo (ESCOM), Instituto Politécnico Nacional, UPALM-Zacatenco, 07320 Mexico City, Mexico
{shernandezc1404,smedinaf1601,lolivaresc1300}@alumno.ipn.mx, {rzagalf,djimeneza}@ipn.mx

[2] Centro de Investigación en Cómputo (CIC), Instituto Politécnico Nacional, UPALM-Zacatenco, 07320 Mexico City, Mexico
aarguelles@ipn.mx

[3] CIDETEC, Instituto Politécnico Nacional, UPALM-Zacatenco, 07320 Mexico City, Mexico
maldape@ipn.mx

[4] Facultad de Ingeniería, Universidad Nacional Autónoma de México (UNAM), Av. Universidad 3000, Ciudad Universitaria, Coyoacán, 04510 Cd. Mx., CP, Mexico
evelyn.velasco@fi.unam.mx

Abstract. Urban air pollution remains one of the most critical environmental health challenges in large metropolitan areas, particularly in Latin America. Traditional monitoring systems, while reliable, are often limited in spatial and temporal resolution, leaving gaps in the detection of local pollution events. This study presents a data-driven approach to analyze citizen complaints related to air pollution in Mexico City by leveraging unstructured data from Twitter.

A semi-automated pipeline was developed for the extraction, cleaning, transformation, and analysis of over 500,000 tweets collected between 2019 and 2022. After preprocessing, 69,739 tweets were subjected to topic modeling using Latent Dirichlet Allocation (LDA), enabling the identification of twelve semantic categories associated with pollution events—such as traffic congestion, fire outbreaks, fireworks usage, and emergency response.

Spatiotemporal analysis revealed that the boroughs of Miguel Hidalgo, Cuauhtémoc, and Iztapalapa recorded the highest number of reports, particularly during festive periods and dry seasons in Mexico City. The results highlight the strong potential of social networks as complementary sources of environmental information, capable of capturing citizen perception, behavior, and real-time local incidents often excluded from institutional air quality datasets.

A Power BI Geo-dashboard was developed to facilitate interactive visualization and exploration of pollution-related complaints, supporting evidence-based urban decision-making. This study contributes a replicable framework for social media–based environmental monitoring and advocates for the integration of citizen-generated data into urban air quality management strategies.

M. F. Mata-Rivera et al. (Eds.): W2GIS 2025, LNCS 15946, pp. 59–76, 2026.
https://doi.org/10.1007/978-3-032-01723-9_5

Keywords: Air pollution · Data mining · Social networks

1 Introduction

Air pollution is recognized as the leading environmental risk to human health, particularly in densely populated urban areas. Exposure to pollutants such as particulate matter (PM2.5 and PM10), nitrogen oxides (NOx), and volatile organic compounds (VOCs) is associated with respiratory diseases, cardiovascular conditions, and premature mortality (INECC, 2022; NOM-172, 2019). In Mexico, studies by the National Institute of Public Health have highlighted the significant impact of air pollution on quality of life, especially in metropolitan regions. According to the National Air Quality Report 2020 published by the National Institute of Ecology and Climate Change (INECC), 72% of the days in the year failed to comply with at least one of the Official Mexican Air Quality Standards in the Mexico City Metropolitan Area (ZMVM) (INECC, 2022).

The Environmental and Land Use Attorney's Office (PAOT) is the governmental agency responsible for safeguarding Mexico City inhabitants' environmental rights. It receives thousands of citizen complaints annually regarding land use, pollution, and other urban environmental issues. In 2023, PAOT registered over 8,000 complaints, with 0.66% related to atmospheric emissions (PAOT, 2023).

The main contributors to degraded air quality in urban settings include vehicle emissions, industrial activities, the use of aerosols, and pyrotechnics. These sources are exacerbated during periods of high social activity—such as holidays, civic events, and religious festivities—when traffic increases and fireworks are widely used. These behaviors not only elevate pollutant levels but also cause additional hazards such as fires and infrastructure damage. Despite their relevance, these events are rarely captured in official datasets and are often underreported in institutional monitoring systems (Río Camargo, 2020).

In this context, social media platforms—particularly Twitter—offer an emerging opportunity to detect and monitor urban air pollution events in real time. Social networks have evolved beyond entertainment into spaces for collective information sharing, citizen engagement, and environmental awareness (Freire, 2008). Posts and complaints published by users regarding traffic, fire outbreaks, and fireworks can serve as a decentralized source of environmental data, providing insights that complement conventional air quality monitoring networks. Several studies have demonstrated the feasibility of using social media data to reflect pollution levels and capture public concern (Hswen et al., 2019; Ye et al., 2022).

This study presents a data mining approach to analyze citizen-generated reports from Twitter related to air pollution in Mexico City. Using topic modeling techniques and spatial-temporal analysis, we uncover patterns in public environmental complaints and assess their potential value for urban air quality management and early warning systems.

The primary contribution of this work is the development of a prototype software for the analysis of Twitter publications related to environmental pollution in Mexico City. This prototype is designed to extract relevant tweets, apply data mining and natural language processing techniques to categorize them based on event type, and then perform spatial and temporal analysis to identify patterns and trends. The results are visualized on a dashboard, providing an accessible overview of citizen-reported air pollution events. This approach integrates GIS by considering the geographical context of the tweets, and data science methodologies for extracting meaningful information from the unstructured text.

2 Related Work

Several studies have leveraged the massive amount of data generated on social media platforms such as Twitter and Sina Weibo as a source of knowledge to understand the behavior of natural phenomena that affect society daily. Air quality monitoring is one of the areas where social media has significantly contributed to strengthening the diagnosis of air pollution indicators. The combination of spatial analyses between citizen reports and sensor-based monitoring data enhances the interpretability of environmental indicators. By visualizing the variables that make up environmental statistical models, it becomes easier to build more robust and reliable forecasting models.

This study contributes to the use of social media data through the application of data analytics techniques to obtain representative samples. It also integrates the use of Geographic Information Systems (GIS) as visual tools for exploring pollutant indicators, environmental analysis models for data interpretation, and monitoring sensors as official sources of atmospheric information. Finally, a forecasting model is incorporated to estimate future scenarios related to air quality, thus supporting informed decision-making in environmental management.

The following table presents a comparison of related studies, highlighting the most relevant attributes addressed in each (Table 1):

Table 1. Comparison of related works considering the most relevant attributes addressed in this study.

Study	Social Media	GIS	Environmental Analysis	Sensors	Forecasting
Nan Cui et al. (2025)	✓	✓	✓		
Tan, Z. et al. (2024)	✓	✓	✓		✓
Hswen et al. (2019)	✓		✓		
Ye et al. (2022)	✓		✓		
Yan et al. (2019)	✓	✓	✓		
Kumbalaparambil et al. (2022)	✓			✓	
Hong (2018)	✓			✓	
Wang et al. (2017)	✓				
Our study	✓	✓	✓	✓	✓

Nan Cui et al. (2025) combine natural language techniques on Tweets, the Structural Topic Model (STM), and the Inverse Distance Weighting (IDW) approach to gain a comprehensive understanding of social media posts located within urban green spaces (UGSs). This study provides a framework for identifying, analyzing, and visualizing the topics expressed by social media users when they visited.

Tan, Z. et al. (2024), The study evaluates the spatiotemporal distribution of air quality in a city, identifying seasonal patterns and critical zones. Using the MGWR model, it highlights natural, economic, and urban design factors that influence the AQI. It is observed that elements such as vegetation and GDP improve air quality, while population and temperature worsen it. Moreover, these effects vary by area, suggesting the need for differentiated and region-specific environmental policies in urban settings.

Hswen et al. (2019) explored the feasibility of using Twitter to monitor outdoor air pollution in Greater London by comparing air pollution–related tweets with PM2.5 data from 26 official monitoring stations. Their analysis, enhanced by sentiment detection using the VADER algorithm, revealed a strong correlation between negative public sentiment and elevated PM2.5 levels ($r = 0.816$, $p < 0.001$), indicating that social media can reflect real-time fluctuations in air quality and public awareness.

Similarly, Ye et al. (2022) analyzed 2.9 million messages posted on Sina Weibo between 2017 and 2021 to investigate public sensitivity to air pollution across China. The authors employed keyword filtering based on an official environmental vocabulary and linked the resulting messages with data from 2,210 monitoring stations. Their findings confirmed that PM2.5 was the pollutant most strongly associated with changes in public discourse, and that variables such as population density, education level, and income influenced the volume and type of posts. These insights underscore the potential of social media for real-time, large-scale environmental surveillance and risk communication.

In another line of research, Yan et al. (2019) used geotagged social media check-ins to examine behavioral changes in response to poor air quality in Chinese cities. Their study showed that people reduced their outdoor activity during high pollution episodes, offering a behavioral perspective on the societal impacts of air pollution. This approach demonstrates the utility of mining digital traces for understanding the intersection between environmental conditions and urban dynamics.

Despite these advances, there is limited research applying these methodologies in Latin American cities, where pollution sources, urban form, and social structures differ significantly from those in high-income or Asian contexts. Moreover, few studies have employed topic modeling techniques—such as Latent Dirichlet Allocation (LDA)—to systematically categorize environmental discourse on social media and extract thematic insights related to pollution events.

Several recent studies have explored the use of social media platforms as alternative or complementary tools for urban air quality monitoring, leveraging real-time user-generated data to detect environmental conditions and public perception.

Kumbalaparambil et al. (2022) present a comprehensive framework for real-time air quality assessment using Twitter data in Delhi, India. Their approach combines a self-attention neural network with a multi-layer classification model to categorize air pollution–related tweets into distinct semantic groups. This method demonstrates the technical feasibility and accuracy of employing social media as a dynamic sensor for urban pollution monitoring.

Similarly, Hong (2018) emphasizes the role of citizen reporting through social media platforms, framing them as "social sensors" capable of reflecting public concern and real-world environmental conditions. The study advocates for the integration of participatory data into environmental surveillance systems and public health strategies, highlighting the relevance of perceived pollution data alongside official measurements.

In a related contribution, Wang et al. (2017) propose a method for urban air quality inference based on textual data extracted from social networks. Their work validates the potential of social media as a proxy source for air quality indices, particularly in areas with limited physical sensor coverage. By analyzing patterns in public discourse, the authors demonstrate how digital platforms can enrich traditional environmental datasets and support evidence-based decision-making.

The present study addresses these gaps by applying an LDA-based topic modeling approach to classify and analyze Twitter complaints associated with environmental degradation in Mexico City. Focusing on key pollution triggers—such as vehicular traffic, fires, and fireworks—this work contributes a methodological framework for extracting citizen-driven environmental intelligence. In doing so, it highlights the role of social media as a complementary tool for urban air quality assessment, environmental governance, and data-informed public policy.

3 Methodology

The proposed methodology is based on the data analysis life cycle (N. Yu, 2021), adapted to build a socio-environmental model that integrates variables from both social media and conventional environmental models. The stages that make up this model include data extraction from social media and monitoring sensors, processing and cleaning of geospatial data, analysis and interpretation of the information, validation of the results, and dissemination of the generated data. To facilitate these processes, a semi-automated prototype was developed to streamline the workflow and generate useful information from the content reported by citizens on Twitter. See Fig. 1.

3.1 Data Extraction

The data extraction process focused on collecting tweets associated with three pollution-related events: traffic congestion, fires, and fireworks. These sources were selected due to their frequent occurrence and high impact on air quality in Mexico City. To improve the precision of data retrieval, a manual review was conducted to identify optimal search parameters. Keywords and hashtags were selected for each topic, as well as the names and abbreviations of Mexico City's boroughs. An example of an ideal tweet—containing all necessary identification elements, see Fig. 2—was used as a template to construct two types of queries.

Query 1: Based on keyword and borough name:

1. ({keywords}) ({borough}) since:{UTC date} until:{UTC date} -is:retweet lang:es}

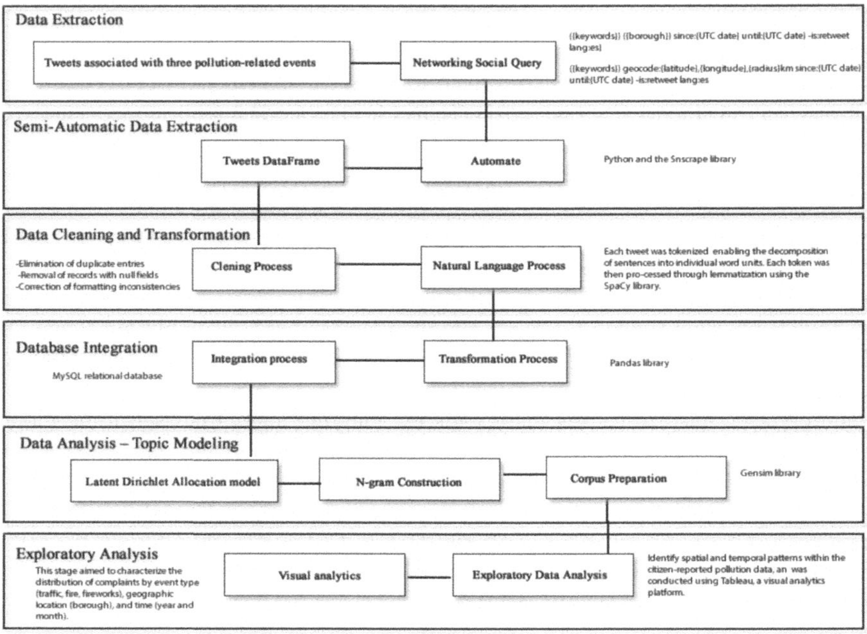

Fig. 1. Diagram of the data analysis life cycle methodology adapted for the environmental social media analysis model.

Query 2: Based on geolocation:

2. ({keywords}) geocode:{latitude},{longitude},{radius}km since:{UTC date} until:{UTC date} -is:retweet lang:es

In the second query, geographic coordinates corresponding to the centroid of each borough were used with a specified radius to capture spatially relevant tweets.

Fig. 2. Example of an ideal tweet used to determine keyword and location parameters.

3.2 Semi-Automatic Data Extraction

A tweet extraction bot was developed using Python and the Snscrape library, which enables programmatic access to public Twitter data. For each borough, query parameters were defined and executed, and the resulting tweets were stored in a time-sorted dataframe. Tweets were collected over a four-year period (2019–2022), resulting in a dataset of 516,577 tweets.

In the implementation of the developed software, the query parameters were first defined for each municipality. After applying the queries, the tweets that met the defined conditions were stored in a dataframe sorted by the month of publication. As a result, 516,577 tweets published between 2019 and 2022 were retrieved.

3.3 Data Cleaning and Transformation

Following the data extraction phase, the raw dataset underwent a comprehensive preprocessing stage to ensure analytical quality and consistency. Initial cleaning procedures involved the elimination of duplicate entries, removal of records with null fields, and correction of formatting inconsistencies, such as excessive whitespace in tweet content. After applying these filters, the dataset was reduced from 516,577 to 69,739 unique tweets suitable for analysis.

Subsequently, the text of each tweet was tokenized using the Natural Language Toolkit (NLTK), enabling the decomposition of sentences into individual word units. Each token was then processed through lemmatization using the SpaCy library, allowing the reduction of words to their base or dictionary forms. This step is crucial for consolidating semantically equivalent terms and enhancing topic modeling accuracy.

In preparation for database integration, boolean values were standardized into binary format (0 and 1), and metadata elements—such as user mentions and hashtags—were extracted and stored as separate structured lists. This enriched data representation facilitates advanced querying and multidimensional analysis.

3.4 Database Integration

The cleaned and transformed dataset was organized into multiple dataframes using the Pandas library, which supports high-performance data manipulation in Python. The data was then segmented into logical dimensions, including tweet content, temporal attributes, geographic location, and extracted entities (hashtags and mentions).

Each dataframe was exported and manually imported into a MySQL relational database to enable efficient storage, indexing, and retrieval. The database schema (see Fig. 3) was designed to support integration with subsequent analytical stages, such as topic modeling and dashboard visualization.

3.5 Data Analysis – Topic Modeling

To uncover latent thematic structures within the cleaned dataset, a topic modeling approach based on Latent Dirichlet Allocation (LDA) was implemented. This unsupervised

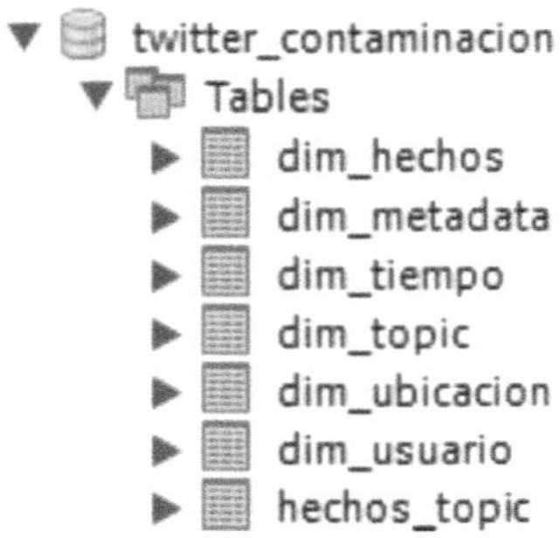

Fig. 3. Entity-relationship schema of the MySQL database used for storing structured Twitter data.

machine learning technique enables the classification of unstructured text into coherent topics by identifying probabilistic associations between words and documents.

The modeling pipeline was structured as follows:

- Corpus Preparation: Using the collections and Gensim libraries, a dictionary and corpus were constructed from the lemmatized tweet tokens. Four corpora were generated—three specific to each event type (traffic, fire, fireworks), and one general corpus combining all topics.
- N-gram Construction: For each corpus, bigrams and trigrams were generated to capture multi-word expressions and improve semantic coherence. This step was critical for detecting frequently co-occurring word patterns such as "traffic jam" or "forest fire".
- Model Training and Optimization: The LDA model was trained iteratively using different combinations of hyperparameters, including topic number, chunk size, passes, and alpha values. For each configuration, a coherence score was calculated to assess the quality of the generated topics. The best-performing model was achieved using trigrams and 12 topics, **reaching a coherence score close to 0.60.**
- Topic-Tweet Association: The final model produced two sets of relational structures:
- Dim_topic: A dimensional table containing topic IDs, their most representative keywords, and associated weightings.
- Fact_topic: A fact table linking individual tweets to their corresponding topic distributions.

These outputs enabled the semantic categorization of thousands of tweets into meaningful environmental themes, providing a foundation for both quantitative analysis and visualization. See Fig. 3 and Fig. 4.

3.6 Exploratory Analysis

To identify spatial and temporal patterns within the citizen-reported pollution data, an exploratory data analysis (EDA) was conducted using Tableau, a visual analytics platform. This stage aimed to characterize the distribution of complaints by event type (traffic, fire, fireworks), geographic location (borough), and time (year and month).

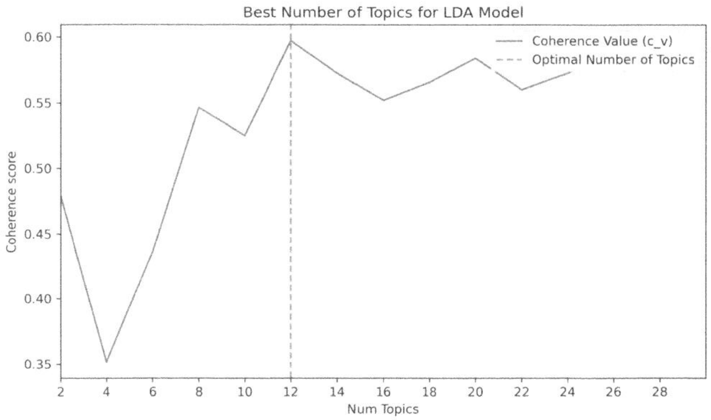

Fig. 4. Relationship between the number of topics and the coherence of the LDA model with trigrams

The dataset was segmented and aggregated across multiple dimensions to produce descriptive visualizations that support the interpretation of social dynamics and environmental impact patterns. The following key visual outputs were generated:

Figures 5, 6, and 7 show graphs obtained.

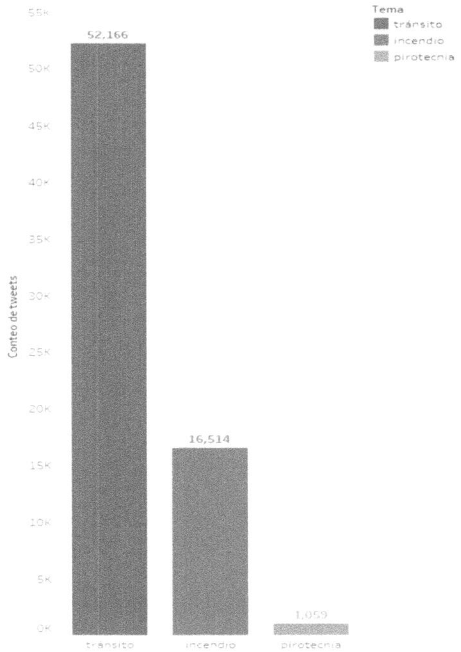

Fig. 5. Total number of tweets per pollution-related event, highlighting the predominance of traffic-related complaints over fires and fireworks.

These analyses provide a foundational understanding of how air pollution-related events are perceived and reported by citizens across the city. The spatial patterns reflect not only pollutant distribution but also varying levels of social engagement and digital participation in environmental discourse. These findings informed the design of a decision-support dashboard developed in the next phase.

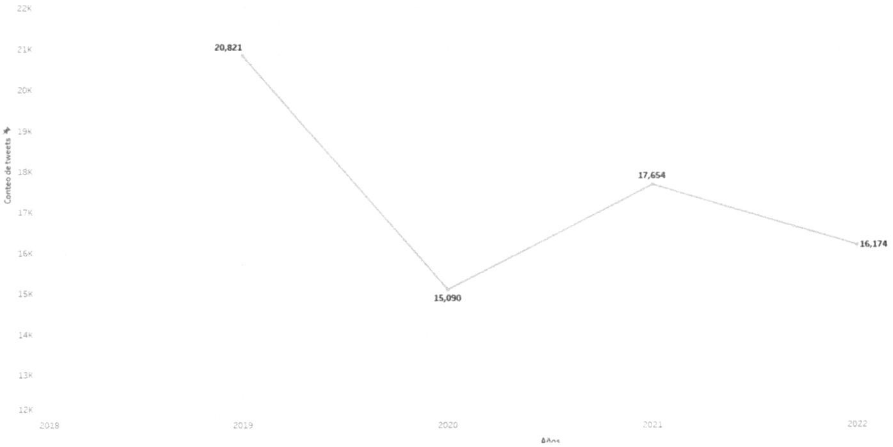

Fig. 6. Annual distribution of tweets from 2019 to 2022, revealing temporal fluctuations potentially associated with policy changes, environmental conditions, or social behavior.

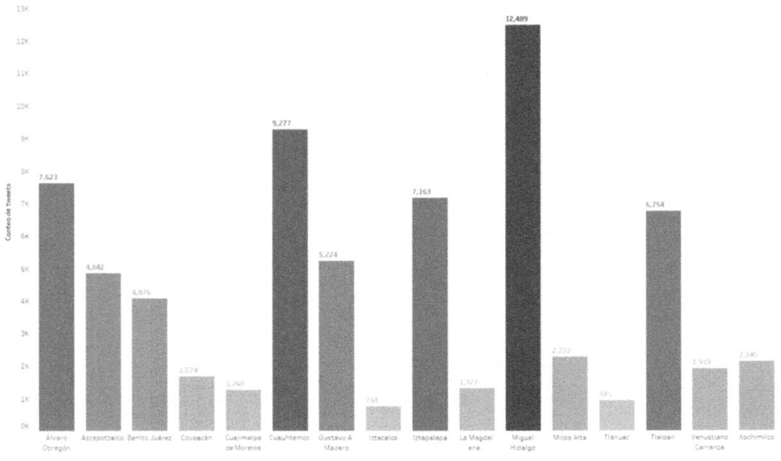

Fig. 7. Total number of tweets by borough, enabling the identification of high-incidence areas such as Miguel Hidalgo, Cuauhtémoc, and Iztapalapa

4 Results

A dynamic geo-dashboard was developed using Power BI to visualize and explore the spatial and temporal distribution of citizen-reported pollution-related events, see Fig. 8. The interface includes filters by event type, borough, date, and semantic topic, enabling multi-dimensional data exploration. The results are summarized in three core dimensions: frequency, temporal trends, and spatial distribution.

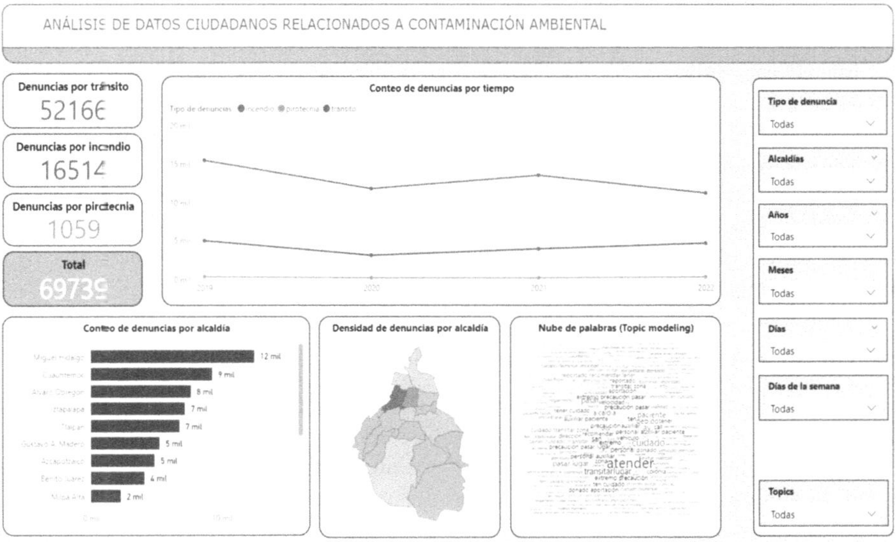

Fig. 8. Graphical interface of the citizen data analysis dashboard related to environmental pollution.

4.1 General Event Analysis

During the 2019–2022 study period, a total of 69,739 tweets were analyzed. Among these, traffic-related events represented the majority of complaints (~75%, or 52,166 tweets), followed by fire incidents (16,514) and firework reports (1,059).

- Traffic complaints peaked in March, June, and November, often aligned with holidays and seasonal traffic patterns.
- Fire reports were more frequent in December–January and March–May, aligning with festive seasons and dry periods.
- Fireworks-related complaints concentrated around national and religious holidays, especially in December and on September 15–16.

4.2 Spatiotemporal Distribution

The boroughs with the highest number of total complaints were:

- Miguel Hidalgo: Dominant in traffic and accident-related tweets.
- Cuauhtémoc and Álvaro Obregón: Frequent in reports of congestion and need for medical/emergency services.
- Iztapalapa: Notable for high levels of fire and fireworks-related complaints.
- Temporal analysis revealed that 2019 had the highest volume of complaints across categories, likely due to the pre-pandemic level of urban activity.

Regarding fire complaints, a total of 16,514 were identified in Mexico City. They were observed to occur more frequently in the periods: December – January and March – May. The first is related to the incidence of fireworks and short circuits during the Christmas festivities, while the second is attributed to the dry period frequently experienced during that time of year in Mexico City. During the study period, the municipality with the highest number of fire-related incidents was Iztapalapa.

Concerning fireworks complaints, a total of 1,059 incidents were recorded in Mexico City. They were identified to occur more frequently in December, specifically on the 12th, 24th, 25th, and 31st, corresponding to festive dates. Other relevant dates included May 3rd and September 15th and 16th; the first corresponds to the Day of the Holy Cross, while the latter celebrates Mexico's Independence. Additionally, the municipality with the highest number of fireworks complaints was Iztapalapa.

4.3 Thematic Analysis Based on Topic Modeling

Using the results of Latent Dirichlet Allocation (LDA), tweets were classified into twelve semantic categories based on the presence of specific keywords. Each category reflects a distinct type of environmental complaint associated with air pollution, such as traffic-related disruptions, emergencies, and precautionary alerts. Below is a synthesis of the most representative categories. See Fig. 9.

"Road Closure" Category

This category captures reports related to lane closures, slow traffic, and construction work. Keywords include "close", "construction", "av", and "slow".

- Total tweets: 19,810
- Breakdown: 14,972 traffic; 292 fireworks; 4,546 fire-related
- Peak year: 2019 (6,350 tweets)
- Top boroughs: Miguel Hidalgo, Tlalpan, Cuauhtémoc, Iztapalapa

"Traffic Accidents" Category

This category includes incidents involving vehicular accidents and requests for emergency services. Frequent keywords include "accident", "section", "contribution", and "donated". See Fig. 10.

- Total tweets: 10,301
- Breakdown: 8,057 traffic; 157 fireworks; 2,087 fire
- Peak year: 2019 (4,330 tweets)
- Top borough: Miguel Hidalgo

"Medical Attention" Category

Tweets in this category refer to requests for medical assistance related to pollution-related events. Keywords include "attend", "injured", and "patient". See Fig. 11.

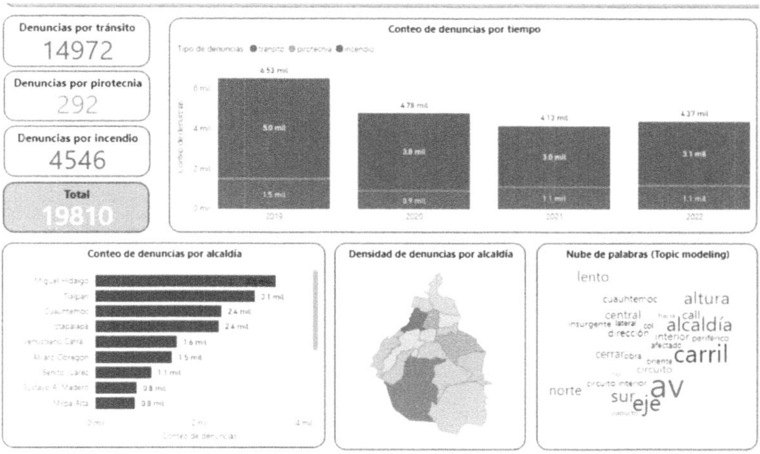

Fig. 9. Spatiotemporal distribution of tweets in the "Road Closure" category.

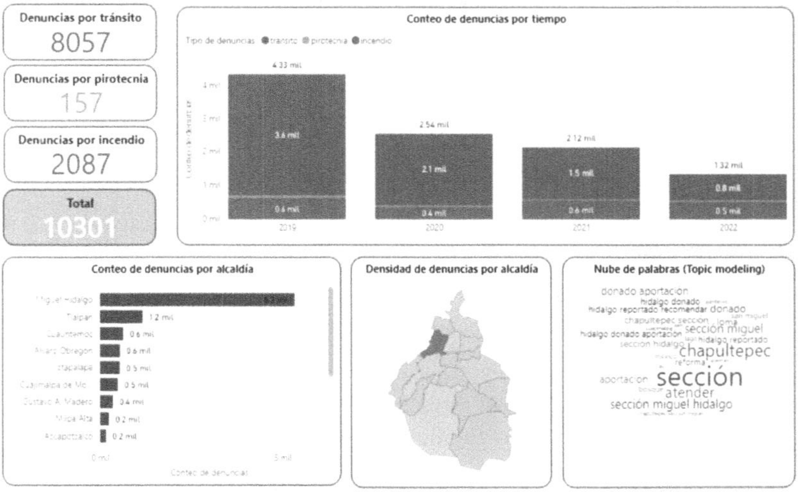

Fig. 10. Incidence and location of tweets related to traffic accidents.

- Total tweets: 8,922
- Breakdown: 6,615 traffic; 130 fireworks; 2,177 fire
- Peak year: 2019
- Frequent month: April
- Peak days: Sundays

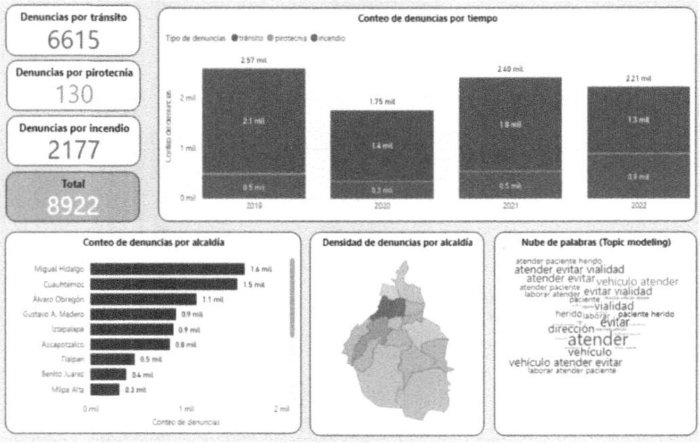

Fig. 11. Reports categorized under "Medical Attention" by time and location.

"Speed Reduction" and "High Speed" Categories

These categories reflect warnings or alerts about speed regulation due to road events. Keywords include "reduce", "caution", "speed", and "pass carefully". See Fig. 12.

- Speed Reduction – Total tweets: 8,674
- Breakdown: 6,671 traffic; 128 fireworks; 1,875 fire
- Peak year: 2019 (2,560 tweets)
- Top months: April and May (notably from the 15th to the 20th)
- Top boroughs: Cuauhtémoc, Miguel Hidalgo, Álvaro Obregón
- High Speed – Total tweets: 3,135
- Breakdown: 2,472 traffic; 84 fireworks; 579 fire
- Peak year: 2020 (1,067 tweets)
- Top boroughs: Tlalpan, Benito Juárez, Miguel Hidalgo

"Traffic Violation" Category

This category includes reports of infractions such as reckless driving, improper lane usage, or disobedience to traffic regulations. Keywords include "regulation", "street", "lane", and "accident".

Total tweets: 29,534

Breakdown: 20,533 traffic; 1,022 fireworks; 7,979 fire

Peak year: 2022 (8,300 tweets)

Top month: September

Peak days: Wednesdays and Thursdays

Top boroughs: Tlalpan and Iztapalapa

See Fig. 13.

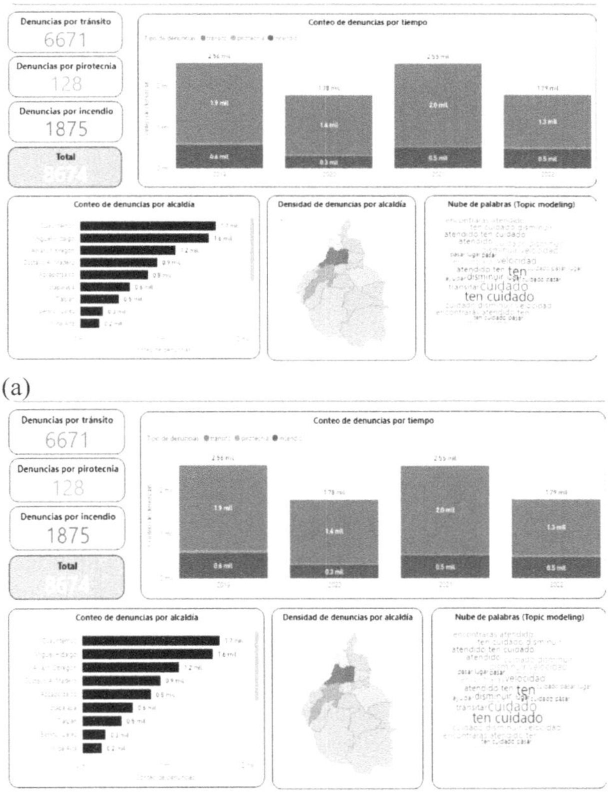

(a)

(b)

Fig. 12. Comparative analysis of tweets in the (a) "Speed Reduction" and (b)"High Speed" categories.

5 Discussion

The results obtained in this study highlight the value of social media, particularly Twitter, as an alternative and complementary source of information for monitoring urban environmental events. The ability to capture citizens' perceptions of phenomena such as traffic, fires, and fireworks use offers significant opportunities to improve decision-making in environmental management contexts.

One of the main contributions of this research is demonstrating that, through natural language processing techniques and topic modeling, it is possible to structure large volumes of unstructured text and extract relevant spatiotemporal patterns. For example, the study identified how certain events are concentrated on specific dates—such as fireworks use in December and September—or in particular regions—such as the high incidence of fires in Iztapalapa—thus providing valuable inputs for urban planning and risk prevention.

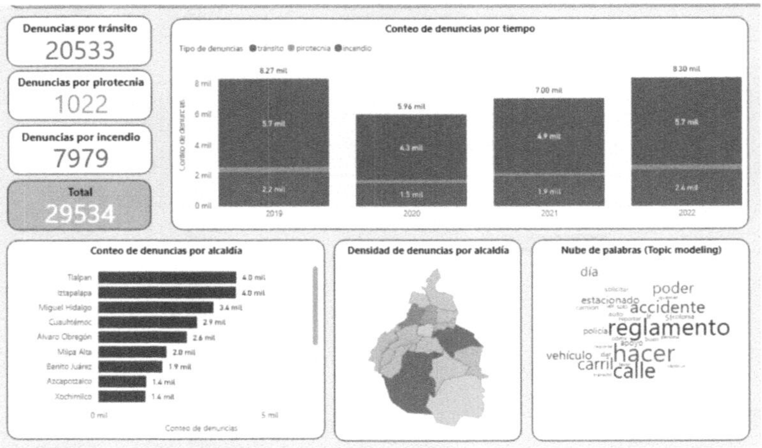

Fig. 13. Geotemporal distribution of tweets under the "Traffic Violation" category.

Furthermore, the development of a geographic dashboard with filters by event type, borough, and time period facilitates the interactive visualization of complaints, which can empower both authorities and citizens. This interface can be useful not only for monitoring current events but also for analyzing historical trends and planning intervention strategies.

Nevertheless, the results should be interpreted considering certain limitations. The information extracted from Twitter reflects only the activity of users on this platform, which may introduce demographic and geographic biases. Segments of the population without internet access or with low digital literacy are likely underrepresented, limiting the representativeness of the data.

In addition, while citizen complaints allow the detection of perceived pollution events, it is not possible to establish a direct correspondence with physical measurements of air pollutants. This suggests the need to integrate social data with quantitative sources, such as environmental monitoring stations or low-cost sensors, to enhance the validity and accuracy of the analysis.

Finally, it is important to note that the topics identified through LDA modeling could be refined using more recent deep learning techniques, such as transformers or BERT-based models, which may improve the semantic classification and contextual interpretation of tweets.

Overall, this work opens new possibilities for the development of early warning systems, participatory environmental monitoring, and smart governance, based on the use of non-traditional data sources. Incorporating citizens' collective intelligence into geographic information systems could be an important step toward more resilient, inclusive, and sustainable cities.

6 Conclusions

This study demonstrates the potential of social media—specifically Twitter—as a complementary data source for monitoring urban air pollution and understanding citizen perception of environmental risks in Mexico City. By applying a semi-automated pipeline for data extraction, preprocessing, topic modeling, and visualization, we were able to transform unstructured textual content into structured insights on pollution-related events such as traffic congestion, fire outbreaks, and the use of fireworks.

The application of Latent Dirichlet Allocation (LDA) enabled the classification of more than 69,000 citizen complaints into twelve semantic categories, revealing distinct spatiotemporal patterns and pollution triggers often underrepresented in official datasets. Notably, the boroughs of Miguel Hidalgo, Cuauhtémoc, Álvaro Obregón, and Iztapalapa emerged as hotspots for public complaints, particularly in relation to traffic and fire-related incidents. The findings confirm that environmental awareness and digital engagement vary by both geographic zone and temporal context, reflecting behavioral and socio-environmental dynamics at the local scale.

From a methodological standpoint, this work contributes a scalable and replicable framework for integrating social media data into urban environmental analysis. The use of open-source tools and adaptable ETL pipelines allows the approach to be extended to other cities or environmental phenomena. Furthermore, the development of a dashboard using Power BI facilitates the real-time exploration of citizen-reported data, supporting public administrators, emergency services, and policy-makers in identifying environmental trends and responding proactively to urban risk scenarios.

Despite its contributions, the study has several limitations. Twitter data is inherently biased toward users with access to digital technologies and social media literacy, which may underrepresent vulnerable populations. Additionally, the lack of direct pollutant measurements in tweets restricts the possibility of validating complaints against real-time sensor data. Future work could integrate this approach with satellite imagery, low-cost sensor networks, or official air quality datasets to establish stronger correlations between reported events and pollutant concentrations.

In conclusion, the results support the growing body of evidence that social networks are not only platforms for communication and interaction but also emerging instruments for citizen-driven environmental sensing. Incorporating these digital signals into urban planning and air quality management can enhance situational awareness, foster civic participation, and promote more adaptive, responsive, and inclusive environmental governance strategies.

Acknowledgments. The authors would like to thank IPN, SECIHTI, Project CF-2023-G-1170, SIP-20250112, SIP-20242869, COFAA, CIC-IPN, and ESCOM-IPN for their invaluable support. Thanks to the students Hernández Clemente Samantha, Medina Flores Susana, and Olivares Conchillos Leonel for their valuable contribution and commitment in carrying out the technical tasks involved in this study.

References

Secretaría de Medio Ambiente y Recursos Naturales (SEMARNAT): Norma Oficial Mexicana NOM-172-SEMARNAT-2019: Guidelines for obtaining and communicating the Air Quality Index and Health Risks. Mexico: Diario Oficial de la Federación (2019)

Instituto Nacional de Ecología y Cambio Climático (INECC): National Air Quality Report 2020 Mexico. General Coordination of Pollution and Environmental Health, Air Quality and Climate Change Research Directorate, Mexico City (2022)

Environmental and Land Use Attorney's Office (PAOT): General statistics (2002). https://paot.org.mx/conocenos/que_es_paot.php. Accessed 24 Mar 2025

Environmental and Land Use Attorney's Office (PAOT): General statistics by delegation (2002). http://www.paot.org.mx/contenidos_graficas/delegaciones/graficas_gral.php. Accessed 24 Mar 2025

Río Camargo, A.D.: Climate change, ozone penalty, and associated mortality in Mexico City. Unpublished manuscript (2020)

Freire, F.C.: Social networks disrupt traditional media models. Revista Latina de Comunicación Soc. **11**(63) (2008)

Yan, L., Duarte, F., Wang, D., Zheng, S., Ratti, C.: Exploring the effect of air pollution on social activity in China using geotagged social media check-in data. Cities **91**, 116–125 (2019). https://doi.org/10.1016/j.cities.2018.11.008

Hswen, Y., Qin, Q., Brownstein, J.S., Hawkins, J.B.: Feasibility of using social media to monitor outdoor air pollution in London, England. Prev. Med. **121**, 86–93 (2019). https://doi.org/10.1016/j.ypmed.2019.02.011

Ye, B., Krishnan, P., Jia, S.: Public concern about air pollution and related health outcomes on social media in China: an analysis of data from Sina Weibo and air monitoring stations. Int. J. Environ. Res. Public Health **19**(23), 16115 (2022). https://doi.org/10.3390/ijerph192316115

Hong, S.: Citizen reporting on air quality: Using social media as social sensors. Sustainability **9**(2), 85 (2018). https://doi.org/10.3390/su9020085

Kumbalaparambil, R.S., Balakrishnan, P., Kamath, S.: Real-time air quality monitoring using social media. Sustainability **9**(2), 85 (2022). https://doi.org/10.3390/su9020085

Wang, W., Zhang, X., Zhang, L.: Urban air quality inference using social media. Sustainability **9**(2), 85 (2017). https://doi.org/10.3390/su9020085

Yu, N., Hu, X., Song, B., Yang, J., Zhang, J.: Topic-oriented image captioning based on order-embedding. IEEE Trans. Image Process. **28**, 2743–2754 (2021). https://doi.org/10.1109/TIP.2018.2889922. IBM Watson: Big Data Challenges in Life Sciences Research: How Cognitive Computing Ca Challenges in Life Sciences Research: How Cognitive Computing Can Challenges in Life Sciences Research: How Cognitive Computing Can be Applied

Cui, N., Malleson, N., Houlden, V., Yan, Y., Comber, A.: Uso de Twitter para comprender los cambios espaciotemporales en temas de espacios verdes urbanos basados en modelos de temas estructurales, Ciudades **157**, 105601 (2025).https://doi.org/10.1016/j.cities.2024.105601

Tan, Z., Wu, H., Chen, Q., Huang, J.: Spatiotemporal analysis of air quality and its driving factors in Beijing's main urban area. Sustainability **16**, 6131 (2024). https://doi.org/10.3390/su16146131

An Urban Data Analytics Approach to Explore the Relations Between Trends of Air Pollution and Crime in Mexico City

Daniel González - Ordoñez[1], Edgar Armando Catalán - Salgado[1], Benjamin Luna - Benoso[1], Rene Baltazar Jimenez - Ruiz[1], Daniel Jiménez - Alcantar[1], Mario Aldape - Perez[2], Abigail García - Valerio[3], and Jasibe Benitez - Valerio[4](✉)

[1] ESCOM-IPN, Instituto Politécnico Nacional, Escuela Superior de Cómputo I.P.N, Ciudad de México, Mexico
dgonzalezo1500@alumno.ipn.mx, {ecatalans,blunab, rbjimenez}@ipn.mx

[2] CIDETEC, Instituto Politécnico Nacional. UPALM-Zacatenco, 07320 Mexico City, Mexico
maldape@ipn.mx

[3] Consejo Mexiquense de Ciencia y Tecnología/Universidad Autónoma del Estado de Mexico, Toluca de Lerdo, Estado de Mexico, Mexico
agarciav017@alumno.uaemex.mx

[4] Facultad de Geografía, Universidad Autónoma del Estado de México, 50110 Toluca de Lerdo, Estado de Mexico, Mexico

Abstract. Mexico City has more than nine million inhabitants living in marginalized regions characterized by high crime rates and significant air pollution. According to data provided by the Government of Mexico City, the areas with the highest reported crime rates since 2014 are located in the central, northern, and eastern parts of the city; these same areas also record historically high levels of fine particulate matter (PM10 and PM2.5). Current studies are focusing on the psychological dimension and the possible link between air pollution and criminal behavior, suggesting that ongoing exposure to elevated levels of PM10, CO, and ozone may lead to cognitive deterioration, increased anxiety, depression, and aggressive conduct. In this context, how can we integrate, analyze, and explore crime and air quality data to identify correlations between these phenomena? This paper proposes an advanced urban data analytics framework that outlines phases for integrating datasets and detecting correlations between rising air pollution and the crimes recorded at the borough level in Mexico City. Using data mining techniques, we integrated and analyzed trends in PM10, PM2.5, CO, ozone, and both violent and non-violent crimes from 2016 to 2020, drawing on open data sources from the city. We included records of crimes such as robberies with violence, theft in public transportation and urban spaces, domestic violence, and homicides. These data were examined in greater depth using Pearson correlation and linear regression. The results indeed suggest a positive and statistically significant relationship between boroughs with higher crime rates and elevated air pollution.

Keywords: Air Pollution · Crime · Spatio-Temporal Analysis · GIS · Data Science · Mexico City

M. F. Mata-Rivera et al. (Eds.): W2GIS 2025, LNCS 15946, pp. 77–89, 2026.
https://doi.org/10.1007/978-3-032-01723-9_6

1 Introduction

Air pollution and crime represent significant challenges for urban populations worldwide. The detrimental effects of air pollution on physical health are well-documented, and emerging research suggests a link between air quality and mental health issues, potentially influencing behaviors such as criminal activity. Similarly, high crime rates undermine social well-being and economic development in urban centers. While studies in various countries have explored the association between air pollution and crime, research focusing on the local level within Mexico City has been limited.

This study addresses this gap by conducting a spatio-temporal analysis of the relationship between air pollution (specifically PM2.5 and ozone concentrations, represented by the Air Quality Index - AQI22...) and crime incidence across the 16 alcaldías (boroughs) of Mexico City from 2016 to 2020. Utilizing daily crime data and air quality measurements from public data portals, we employed data mining techniques, including Extraction, Transformation, and Loading (ETL), Exploratory Data Analysis (EDA), linear regression analysis, correlation analysis, and Geographic Information Systems (GIS) for visualization.

The primary contribution of this work lies in providing a localized analysis of the potential association between air pollution and crime in Mexico City, a megacity facing significant challenges in both areas. Our findings suggest a positive correlation between higher levels of air pollution and an increase in violent crime in several alcaldías, although the strength of this relationship varied across different boroughs and years. Notably, no significant relationship was found between air pollution and non-violent crime. Alcaldías such as Azcapotzalco, Iztacalco, and Iztapalapa exhibited a more consistent historical relationship between these phenomena. These results, visualized through heatmaps and GIS tools, offer a spatially nuanced understanding of this complex interaction and lay the groundwork for future research incorporating additional socio-economic and environmental factors.

2 State of the Art

While the provided document extensively reviews existing literature, several other studies not explicitly mentioned offer relevant insights into the relationship between air pollution and crime, particularly employing spatio-temporal analysis. The following describes the research related to this study.

Moretti *et al.* (2011), this study uses micro-level data on daily crime incidents and air pollution concentrations in California. Their findings indicate a robust positive correlation between same-day changes in air pollution and violent crime, suggesting a potential causal link. While focusing on a different geographical context and using microdata, the study's methodology and findings on the contemporaneous relationship between pollution and violent crime are highly relevant to our work.

Borrego-Hernández *et al.* (2014), evaluated the retrospective health impact of ozone in the ZMVM in the Metropolitan Area of the Valley of Mexico (ZMVM) during the period 1991–2011. The methodology used was through a retrospective study design (HIA) where hourly ozone concentrations recorded between January 1, 1991, and

December 31, 2011, at approximately 22 monitoring stations were analyzed. The Cressman objective analysis method was applied to interpolate ozone values to an appropriate spatial grid, considering unmeasured locations. A dynamic exposure model based on variable spatial population distributions during the day was introduced to accurately reflect real urban mobility patterns. The assessment was stratified by age groups: children (0–5), school-age children (5–18), active adults (18–64), and older adults (>64), with differentiated vulnerability analysis. As results, it was confirmed that people tend to move to areas with lower ozone concentrations during the day, and the implemented policies were successful in reducing ozone exposure in various population segments, providing significant health benefits.

The findings support the continuation and improvement of ozone regulation strategies, considering both air quality and urban mobility, to optimize public health outcomes.

In Reyes *et al.* (2015), although not exclusively focused on air pollution, this research explores the broader concept of environmental inequality, including exposure to pollutants, and its association with crime rates across neighborhoods. The study suggests that communities disproportionately burdened by environmental hazards tend to experience higher levels of crime. This broader perspective on environmental factors and crime complements our focused analysis on air pollution.

This recent study investigates the spatio-temporal relationship between air pollution and crime in Dhaka, Bangladesh, using various statistical methods and GIS techniques. Their analysis reveals significant spatial clusters of both high pollution and high crime rates, along with temporal correlations. This study, conducted in another densely populated urban environment, highlights the utility of spatio-temporal methods in understanding the co-occurrence of these issues, echoing the approach taken in our research.

Moreover, Lu et al. (2018), examine the relationship between air pollution and increased crime and unethical behavior. The study proposes that exposure to high levels of air pollution impairs cognition and emotions, reducing self-control and adherence to social norms, increasing the propensity for antisocial behavior.

The study employs a mixed-methods approach, combining observational analyses with controlled experiments to strengthen the causal and external validity of the findings. Historical and geographical data on air pollution indices (PM2.5 particles, nitrogen dioxide, among others) and crime records from various cities and regions were collected. Multivariate regression models were used to control for socioeconomic, demographic, and environmental factors, thereby isolating the impact of pollution on crime incidence. Temporal patterns were analyzed to correlate pollution peaks with changes in crime rates.

This study provides a solid theoretical framework linking air pollution to increased crime and unethical behavior, arguing that pollution affects cognition and emotions, which decreases self-control and adherence to social norms. This psychological and social perspective is highly relevant for analyzing crime dynamics in a complex urban context such as Mexico City.

Additionally, Sánchez-Pérez & Arista-Jalife (2018), present the design and development of a computational system, based on mobile devices and GIS technology, focused on monitoring and controlling urban crime in Mexico City. The main objective is to create georeferenced crime indicators accessible through an interactive map. This allows users to identify, visualize, and avoid risk zones, while also participating in data collection for crime prevention. This system uses (i) Geographic Information Systems (GIS) for the visualization and spatial analysis of crime incidents, (ii) geolocation and mobile positioning as a basis for real-time event reporting, and (iii) a crowdsourcing platform where users can contribute information on crimes.

It offers a visual model that highlights crime hotspots, useful for designing preventive strategies. It proposes a tool that can be scaled or adapted to other cities, thanks to its mobile and collaborative structure. This work provides a solid foundation for an urban data analysis approach in Mexico City, enabling the adoption of GIS methodologies and technologies for mapping and analyzing crime.

Besides, Bryshnikova, Wesselbaum, & Davidson (2019), investigated whether air pollution has a causal impact on crime, focusing on the United States. They used a methodology that integrated daily data on crimes (violent and non-violent categories) and environmental pollutants ($PM_{2.5}$ and ozone) at the county level for a period of 2006–2013. Satellite and interpolated data were used to mitigate the lack of direct coverage by monitoring stations. Evidence supported that air pollution increases violent crime and estimated an additional societal benefit: a 10% reduction in $PM_{2.5}$ or ozone could save between USD 1.4 billion per year in costs associated with violent crimes. High-dimensional econometric models with fixed effects were used, controlling multiple climatic, spatial, and temporal factors. This approach can be replicated or adapted in your study in Mexico City, where there are also significant microclimatic and urban variations.

As found by Berman et al. (2019), they evaluated the relationship between short-term exposure to air pollutants ($PM_{2.5}$ and ozone) and the risk of violent behavior in the US, using rigorous statistical designs to establish temporal and spatial links. They designed a two-stage hierarchical time series model applied to daily pollution and crime data in 301 counties in 34 states, between 2000 and 2013; using $PM_{2.5}$ and ozone pollutants, obtained from the EPA. They differentiated between violent crimes (mainly assaults, inside and outside the home) and non-violent crimes; using a statistical model through fixed effects by county and date, controls for climate, demographics and community characteristics (urbanicity, poverty, race, age) and an evaluation of the dose-effect response, that is, the increase in pollutant is associated with percentage variations in the dynamic relative risk of violent occurrence.

They found that the effect remained valid in most community settings, except in rural areas. Dose-response curves revealed that even levels below the regulatory standard increase the risk of violence.

Zeng et al. (2019), found that exposure to air pollutants is associated with an increased risk of depression; they assessed the association between exposure to ambient air pollution and the presence of depression through a systematic review and meta-analysis of observational studies. Methodologically, they reviewed five academic databases, identifying 15 original studies ("observational studies") on outdoor pollution and depression. They included common pollutants ($PM_{2.5}$, PM_{10}, NO_2, SO_2, CO, O_3) and different types of exposure (short and long term); by (i) calculating the combined risk (pooled odds ratios) for each pollutant and duration of exposure; (ii) stratified analyses were performed by study design, type of population, pollutant level and presence of confounding variables and 39 studies were included using a random-effects model with sex: I^2, Q-test and REML. A significant increase in the risk of depression was observed associated with $PM_{2.5}$ (OR $\approx$1.07) and NO_2 (OR $\approx$1.04); in Dose-response effect: The higher the level of pollutant, the greater the risk of depression. This highlights the importance of controlling environmental pollution as a strategy to reduce mental health disorders.

On the other hand, Piña-García and Ramírez-Ramírez (2019), analyzed crime patterns in Mexico City using official data and online sources, applying ARIMA models with Google Trends variables using a Big Data approach. The methodology was based on (i) Coverage and data used, that is, official records of 13 types of crimes from January 2013 to September 2016, obtained from the Mexico City Police; time series from Google Trends and geolocation data from Twitter. (ii) Spatial-descriptive analysis: Official incidents were georeferenced to identify areas with high crime concentration ("hot spots") and the spatial distribution of crime was compared between official data and Twitter reports. And (iii) Predictive modeling of time series; Weekly ARIMA models were fitted with covariates from Google Trends, selected using LASSO (e.g., "complaint," "robbery," "murder"), and the predictive ability of the model at 1 week was assessed using AIC criteria, interval length, and hit rates in the prediction intervals.

The results obtained were: (i) ARIMA+Google Trends models achieved reliable weekly forecasts for the total frequency of crimes, although with variations in accuracy depending on the criminal category, (ii) the correlation between Official Data and Google Trends was limited, but the model still retained predictive capacity and (iii) Twitter proved to be useful for detecting spatial patterns of crime in different areas of the city.

Also, P.-F, Kuo., & I. G. Putra. (2021), they evaluate the hypothesis that an increase in air pollution, as measured by the Air Quality Index (AQI), is differentially associated with types of crime: it is postulated that poor air quality reduces the incidence of outdoor crimes (such as robberies) due to decreased mobility, while it increases indoor crimes (such as domestic violence), due to increased intra-household interaction.

Crime and pollution data from New South Wales, Australia, from 2016 were used. Variables included AQI, crime categories, and socioeconomic and demographic factors. Three statistical modeling approaches were employed: (i) Ordinary linear regression (OLS), (ii) Geographically weighted regression (GWR) and Geographically and time-weighted regression (GTWR), which provided the best fit (lowest AIC). Kuo & Putra's work provides empirical evidence and a clear theoretical framework linking air quality to crime dynamics, supporting the hypothesis that the environmental setting affects social behavior.

Similarly, Hernández et al. (2021), analyzed the geographic risk of crime against women in Mexico City. Their work focused on constructing a spatial crime risk index using data on crime incidence and contextual variables such as land use, accessibility, and safety conditions. The spatial approach in their study, particularly the use of borough-level segmentation and GIS tools for visualization, aligns closely with the methodological framework of our study, which seeks to uncover localized relationships between air pollution and crime.

Other contribution is by Zagal Flores et al. (2022) who conducted a geo-social characterization of the health impacts of air pollution in the Valley of Mexico. Their study applied geospatial data mining and social analysis techniques to identify exposure patterns among populations affected by high levels of pollutants. The authors emphasize the importance of incorporating territorial and demographic factors when assessing environmental risks. The methodology they proposed, integrating spatial and socio-environmental data, provided a conceptual foundation for the correlation model developed in our research.

These studies, along with those cited in the original document, underscore the growing interest in understanding the complex interplay between environmental quality and social behavior, and the importance of localized spatio-temporal analyses.

3 Methodology

This research adopted the CRoss-Industry Standard Process for Data Mining (CRISP-DM) methodology, a cyclical process guiding the data analysis from business understanding to deployment.

Data Understanding: Daily data on air quality (PM2.5, PM10, CO, and Ozone) and crime incidents in Mexico City from 2016 to 2020 were obtained from the city's public data portal. The air quality data included measurements from various monitoring stations across the city, while the crime data contained information on the date, time, type of crime, and alcaldía of occurrence.

Data Preparation: The raw datasets underwent an extensive ETL process using Python and SQL Server, Fig. 1 shows the data model to store integrated data. Air quality data, initially in separate files per year and pollutant, were restructured and integrated. The Air Quality Index (AQI) was calculated based on US EPA standards, prioritizing the highest AQI value among the measured pollutants (primarily PM2.5 and ozone) for each spatio-temporal point. Crime data were filtered to include only incidents within Mexico City's alcaldías and categorized into violent and non-violent crimes. Both datasets were aggregated at the daily level per alcaldía to facilitate spatio-temporal matching. A unique identifier combining day, month, year, and alcaldía was created to merge the air quality and crime data.

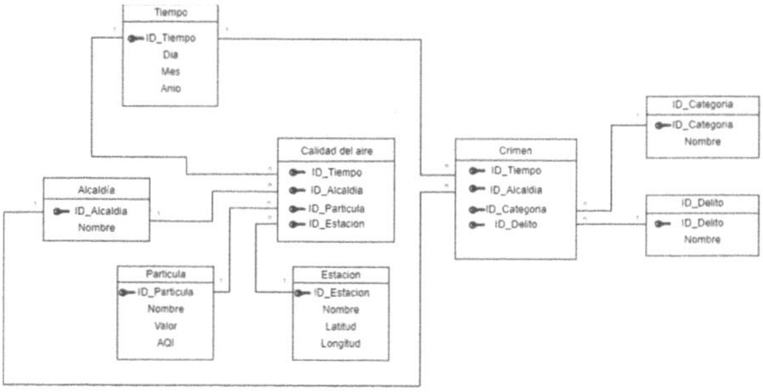

Fig. 1. Data model to explore the relationship between the AQI crimes

Modeling: Linear regression analysis was employed to explore the relationship between the average daily AQI and the number of crimes (both violent and non-violent) per alcaldía for each year. The Pearson correlation coefficient (r) and p-values were calculated to assess the strength and statistical significance of the linear relationships. Evaluation criteria, based on existing literature, were defined to interpret the significance of the correlation. Attempts were also made to develop predictive models using linear and logistic regression with k-means clustering on crime data to forecast future crime incidence based on AQI levels.

Evaluation: The results of the regression analyses were evaluated based on the defined criteria (r, p-value, and percentage increase in crime per 10 AQI points). The predictive models were assessed using accuracy metrics. See Table 1.

Table 1. Classification of correlation (r) and significance (p) values

r		P value		% / 10 AQI Points	
Value	Classification	Value	Classification	Value	Classification
−1 to 0	−1	0.65 to 1	−1	−2 to 0	−1
0 to 0.083	0	0.4 to 0.65	0	0 to 0.6	0
0.083 to 0.17	1	0.1 to 0.4	1	0.6 to 1	1
0.17 to 1	2	0 to 0.1	2	1 to 3	2

Deployment: The findings were visualized using heatmaps to illustrate the spatio-temporal patterns of correlation strength across alcaldías and years. GIS tools (QGIS and ArcGIS) were used to create choropleth maps and cluster maps to further explore the spatial distribution of air pollution and crim. A web-based dashboard was developed using Dash (Python framework) to allow interactive exploration of the results.

4 Results

The spatio-temporal analysis revealed varied relationships between air pollution and crime across the alcaldías of Mexico City. While the overall correlation at the city level was weak, analyses conducted at the individual alcaldía level yielded more nuanced findings.

Linear regression analysis indicated a suggestive positive correlation between the average daily AQI (primarily influenced by PM2.5 and ozone) and the incidence of violent crime in several alcaldías, including Azcapotzalco, Iztacalco, and Iztapalapa. This suggests that, in these areas, days with higher air pollution levels tended to coincide with a greater number of reported violent crimes. The percentage increase in violent crime for every 10-point rise in AQI varied by alcaldía and year, with some instances showing increases ranging from 0.6% to 3.34%.

Conversely, no statistically significant or consistent relationship was observed between air pollution levels and the incidence of non-violent crime across the alcaldías.

Heatmaps visually represented the spatio-temporal variations in the correlation strength (r-value), statistical significance (p-value), and percentage increase in crime across the alcaldías from 2016 to 2020. See Fig. 2.

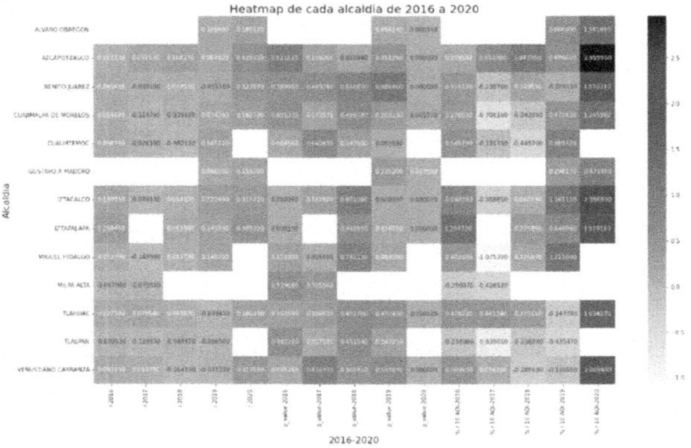

(a)

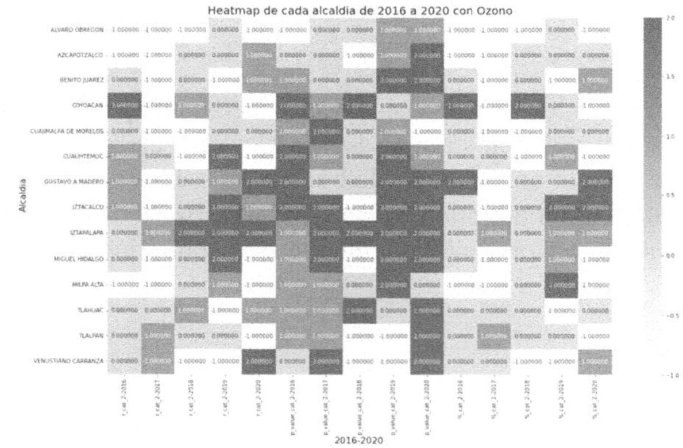

(b)

Fig. 2. (a) Heatmap of each borough from 2016 to 2020; (b) Categorized heatmap combining PM2.5 and ozone levels

These visualizations highlighted the alcaldías with more pronounced and consistent positive correlations over the study period.

The inclusion of ozone data alongside PM2.5 in the AQI calculation led to a more comprehensive spatial coverage in the analysis.

The model was trained using four variables: day, month, year, and AQI. Eighty percent of the dataset was allocated for training, 10% for testing, and 10% for validation. It is important to note that each borough had its own dedicated model. An experiment was conducted for each borough, where the model was evaluated to determine its accuracy, and crime predictions over time were generated accordingly

Attempts at developing accurate predictive models using linear and logistic regression with clustering yielded limited success, with accuracy rates around 35% for linear regression with clustered crime data. These preliminary modeling efforts suggest the complexity of predicting crime based solely on air pollution data and highlight the need for incorporating additional influencing factors. See Fig. 3.

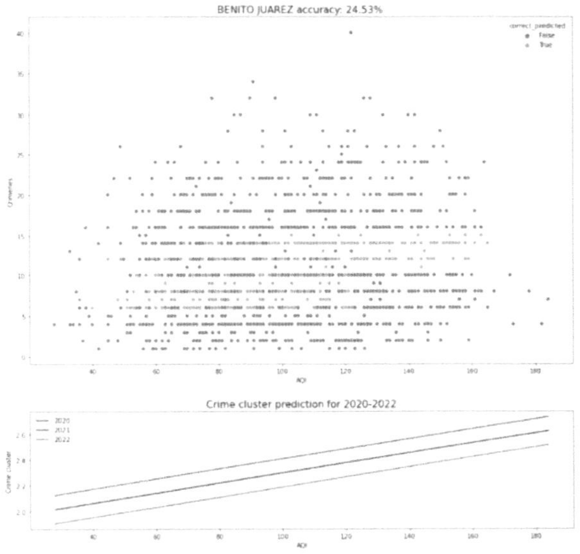

Fig. 3. Predictive model performance for testing phase in the "Benito Juárez" borough

GIS mapping, including choropleth maps and cluster analysis, corroborated the spatial heterogeneity of air pollution levels and crime incidence across Mexico City, further supporting the localized nature of the observed relationship.

These findings suggest a localized and potentially time-dependent relationship between air pollution and violent crime in specific areas of Mexico City, warranting further investigation into the underlying mechanisms and the influence of other socio-environmental factors.

For example, the figure shows a choropleth map combining PM2.5 and ozone levels in 2020 to visualize the percentage increase in crime for every 10-point rise in the AQI. It can be observed that the boroughs with the highest increases in both pollution and crime are mainly located in the northeastern area of Mexico City. See Fig. 4.

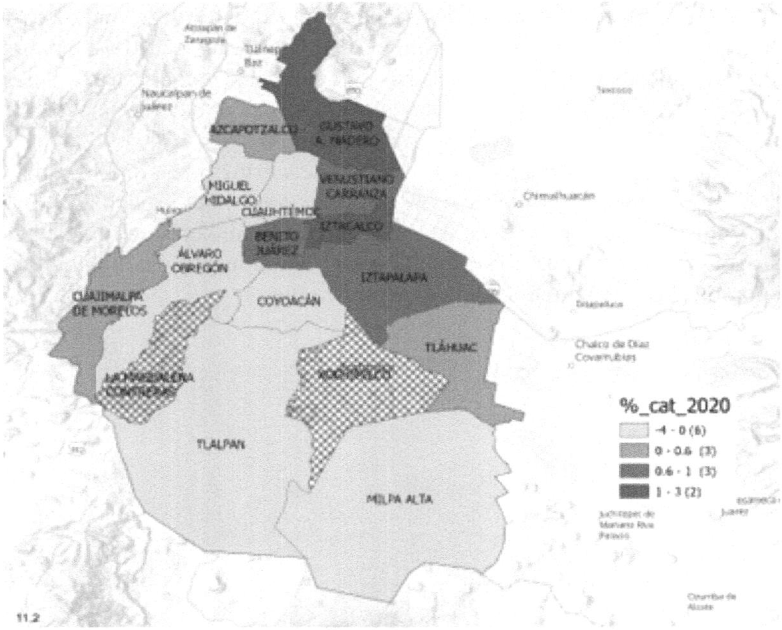

Fig. 4. PM2.5 and ozone levels in 2020 to visualize the percentage increase in crime for every 10-point rise in the AQI.

5 Discussion

The results obtained in this study reveal significant and localized patterns in the relationship between air quality and the incidence of violent crimes in Mexico City, providing empirical evidence for an emerging line of research on the effects of environmental factors on social behavior.

Unlike previous studies that have addressed this relationship at aggregated scales or using purely temporal approaches, our spatio-temporal analysis at the borough level showed that the correlation between the Air Quality Index (AQI) and violent crimes is not uniform across the city. Boroughs such as Azcapotzalco, Iztacalco, and Iztapalapa exhibited consistent positive correlations, suggesting that days with higher air pollution levels tend to coincide with a greater incidence of violence in these areas.

However, the study also found no statistically significant relationship between air pollution and non-violent crimes, reinforcing the idea that certain types of antisocial behavior may be more influenced by adverse environmental conditions than others. This difference could be explained by factors such as the physiological stress induced by pollutants (Dockery et al., 1993), which may exacerbate immediate aggressive responses without necessarily affecting opportunistic or economic crimes.

Another important finding was the limited predictive capacity of models developed based solely on the AQI. Despite the use of techniques such as linear regression, logistic regression, and clustering, the models achieved modest accuracy levels (~35%), suggesting that while air pollution may correlate with violence in certain contexts, it is not a sufficient predictor on its own to anticipate criminal patterns. This underscores the need to incorporate additional variables—such as socioeconomic indicators, police presence, population density, or social events—to develop more robust and reliable models.

Based on what has been gathered, the next step is to more precisely identify the sources of PM2.5 and ozone emissions, as well as the daily quantities released into Mexico City. This study could serve as a starting point for developing strategies to reduce pollutant gases and, at the same time, decrease crime rates caused by pollution. Additionally, it can help formulate policies aimed at maintaining optimal health conditions for residents.

To enrich this research, other pollutants such as nitrogen oxides, carbon dioxide, sulfur dioxide, and carbon monoxide could be included, as they have neurotoxic effects (Bryshnikova, 2019) that may influence criminal activity. Furthermore, variables like temperature, population size, age, gender, a smaller study area, and lifestyle factors could contribute to obtaining more precise information about the causes or increase in criminal activities.

This study is a starting point to emphasize the importance of mental and emotional health, which has been affected by air pollution in large cities like Mexico City. Exposure to high levels of pollutants influences mood, decision-making, and rest among the population. This underscores the urgent need to act swiftly against air pollution.

Moreover, the findings could inform policymakers to develop effective public policies that promote mental health, conserve the natural environment, enforce strict emission regulations, and reduce crime rates.

However, it would be advisable to conduct longitudinal and experimental studies to establish stronger causal relationships and evaluate the impact of environmental policies aimed at reducing urban violence. This could involve designing specific interventions in certain areas, such as campaigns to lower emissions, temporary restrictions on polluting activities, or improvements in public transportation—always with air quality and crime rates monitored before and after these interventions.

Finally, this study highlights the importance of adopting interdisciplinary and data-driven approaches to address complex urban problems. The relationship between air quality and crime cannot be understood without considering the local context, social dynamics, and specific environmental conditions of each area. In this sense, the findings provide a useful empirical foundation for future research and for the formulation of crime prevention strategies with a territorial and environmental focus.

6 Conclusions

This study provides a spatio-temporal analysis of the relationship between air pollution and crime in Mexico City at the alcaldía level. Our analysis indicates a suggestive positive association between higher levels of air pollution (indicated by the AQI, primarily driven by PM2.5 and ozone) and an increase in violent crime in certain alcaldías, particularly Azcapotzalco, Iztacalco, and Iztapalapa. This localized relationship, visualized through heatmaps and GIS tools, highlights the spatial heterogeneity of this phenomenon within a major urban environment. Notably, no significant correlation was found between air pollution and non-violent crime. While city-wide correlations were weak, the alcaldía-level analysis suggests that environmental factors like air pollution may play a role in influencing violent behavior in specific urban contexts. These findings contribute to the growing body of interdisciplinary research examining the complex interplay between environmental quality and social outcomes in urban settings.

Several avenues for future research can build upon the findings of this study, These include:

- Integrating ozone more comprehensively into predictive models to assess its specific impact on crime prediction.
- Conducting geofence-based analysis around air quality monitoring stations to explore the spatial decay of the pollution-crime relationship.
- Exploring multivariate time series forecasting techniques, such as Long Short-Term Memory (LSTM) networks, to improve crime prediction models by incorporating temporal dependencies and other relevant variables.

References

Kuo, P.-F., Putra, I.G.: Analyzing the relationship between air pollution and various types of crime. PLOS ONE **16**(8) (2021). 10 M. Bondy, S. Roth, and L. Sager, "Crime is in the air: The contemporaneous relationship between air pollution and crime," Journal of the Association of Environmental and Resource Economists, vol. 7, no. 3, pp. 555–585, 2020. 11

Lu, J.G., Lee, J.J., Gino, F., Galinsky, A.D.: Polluted morality: air pollution predicts criminal activity and unethical behavior. Psychol. Sci. **29**(3), 340–355 (2018)

Piña-García, C.A., Ramírez-Ramírez, L.: Exploring crime patterns in Mexico City. J. Big Data **6**(1) (2019). 120 Calvillo Saldaña, Yezmín, y "Espacio y delincuencia: un caso de estudio del robo a transeúnte en el Centro Histórico de la ciudad de México" Espacialidades. Revista de temas contemporáneos sobre lugares, política y cultura, vol. 4, no. 2, 2014, pp.112–151. Redalyc, https://www.redalyc.org/articulo.oa?id=419545122005. 121 A. Espinoza-Ramírez, M. Nakano,

Sánchez-Pérez, G., Arista-Jalife, A.: Sistemas de Información Geográfica y su análisis aplicado en zonas de delincuencia en la ciudad de méxico. Información tecnológica **29**(5), 235–244 (2018)

Borrego-Hernández, Ó., García-Reynoso, J.A., Ojeda-Ramírez, M.M. and Suárez-Lastra, M.: Retrospective health impact assessment for ozone pollution in Mexico city from 1991 to 2011. Atmósfera **27**(3), 261–271 (2014)

Carazo Fernández, L., Fernández Alvarez, R., González-Barcala, F.J., Rodríguez Portal, J.A.: Contaminación del aire interior y su impacto en la patología respiratoria, Archivos de Bronconeumología **49**(1), 22–27 (2013)

Clofent, D., Culebras, M., Loor, K., Cruz, M.J.: Contaminación ambiental y Cáncer de Pulmón: El poder Carcinogénico del Aire Que respiramos. Arch. Bronconeumol. **57**(5), 317–318 (2014)

Bryshnikova, N.V., Wesselbaum, D., Davidson, S.F.: Does pollution affect crime? Evidence from US Cities, 2293. (2019). https://ourarchive.otago.ac.nz/bitstream/handle/10523/9813/DP_1910.pdf?sequence=1

Burkhardt, J., et al.: The effect of pollution on crime: evidence from data on particulate Matter and ozone. J. Environ. Econ. Manag. **98**, 102267 (2019)

Berman, J.D., Burkhardt, J., Bayham, J., Carter, E., Wilson, A.: Acute air pollution exposure and the risk of violent behavior in the United States. Epidemiology **30**(6), 799–806 (2019)

Zeng, Y., Lin, R., Liu, L., Liu, Y., Li, Y.: Ambient air pollution exposure and risk of depression: a systematic review and meta-analysis of observational studies, Psychiatry Res. **276**, 69–78 (2019) 132 "IBM EDA". IBM - Deutschland I IBM. https://www.ibm.com/case-studies/ibm-eda. Accedido 3 mayo 2022

Chapman, P., et al.: CRISP-DM 1.0: Step-by-step data mining guide (2000)

Moro, S., Laureano, R.M.S., Cortez, P.: Using data mining for bank direct marketing: an application of the crisp-Dm methodology, Instituto Universitário de Lisboa, 2011. Accedido el 3 de mayo de (2022). http://hdl.handle.net/1822/14838

Cantú M.P, Contaminación ambiental. México: Diana, 1993: Extract, transform, and load (ETL) - Azure Architecture Center, Docs.microsoft.com (2022). https://docs.microsoft.com/en-us/azure/architecture/data-guide/relational-data/etl. [Accessed: 09- Mar- 2022]

PowerData,G.: Data warehouse: todo lo que necesitas saber sobre almacenamiento de datos", Powerdata.es, 2022. 46 "IBM Docs", Ibm.com (2022). https://www.ibm.com/docs/es/spss-modeler/SaaS?topic=dm-crisp-help-overview. Accessed 09 Mar 2022

Frye, J.G., Frontani, K.D., García-Martínez, M., Coulombe, D.B., Plantenga, M.L., Auchincloss, R.F.: Association between ambient air pollution and mental health service use among children and adolescents in Massachusetts. JAMA Netw. Open **2**(6), e196014 (2019)

"Guide To K-means clustering algorithm in Python: Analytics India magazine (2022). https://analyticsindiamag.com/guide-to-k-means-clustering-algorithm-in-python/. Accessed 01 May 2022

"Guide To BIRCH clustering algorithm (with python codes)", Analytics India magazine (2022). https://analyticsindiamag.com/guide-to-birch-clustering-algorithmwith-python-codes/. Accessed: 01 May 2022

What is exploratory data analysis? (s. f.). IBM - Deutschland I IBM. https://www.ibm.com/cloud/learn/exploratory-data-analysis 137 Carrillo, P.E., Lopez-Luzuriaga, A., Malik, A.S.: Pollution or crime: the effect of driving restrictions on criminal activity. Journal of Public Economics, 164, 50–69 (2018). https://doi.org/10.1016/j.jpubeco.2018.05.007

What is Logistic Regression? - Logistic Regression - AWS. Amazon Web Services, Inc. https://aws.amazon.com/what-is/logistic-regression/. Accedido el 20 de noviembre de 2022

Zagal Flores, R., et al.: A Geo-Social Characterization of Health Impact from Air Pollution in Mexico Valley. Mob. Inf. Syst. **2022**, 1–19 (2022). https://doi.org/10.1155/2022/5562317

Hernández, J., Jiménez, D., Zagal, R., Mata, F., Leon Borges, J.A.: Analysis of the level of geographic criminal risk oriented to women. In: Mata-Rivera, M.F., Zagal-Flores, R., Barria-Huidobro, C. (eds.) WITCOM 2021, Communications in Computer and Information Science, vol. 1430, pp. 230–245. Springer, Cham (2021). https://doi.org/10.1007/978-3-030-89586-0_19

Dockery, D.W., et al.: An association between air pollution and mortality in six U.S. cities. New England J. Med. **329**(24), 1753–1759 (1993). https://doi.org/10.1056/NEJM199312093292401

Moretti, E., Neidell, M.: Pollution, health, and avoidance behavior: evidence from the ports of Los Angeles. J. Hum. Res. **46**(1), 154–175 (2011). https://doi.org/10.3368/jhr.46.1.154

Borrego Hernández, Ó., García Reynoso, J.A., Ojeda Ramírez, M.M., Suárez Lastra, M.: Retrospective health impact assessment for ozone pollution in Mexico City from 1991 to 2011. Atmósfera **27**(3), 261–271 (2014). https://doi.org/10.1016/S0187-6236(14)71115-4

Diabetes Disparities in Mexico: A Spatio-Temporal and Marginalization Index Analysis

Carlos Hernandez-Nava[1](✉), James Williams[2,3], Sergio Flores-Hernandez[4], and Miguel-Felix Mata-Rivera[1]

[1] Instituto Politécnico Nacional, UPIITA-IPN, 07340 Ciudad de Mexico, Mexico
hernandeznc@ipn.mx

[2] Computer Science, Faculty of Arts, Society and Professional Studies, Birmingham Newman University, Birmingham, UK

[3] Nottingham Geospatial Institute, University of Nottingham, Nottingham, UK

[4] Instituto Nacional de Salud Pública de Mexico, 62100 Cuernavaca, Morelos, Mexico

Abstract. Understanding the geospatial and temporal distribution of diabetes mellitus in Mexico can be an essential tool in supporting vulnerable populations and addressing health inequalities. This article presents a spatio-temporal investigation of patients aged 18 years and older with diabetes mellitus in Mexico, associated with geographical area and a temporal range from 2005 to 2022. This approach includes calculating diabetes-related hospitalizations and deaths and its association with the margination index segmented into eight geographical areas of Mexico. Furthermore, this research stratifies based upon age group and type of medical institute of the health services in Mexico. The main contribution of this research is to explore the relationship between diabetes-related hospitalizations, deaths, geographical area, age, sex, and margination index of populations to support preventive action. The results highlight that adults between the ages of 45 and 64 years old who live in areas with a high margination index have a greater likelihood of suffering complications related to diabetes. The age-adjusted rate of DRAH shows that the Peninsula has the highest values among geographical areas. Research will now continue to explore mapping interventions to specific states and external datasets, to further extrapolate the results of the analysis.

Keywords: spatio-temporal analysis · margination index · geographical areas · hospitalizations · deaths · diabetes mellitus · regression · association modelling

1 Introduction

Diabetes mellitus is a 21st century challenge in worldwide public health, with the increasing number of individuals with diabetes encouraging an ongoing focus in preventative programs [1]. Based on the worldwide research context, the spatio-temporal analysis in this article enables us to measure the impact of social privations, including education, food, and essential services, on diabetes-related hospitalizations and deaths in Mexico.

M. F. Mata-Rivera et al. (Eds.): W2GIS 2025, LNCS 15946, pp. 90–104, 2026.
https://doi.org/10.1007/978-3-032-01723-9_7

Diabetes is one of the most prevalent non-communicable diseases in the world, with significant increases in occurrence being identified from 1980 to 2014 [2]. Researchers have investigated the effects of various factors, analyzing them temporally from 2005 to 2022 and spatially across the eight geographical areas of Mexico, and associating to the sex, age group, and medical institute where patients are affiliated [3]. This article builds on this existing work to focus on the spatio-temporal context and marginalization to support ongoing preventive action. Defining spatio-temporal is how something evolves in different places over time and the marginalization index serves as a metric that distinguishes localities within the country based on the overall impact of deprivations experienced by the population. This impact arises from inadequate access to education, substandard living conditions, and a lack of essential goods.

The remainder of the paper is structured as follows. The next section briefly introduces the background of the project and related work; Sect. 3 provides the context of the work completed and describes the records of the hospitalization and death datasets. Section 4 develops the CRISP-DM methodology specific to this article, an analysis of Diabetes-relates Avoidable Hospitalizations (DRAH) and Diabetes-Related Deaths (DRD); Sect. 5 reports and presents the findings and results. Finally, Sect. 6 concludes and outlines future work which could be conducted in the spatio-temporal analysis of diabetes.

2 Background

Exploration of the association of diabetes-related hospitalizations and deaths worldwide has garnered increased health systems attention. In 2021, the World Health Organization ranked diabetes mellitus as the 8th leading cause of death worldwide [4], providing significant motivation for a continued focus on evaluating spatial disparities. Researchers have employed diverse methodologies to investigate diabetes through spatial methods, with a growing emphasis on understanding access to basic services, such as healthcare and food [5]. Common health difficulties related to diabetes mellitus include an increased risk of a heart attack or stroke and complications related to the eyes, kidneys, and nerves [6]. A brief overview of recent work and distinctions from the approach presented in this study are provided in the remainder of this section.

Due to the international and national prevalence of diabetes around the world, several researchers and projects have explored the spatio-temporal disparities between geographic regions, countries and states. For example, authors have previously explored the incidence, mortality, and risk factors of type-2 diabetes mellitus across 21 world regions from 1990–2019 through an annual average percentage change regression model [7]. Other studies have also examined the temporal aspects of diabetes to project disease and economic burden through a Bayesian model for 2020–2030 [8]. These articles highlight the impact of socio-economic and temporal changes in diabetes, and open data enables new models to be designed. A systematic review [9] highlights many studies using spatial modelling to understand diabetes outcomes, with Bayesian generalized linear mixed modelling, generalized linear modelling, and geographic information systems being used, with spatial studies being considered effective beyond the USA and Europe [9].

Recent studies have emphasized the impact of diabetes mellitus in Mexico, for example, an article on the socio-spatial vulnerability of type-2 diabetes in Mexico during 2020 found several clustered areas with high and low vulnerability to diabetes through a multiple linear regression model [10]. Similarly to worldwide approaches, authors have also investigated the spatio-temporal trends and effect of marginalization between 1990 and 2019 finding that the highest marginalization quintiles had double the risk of dying from diabetes as the lowest through the analysis of death certificates [11]. Using this existing literature as an impetus the work conducted in this article instead focuses on understanding the association between diabetes hospitalization and death alongside the margination index of Mexico.

3 Context and Data Selection

Diabetes mellitus is an Ambulatory Care Sensible Condition (ACSC), a health condition for which adequate treatment and timely intervention in the ambulatory care system could potentially avoid hospitalizations [12]. This noncommunicable disease can be managed by ensuring that individuals needing care are given access to the best information, support and education, this includes the effective measure of outcomes [13] and overall educational programs [14]. Complications of diabetes can include both short-term and long-term issues, for example, heart attacks or strokes, eye damage, and foot problems [6]. This context highlights the importance of a multi-disciplinary approach to spatially understanding diabetes mellitus, its occurrences, and disparities in care, providing impetus for the spatio-temporal analysis conducted in this article.

3.1 Data Selection

The diabetes-related International Codes of Diseases (ICD-10-CM) are listed in the specification of the prevention quality diabetes composite indicator prepared by the Agency for Healthcare Research and Quality (AHRQ) [15], PQI #93, which includes PQI #1, PQI #3, PQI #14, and PQI #16. The datasets of hospitalizations and deaths contain a variable named "principal condition", enabling the filtering of conditions in PQI #93. The research conducted in this study utilizes 26 prevention of quality ICD-10-CM codes: E101-E106, E108-E116, E118-E119, E130-E136, E138, and E139.

As part of the data selection process, medical institutes of Mexico were selected to enable analysis and comparison between varying institutes. These include: SS (Secretaría de Salud) is the public medical institute dependent on the Ministry of Health of Mexico; IMSS (Instituto Mexicano del Seguro Social) is the most extensive medical system in Mexico, which treats all officially registered employees; ISSSTE (Instituto de Seguridad y Servicios Sociales de los Trabajadores del Estado) is the medical system for government workers, accounting for more than 97% of hospitalizations; IMSS-Bienestar is a federal government program that offers free medical access to IMSS facilities; PEMEX (Petroleos Mexicanos) provides medical units for PEMEX workers; SEMAR (Secretaría de la Defensa Nacional y Secretaría de Marina) serves as the medical institute for soldiers and maritime personnel. Lastly, other public and private medical units and DIF (Sistema de Desarrollo Integral de la Familia) are classified.

4 Methodology

The methodology developed in this study represents an adaptation of the widely recognized data mining (DM) approach, specifically tailored for health data in this work. As illustrated in Fig. 1, the Cross Industry Standard Process for Data Mining (CRISP-DM) methodology comprises six stages within its data flow framework: (1) problem understanding; (2) data understanding; (3) data preparation; (4) modelling; (5) evaluation; and (6) deployment [16]. Each of these stages is adapted to the context of investigating diabetes and marginalization in the subsequent sections of this article.

The margination index measures the intensity of deprivation and social exclusion in the population. It comprises education level, access to quality housing, income levels, and access to essential services (including electric power and drainage). Each geographical area has one of the four possible margination indexes: low, medium, high, or very high, according to the National Population Council of Mexico (CONAPO, in Spanish) [17], responsible for evaluating the marginalization in Mexico. This represents a vital understanding of the problem, representing the first stage of the CRISP-DM methodology represented in Fig. 1 at point 1.

In Mexico, the Ministry of Health publishes hospitalization and death records from 2005 to 2022 through the General Department of Health Information in its open data repositories [18]. Although some records for 2023, 2024, and 2025 exist, they were excluded for being incomplete for all geographical areas, months, and medical institutes, whether public or private. Hospitalization records comprise more than 50 variables, which have increased over the years. Key variables include the identification of residence state, sex, age or age group, and ICD-10-CM code for the cause of hospitalization, rising from 1,048,576 records in 2005 to over 1,500,000 in 2022 [19]. Death records also contain more than 50 variables, and those selected for this study are residence state, sex, age, ICD-10-CM code for the cause, and place of death, increasing from 495,241 records in 2005 to 847,717 records in 2022 [20], as shown in point 2 of Fig. 1.

4.1 Data Gathering, Pre-processing, and Preparation

The first two stages were conducted with open government data, extracting health from the General Department of Health Information of Mexico. The records were merged with the margination index per geographical area by the identifier of the residence state, according to the National Health and Nutrition Survey of Mexico in 2022 (ENSANUT, in Spanish). The 8 geographical areas and corresponding states are: (1) Pacífico Norte: Baja California, Baja California Sur, Nayarit, Sinaloa and Sonora; (2) Frontera: Chihuahua, Coahuila, Nuevo León and Tamaulipas; (3) Pacífico-Centro: Colima, Jalisco and Michoacán; (4) Centro-Norte: Aguascalientes, Durango, Guanajuato, Querétaro, San Luis Potosí and Zacatecas; (5) Centro: Hidalgo, Tlaxcala and Veracruz; (6) Ciudad de México/Estado de México: Ciudad de México and Estado de México; (7) Pacífico Sur: Guerrero, Morelos, Oaxaca and Puebla; and (8) Península: Campeche, Chiapas, Quintana Roo, Tabasco and Yucatán. Each area was associated with its corresponding margination index; therefore, only the margination indexes were taken in the association analysis due to the imminent correlation between the variables in this pre-processing stage.

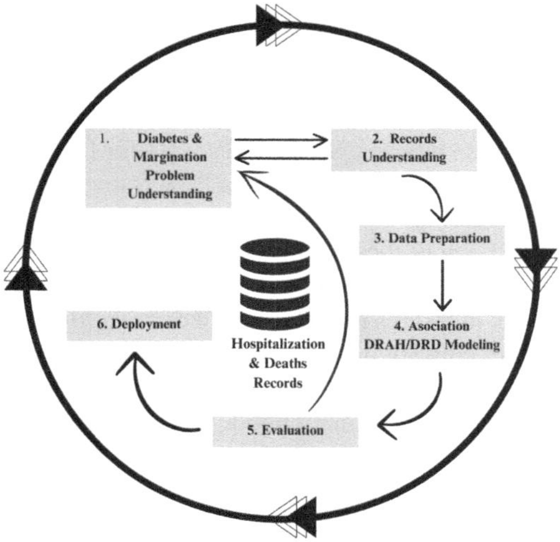

Fig. 1. A diagram representing the Cross Industry Standard Process for Data Mining (CRISP-DM) methodology which was adapted and applied to this work (Adapted from: [16]).

In the data cleansing and preparation stage, point 3 in Fig. 1, records with outlier data and unknown sex, residence, medical institute, age, or age group were removed, averaging between 1% and 5% of rows being removed per dataset.[1]

4.2 Data Integration, Statistical Analysis, and Exploration

This fourth stage of the CRISP-DM methodology (point 4 in Fig. 1) involves modelling the association using a binomial regression, where Diabetes-Related Avoidable Hospitalization (DRAH) is the dependent variable. The data is coded as "1" if classified as an avoidable hospitalization and "0" if it is not. For Diabetes-Related Deaths (DRD), the coding is classified as "1" if the death is due to a preventable condition related to diabetes and "0" if it is not.

Data was collected and categorized as part of the data integration and exploration stages. Figure 2 presents bar plots of DRAH per year from 2005 to 2022, displayed as a stacked bar chart with cases represented per medical institution. Beneath each bar plot, the margination index is illustrated using grey tones; the darkest square indicates a very high margination, while the lightest square represents a low index. Figure 3 depicts DRD at home or public places, stratified by sex and year, along with the corresponding geographical area and margination index also represented in grey tones.

The results of the statistical analysis conducted through a binomial regression of DRAH and DRD are presented in odds ratios (OR) in Table 1, including the age group of the patients, the margination indexes, and the medical institute treating the patients. To interpret these results, it is necessary to understand the baseline; for instance, in the column of characteristics in Table 1, the first entry is women, and the OR column for

[1] Final dataset available at https://github.com/carloshnava/w2gis25.

2019 results in 0.66, with a confidence interval of 95%, having a lower limit of 0.65 and an upper limit of 0.67, along with a p-value < 0.0001, indicated by three asterisks (***). The baseline or exposure is men, due to the OR being a relative measure. Therefore, women are 33% less likely than men to experience the condition, with a 95% confidence

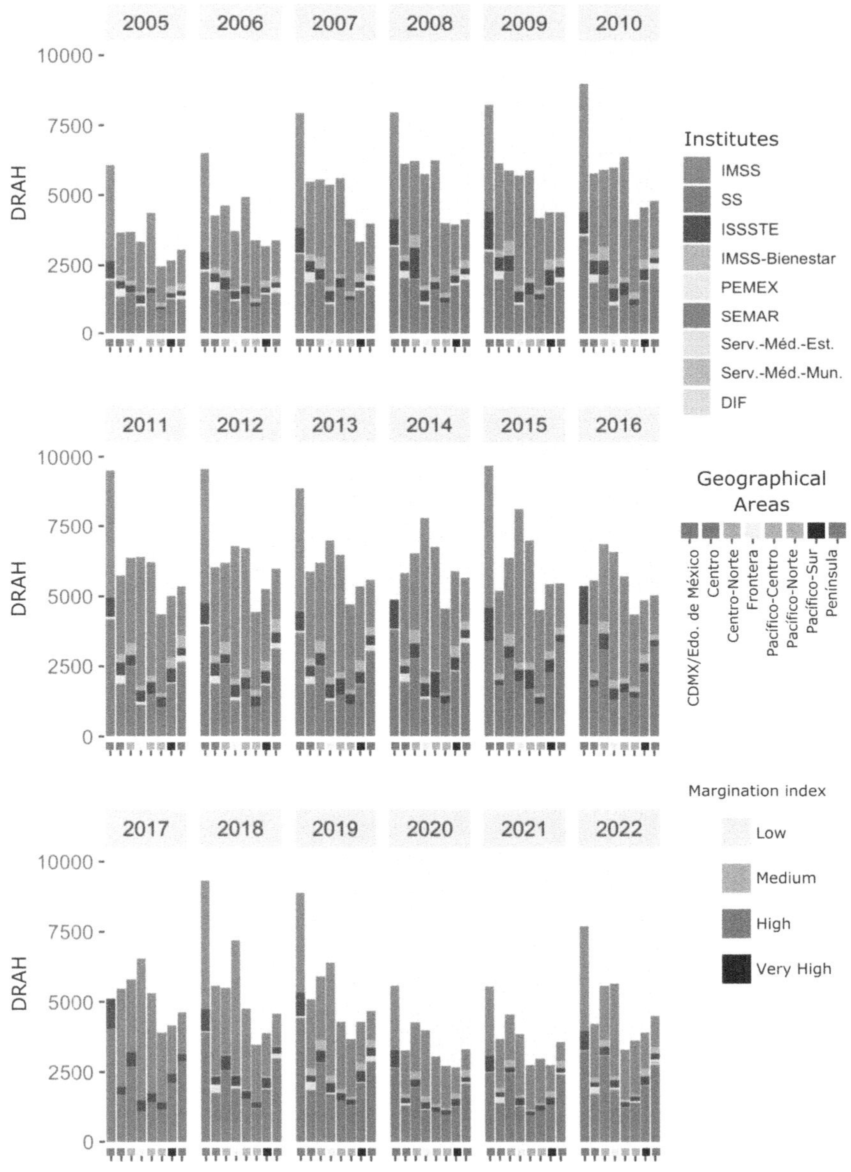

Fig. 2. Stacked spatio-temporal bar charts representing Diabetes-Related Avoidable Hospitalizations (DRAH) per year, geographical area (margination index), and medical institute.

level, and this is statistically significant because the p-value is less than 0.05. Table 1 displays odds ratios for DRAH and DRD for 2019 and 2020, which marks the COVID-19 breakpoint for the pandemic; beneath each value of the odds ratio are the lower and upper limits of the confidence interval to achieve a 95% confidence level.

Another example is the medical institute IMSS, which has the highest number of patients in Mexico. The baseline for this ratio is SS. The OR value for 2019 is 1.79,

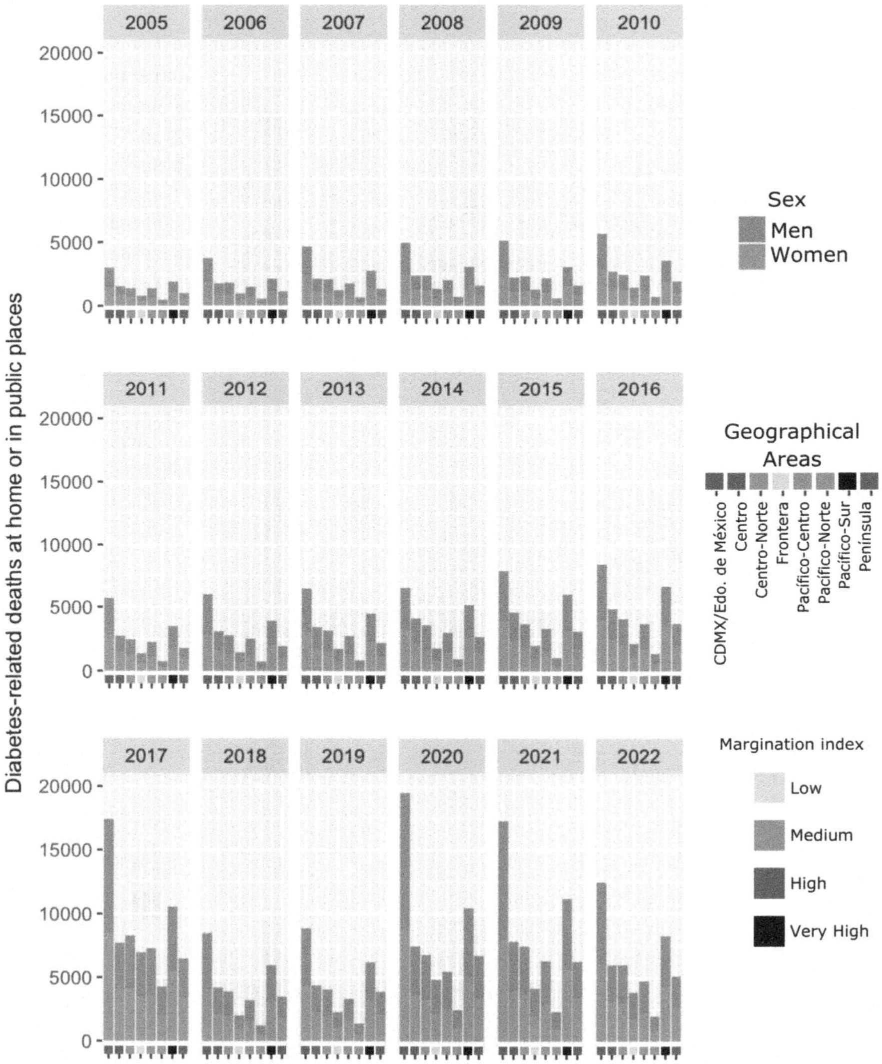

Fig. 3. Stacked spatio-temporal bar charts representing Diabetes-Related Deaths (DRD) at home or public places per year, geographical area (margination index), and institute.

indicating that IMSS patients are 79% more likely than SS patients to be statistically significant.

Hospitalization records are from all health institutions in Mexico, excluding private institutions. According to the Consejo Nacional de Evaluación de la Política de Desarrollo Social (National Council for the Evaluation of Social Development Policy), in 2022 39% of people in Mexico lacked access to health services.

Table 1. Association of Diabetes-related Avoidable Hospitalizations (DRAH) and Diabetes-related Deaths (DRD) in pre-pandemic COVID-19 and the beginning of the pandemic COVID-19 period.

Characteristic	Diabetes-related Avoidable Hospitalizations		Diabetes-related Deaths	
	OR 2019	OR 2020	OR 2019	OR 2020
Women	0.66*** 0.65,0.67	0.68*** 0.67, 0.70	1.23*** 1.20, 1.26	1.21*** 1.18, 1.23
Age-group (years old)				
18–44	—	—		—
45–64	7.03*** 6.89, 7.17	6.50*** 6.34, 6.66	4.18*** 3.93, 4.46	3.47*** 3.31, 3.63
+ 65	6.63*** 6.49, 6.77	6.17*** 6.01, 6.33	2.97*** 2.80, 3.16	2.46*** 2.35, 2.57
Margination index				
Low	—	—	—	—
Medium	0.79*** 0.77, 0.81	0.94*** 0.91, 0.96	1.28*** 1.21, 1.35	1.18*** 1.13, 1.22
High	0.98* 0.96, 1.00	1.06*** 1.03, 1.09	1.83*** 1.74, 1.92	1.88*** 1.82, 1.95
Very High	1.05*** 1.02, 1.08	1.08*** 1.04, 1.12	1.74*** 1.65, 1.84	1.64*** 1.57, 1.70
Institute				
SS	—	—	—	—
IMSS bienestar	0.63*** 0.62, 0.64	0.72*** 0.71, 0.73	1.24*** 1.20, 1.28	1.10*** 1.08, 1.12
IMSS	1.79*** 1.73, 1.85	1.91*** 1.83, 1.98	1.19*** 1.13, 1.25	1.07*** 1.04, 1.11
ISSSTE	0.48*** 0.47, 0.50	0.61*** 0.59,0.63	0.98 0.85, 1.13	0.78*** 0.70, 0.87

(continued)

Table 1. (*continued*)

Characteristic	Diabetes-related Avoidable Hospitalizations		Diabetes-related Deaths	
	OR 2019	OR 2020	OR 2019	OR 2020
PEMEX	0.58*** 0.54, 0.61	0.52*** 0.48, 0.57	1.43*** 1.22, 1.67	1.02 0.90, 1.16
SEDENA		0.32*** 0.18,0.52	1.11 0.81, 1.49	0.94*** 0.74, 1.19
SEMAR	0.21*** 0.14, 0.30		1.18*** 1.15, 1.22	1.04* 1.01,1.07
Other (public)		0.06*** 0.01, 0.20	1.16** 1.06, 1.27	1.08* 1.01, 1.14
Other (private)		5.19*** 1.84, 11.4	0.85	0.74*** 0.64, 0.84

5 Results

The analysis produced using the adapted CRISP-DM methodology presented several interesting findings related to DRAH. When analyzing the data per year, geographical area, and medical institute; we observe that for CDMX/Edo. de México, being the most crowded metropolitan area, with more than 20 million people, presents through the years the highest numbers of avoidable hospitalizations among the geographical areas analyzed. Stacked bar plots of DRAH are shown in Fig. 4 with the number of cases per medical institute; for example, Península, an area geographically with a high margination index, shows that most people have SS as medical services (red area in bar stacked in bottom-right at Fig. 4), representing the key variations of the data analyzed during this study.

Observing the behavior before and after COVID-19 is of note. From 2005, there were upward trends generally until 2015, and then, in 2018, beginning with downward trends until 2020. A possible explanation is COVID-19, but some years before, the trends decreased for other reasons, possibly due to other public health campaigns or programs. Figure 4 presents that DRD in 2020 at home or in public places across all geographical areas increased, possibly due to the impact of COVID-19. Therefore, deaths increased while DRAH decreased. As illustrated in Fig. 4, DRD showed a gradual increase in equal proportions for both men and women from 2005 to 2020. It abruptly increased with the onset of the COVID-19 pandemic, followed by a decline that continued until 2022. The results from this study encourage the further exploration of these associations upon more recent datasets becoming available.

Temporally, Table 2 displays ORs for five-year periods: 2005, 2010, 2015, and 2020, while also including 2019 and 2022 to illustrate the trends of the DRAH with its associated factors. For women, the likelihood of being hospitalized due to a diabetes-related condition is lower than for men, ranging from 10% to 38% (OR values 0.90–0.62). For the age group, people between 45 and 64 have a higher likelihood of being a DRAH than younger people while showing similar results to those older. For example, in the year 2005, the impact of the margination index reveals that a high index generates 40% (OR value of 1.39) more likelihood than those areas with a low index. In the same year, for the medical institute, people affiliated with the IMSS have a 34% (OR value 1.34) higher likelihood than people who use SS medical services. All other medical services analyzed in this article have a lower likelihood.

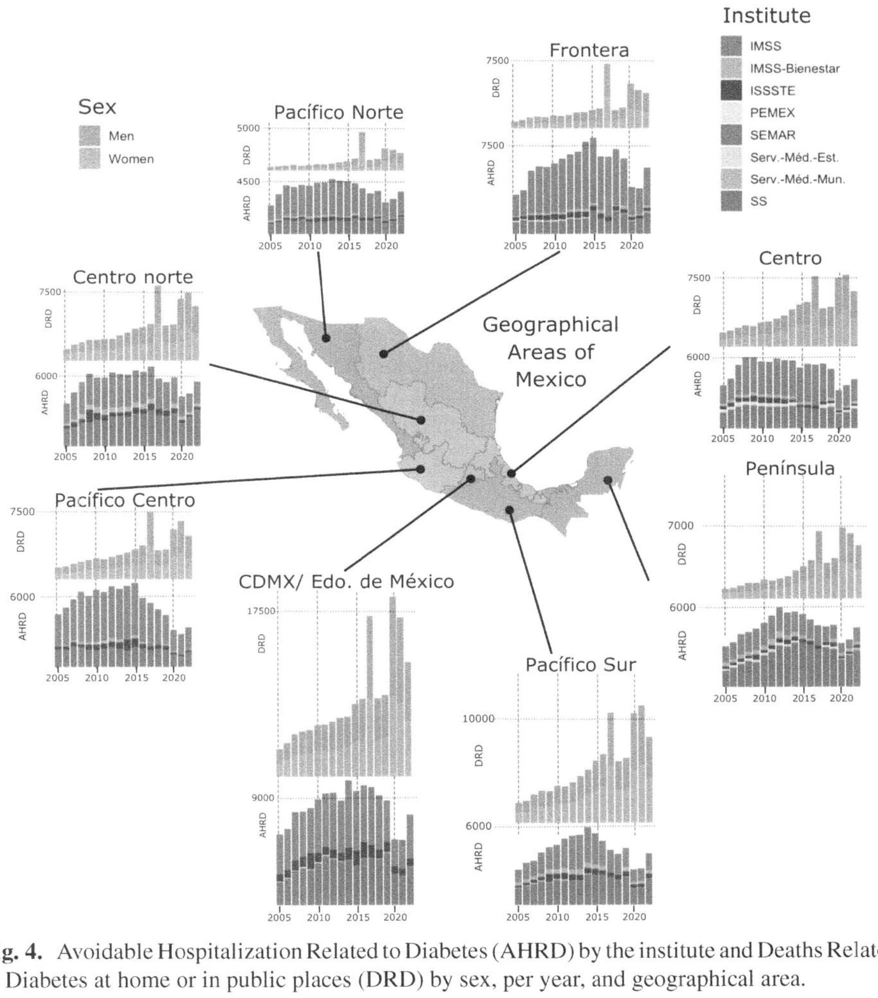

Fig. 4. Avoidable Hospitalization Related to Diabetes (AHRD) by the institute and Deaths Related to Diabetes at home or in public places (DRD) by sex, per year, and geographical area.

In the case of DRD, for women, the likelihood is more significant than for men, on average 25% more (OR value from 1.21 to 1.30). For age groups, this is similar to DRAH; people aged between 45 to 64 years old have a 300% (all OR values are higher than 4.0, except 3.47) likelihood over younger people and double (OR value a little bit higher than 2.0) that of older people. For the margination index, individuals who live in an area with a high or very high index of margination have an 83% (OR values at least 1.83) more likelihood than the remaining lower index areas. Finally, for medical institutes, SS is the baseline and people affiliated with other medical services have a higher likelihood, on average 50%. These medical services have a higher impact on DRD than DRAH.

6 Conclusions

This article investigated the association of diabetes mellitus with DRAH and DRD, incorporating health records of open datasets of hospitalizations and deaths. The work highlighted the spatio-temporal differences of the pre-pandemic and pandemic COVID-19 period, revealing that DRD increased in almost all geographical areas. At the same time, the DRAH decreased at the beginning of the pandemic, years 2020 and 2021. Also, the margination index, which is related to poverty, is a determinant factor contributing to the cases of DRAH or DRD. It is crucial to observe that hospitalization has decreased, in general, since 2017, and abruptly in the first months of 2020, possibly due to COVID-2019. It is essential to highlight the high association between DRAH and DRD for people aged between 45–64 years old with a high margination index. In other words, based on this analysis, if your residence is the Península, Pacífico Sur or CDMX/Edo. de México; you are 45–64 years old; and you are affiliated with IMSS you have a higher likelihood of requiring the hospital or suffering a death related to diabetes.

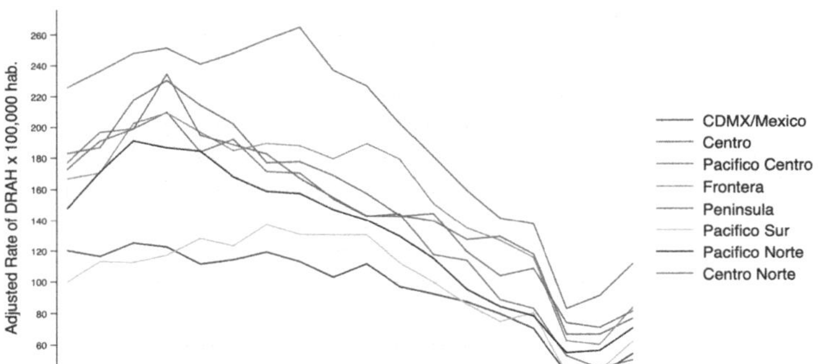

Fig. 5. Age-adjusted Rate Diabetes-related Avoidable Hospitalization (DRAH) for women.

This research also opens opportunities for further investigation by incorporating additional variables, such as environmental factors and specific air and water contamination indexes, to evaluate the impact on preventable hospitalizations and deaths across geographical areas. Additionally, the implementation of classifiers and prediction algorithms is being considered to further supplement the analysis in this study.

For further work, one way to compare the results fairly for physicians, researchers and policymakers is crucial to the data standardization process; Fig. 5 and 6 show the age-adjusted rate of avoidable hospitalization per geographical area for women and men, respectively. These are adjusted by age group: 18–44, 45–64, and 65 years old and over.

The classification of states into geographic areas is based on the latest methodology from the National Health and Nutrition Survey conducted in 2024 by the Evaluation and Survey Research Center of Mexico. The values of the DRAH and DRD have been calculated for each of Mexico's 32 states. This work presents these values by geographic area for a general overview. The subsequent study aims to conduct a detailed analysis of the states within these regions, focusing on DRAH and DRD and the age-adjusted rates of DRAH with the highest and lowest values or other areas of interest (Table 3).

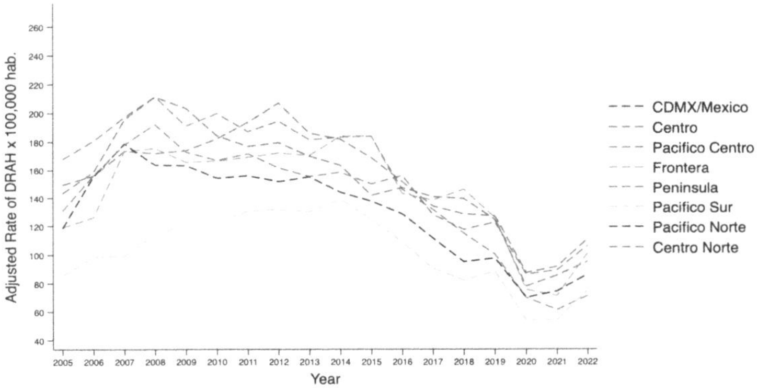

Fig. 6. Age-adjusted Rate Diabetes-related Avoidable Hospitalization (DRAH) for men.

Table 2. Association of age-group, Margination Index and Medical Institute with Diabetes-Related Avoidable Hospitalizations, 2005, 2010, 2015, 2019, 2020 and 2022.

Characteristic	Diabetes-Related Avoidable Hospitalization (DRAH)					
	Odd Ratio (OR)					
	2005	2010	2015	2019	2020	2022
Women	0.90	0.78	0.70	0.66	0.68	0.62
Age-group (years old)						
18–44	—	—	—	—	—	—
45–64	11.4	10.4	9.08	7.03	6.50	5.72
+ 65	11.8	10.5	8.88	6.63	6.17	5.26
Margination index						
Low	—	—	—	—	—	—
Medium	1.32	1.15	0.84	0.79	0.94	0.80

(continued)

Table 2. (*continued*)

Characteristic	Diabetes-Related Avoidable Hospitalization (DRAH)					
	Odd Ratio (OR)					
	2005	2010	2015	2019	2020	2022
High	1.39	1.25	0.92	0.98	1.06	*
Very High	1.28	1.21	*	1.05	1.08	1.16
Institute						
SS	—	—	—	—	—	—
IMSS bienestar	0.76	1.08	0.89	0.63	0.72	0.61
IMSS	1.34	2.06	1.72	1.79	1.91	1.56
ISSSTE	0.44	0.58	0.60	0.48	0.61	0.45
PEMEX	0.73	0.56		0.58	0.52	0.51
SEDENA	0.69	0.77		0.21		1.16
SEMAR					0.32	0.56
Other (public)					0.06	
Other (private)					5.19	

Note: * p-value $> = 0.05$

Table 3. Association of age groups, margination index and medical institute with diabetes-related deaths, 2005, 2010, 2015, 2019, 2020 and 2022.

	Diabetes-Related Deaths (DRD)					
Characteristic	Odd Ratio (OR)					
	2005	2010	2015	2019	2020	2022
Women	1.30	1.29	1.25	1.23	1.21	1.21
Age-group (years old)						
18–44	—	—	—	—	—	—
45–64	4.27	4.64	4.69	4.18	3.47	4.08
+ 65	2.85	2.98	3.08	2.97	2.46	3.02
Margination index						
Low	—	—	—	—	—	—
Medium	1.40	1.33	1.41	1.28	1.18	1.20
High	1.84	1.86	1.92	1.83	1.88	1.75
Very High	1.84	1.83	1.97	1.74	1.64	1.56

(*continued*)

Table 3. (*continued*)

Characteristic	Diabetes-Related Deaths (DRD)					
	Odd Ratio (OR)					
	2005	2010	2015	2019	2020	2022
Institute						
SS	—	—	—	—	—	—
IMSS bienestar	1.69	1.67	1.49	1.24	1.10	1.10
IMSS	1.47	1.48	1.42	1.19	1.07	1.08
ISSSTE	1.31	1.10	1.25	0.98	0.78	0.84
PEMEX	2.12	2.42	1.52	1.43	1.02	1.21
SEDENA	1.32	1.47	1.85	1.11	0.94	1.06
SEMAR	1.47	1.40	1.28	1.18	1.04	1.06
Other (public)	1.28	1.24	1.14	1.16	1.08	1.02
Other (private)			1.02	0.85	0.74	1.05

Note: * p-value > = 0.05

Acknowledgements. The authors would like to thank everyone who contributed to this manuscript for their support, in particular: IPN, SIP-IPN, COFAA, and UPIITA-IPN.

References

1. Zimmet, P.Z., Magliano, D.J., Herman, W.H., Shaw, J.E.: Diabetes: a 21st century challenge. Lancet Diab. Endocrinol. **2**(1), 56–64 (2014). https://doi.org/10.1016/S2213-8587(13)70112-8
2. Standl, E., Khunti, K., Hansen, T.B., Schnell, O.: The global epidemics of diabetes in the 21st century: current situation and perspectives. Euro. J. Prev. Cardiol. **26**(2_suppl), 7–14 (2020). https://doi.org/10.1177/2047487319881021
3. Cervantes, C.A.D., Baptista, E.A.: Mortality from type 2 diabetes mellitus across municipalities in Mexico. Arch. Public Health **82**(1), 196 (2024). https://doi.org/10.1186/s13690-024-01432-z
4. World Health Organization (WHO): The top 10 causes of death (2024). https://www.who.int/news-room/fact-sheets/detail/the-top-10-causes-of-death
5. Lord, J., Odoi, A.: Investigation of geographic disparities of diabetes-related hospitalizations in Florida using flexible spatial scan statistics: an ecological study. PLoS ONE **19**(6), 1–20 (2024). https://doi.org/10.1371/journal.pone.0298182
6. Vinik, A.I., Vinik, E.: Prevention of the complications of diabetes. Am. J. Managed Care **9**(3 Suppl), S63–S80 (2003). https://doi.org/10.1007/hta12090
7. Nanda, M., Sharma, R., Mubarik, S., Aashima, Zhang, K.: Type-2 diabetes mellitus (T2DM): spatial-temporal patterns of incidence, mortality and attributable risk factors from 1990 to 2019 among 21 World Regions. Endocrine **77**(3), 444–454 (2022). https://doi.org/10.1007/s12020-022-03125-5

8. Liu, J., et al.: Projected rapid growth in diabetes disease burden and economic burden in China: a spatio-temporal study from 2020 to 2030. Lancet Reg. Health W. Pac. **33**, 100700 (2023). https://doi.org/10.1016/j.lanwpc.2023.100700
9. Baker, J., White, N., Mengersen, K.: Spatial modelling of type II diabetes outcomes: a systematic review of approaches used. R. Soc. Open Sci. **2**(6), 140460 (2015). https://doi.org/10.1098/rsos.140460
10. Ibarra-Zapata, E., et al.: Socio-spatial vulnerability index of type 2 diabetes mellitus in Mexico in 2020. Geospatial Health **20**(1), (2025). https://doi.org/10.4081/gh.2025.1348
11. Gutiérrez-León, E., et al.: Trends and effect of marginalization on diabetes mellitus-related mortality in Mexico from 1990 to 2019. Sci. Rep. **12**(1), 9190 (2022). https://doi.org/10.1038/s41598-022-12831-z
12. AHRQ: AHRQ QI ICD-10-CM/PCS Specification v2024 Prevention Quality Indicator 93 (PQI 93). AHRQ Quality Indicators. https://qualityindicators.ahrq.gov. Accessed 23 Mar 2025
13. Glasgow, R.E., Osteen, V.L.: Evaluating diabetes education: are we measuring the most important outcomes? Diabetes Care **15**(10), 1423–1432 (1992). https://doi.org/10.2337/diacare.15.10.1423
14. Loveman, E., Frampton, G.K., Clegg, A.J.: The clinical effectiveness of diabetes education models for Type 2 diabetes: a systematic review. Health Technol. Assess. **12**(9), 1–136 (2008). https://doi.org/10.3310/hta12090
15. Fraser, I., et al.: AHRQ Quality Indicators—Guide to Prevention Quality Indicators: Hospital Admission for Ambulatory Care Sensitive Conditions. Agency for Healthcare Research and Quality, Rockville, MD. AHRQ Pub. No. 02-R0203 (2001)
16. IBM: Modeler CRISP-DM Guide: Chapter 1. Introduction to CRISP-DM (2021). https://www.ibm.com/docs/it/SS3RA7_18.3.0/pdf/ModelerCRISPDM.pdf
17. CONAPO: Marginalization in Mexico (2021). https://www.gob.mx/conapo/acciones-y-programas/marginacion-en-mexico
18. DGIS (General Directorate of Health Information): General Directorate of Health Information (DGIS) (2022). https://www.gob.mx/salud/acciones-y-programas/direccion-general-de-informacion-en-salud-dgis (Accessed: 23 Mar 2025)
19. DGIS (General Directorate of Health Information): Database of Hospital Discharges. http://www.dgis.salud.gob.mx/contenidos/basesdedatos/da_egresoshosp_gobmx.html. Accessed 23 Mar 2025
20. DGIS (General Directorate of Health Information): Database of Deaths. http://www.dgis.salud.gob.mx/contenidos/basesdedatos/da_defunciones_gobmx.html. Accessed 23 Mar 2025

Predictive Model for Identifying High-Risk Areas in the Public Transport Network of Mexico City

Braulio Melquisedec Ojeda-Contreras[1](✉), Juan Pablo Suárez-Pérez[1], José Antonio Vázquez-Portuguez[1], Violeta-Shaid Benitez-Valerio[2], Rene Baltazar Jimenez Ruiz[1], Marco Moreno Ibarra[3], and Marcela Virginia Santana Juarez[2]

[1] Escuela Superior de Cómputo (ESCOM), Instituto Politécnico Nacional. UPALM-Zacatenco, 07320 Mexico City, Mexico
{bojedac1700,jsuarezp1701,jvazquezp1602}@alumno.ipn.mx, rbjimenez@ipn.mx

[2] Facultad de Geografía, Universidad Autónoma del Estado de México (UAEMex), Estado de Mexico, 50110 Toluca de Lerdo, Mexico
vbenitezv165@alumno.uaemex.mx, mvsantanaj@uaemex.mx

[3] Centro de Investigación en Cómputo (CIC), Instituto Politécnico Nacional. UPALM-Zacatenco, 07320 Mexico City, Mexico
mmorenoi@ipn.mx

Abstract. The development of smart and healthy cities requires the creation of urban frameworks that comprehensively assess safety levels in transportation systems. Mexico City's subway system (Metro) is the eighth most traveled in the world, while the city's Bus Rapid Transit system (Metrobús) transports approximately 1.8 million passengers daily. However, the Metro has been rated as one of the least secure electric transport systems, underscoring the need for effective strategies to mitigate safety risks. This study proposes a framework based on artificial intelligence and open data to assess security at Metro stations and Metrobús stops. Crime records from 2019 to 2022, georeferenced transport network layers, and passenger flow data were analyzed to identify crime patterns within public transportation environments. Findings reveal that women are the primary victims of harassment and sexual abuse, whereas men are more frequently targeted for street robberies and passenger thefts inside Metro trains. Additionally, crime rates peak at noon, with the most vulnerable age group being individuals aged 21 to 30. Notably, half of the recorded Metro-related crimes occur within the influence zones of Lines 1, 2, and 3. Based on these insights, a predictive model using SARIMA and Support Vector Machines (SVM) was developed to estimate weekly crime risk at transport stations and their surrounding areas. The SVM model achieved 70% accuracy, offering a valuable tool for anticipating high-risk locations and times, which could inform the development of more effective security strategies for public transportation.

Keywords: Spatial Data Science · Crime analysis · Transportation Systems

M. F. Mata-Rivera et al. (Eds.): W2GIS 2025, LNCS 15946, pp. 105–120, 2026.
https://doi.org/10.1007/978-3-032-01723-9_8

1 Introduction

Mexico City is described in the sources as one of the most densely populated urban areas in the world, with an estimated population of approximately 9.2 million inhabitants in 2020. Public transportation is a crucial aspect of the city, with the Sistema de Transporte Colectivo (STC) Metro and the Metrobús being the most heavily utilized systems. The growth of public transportation in Mexico City brings new challenges, including insecurity. There is a need for data-driven processes to understand crime dynamics, analyze patterns, and build predictive models for crime prevention in the Metro and Metrobús systems. These systems are essential for the daily activities of residents within the metropolitan area Mexico City's subway system (Metro) is the eighth most traveled in the world, while the city's Bus Rapid Transit system (Metrobús) transports approximately 1.8 million passengers daily. However, the Metro has been rated as one of the least secure electric transport systems, underscoring the need for effective strategies to mitigate safety risks.

The absence of data-based applications that provide a complete understanding of crime within and near these stations highlights the need for this work. Implementing preventive measures against crime is possible, but the lack of data-driven applications providing a comprehensive understanding of this issue in the Mexico City Metro and Metrobús necessitates the development of an analysis and prediction model.

Understanding the dynamics of crime necessitates considering various risk factors. These factors, as outlined in the report, include high concentration of people (Newman, 1972), the presence of socially vulnerable groups (Shaw & McKay, 1942), and lack of adequate surveillance and control (Clarke, 1980; Eck & Weisburd, 1995). Furthermore, physical vulnerability, related to factors like age and gender, also increases the fear of crime (Pantazis, 2000; Bissler, 2003). These risk factors are crucial considerations in the development of the analysis and prediction model.

This project aims to develop such a model, focusing on low-impact crimes and robberies occurring within and around these stations. It utilizes official crime reports from the Fiscalía General de Justicia (FGJ), geospatial data, and ridership data to find multidimensional patterns and make predictions for both transportation systems, aiding in decision-making for crime prevention by residents and visitors.

This work proposes a framework based on artificial intelligence and open data to assess security at Metro stations and Metrobús stops. Crime records from 2019 to 2022, georeferenced transport network layers, and passenger flow data were analyzed to identify crime patterns within public transportation environments. The purpose is to develop data analysis and prediction model based on low-impact crime and robbery incidents that occurred within and near the stations of the STC Metro and Metrobús of Mexico City from 2019 to 2022. The aim is to find patterns in the dimensions of space, time, and victims, and to make predictions for both modes of transport that jointly contribute to the prevention of these crimes.

2 Related Work

This section reviews existing research on crime related to public transportation. It notes that while previous studies have often been theoretical or descriptive of urban criminality, this project focuses on applying advanced machine learning and data analysis models. These models aim to capture the temporal and spatial aspects of crime at the borough and weekly levels in detail, offering deeper insights than previous approaches. It also explores user satisfaction surveys and the perception of safety in the Mexico City Metro. The use of convolutional neural networks (CNN) to address the spatial aspects is mentioned as a significant approach.

The study of crime in urban environments, particularly within public transportation systems, has been a subject of increasing academic and practical interest. Previous research has explored various aspects, including the theoretical underpinnings of crime occurrence in transit networks, the impact of environmental design on crime, and the application of different policing strategies. Newton (2014) provides a theoretical framework for understanding crime in public transport, highlighting the unique scenarios (places and times) where crime can occur within these networks. Smith and Cornish (2006), as cited by Newton (2014), propose categories of crime in public transport, including crimes against passengers and vandalism. However, this study aligns its crime classification with the standardized system used in the FGJ investigation files, which is based on the National Classification of Crimes for Statistical Purposes (Clasificación Nacional de Delitos para Fines Estadísticos - CNDFE).... The CNDFE offers a unified structure for reporting crime data across Mexico, enhancing the comparability and analysis of crime statistics.

While previous investigations in Mexico City have often focused on theoretical or descriptive analyses of urban crime, this project distinguishes itself by its application of advanced machine learning and data analysis techniques to capture the temporal and spatial dynamics of crime at a detailed level (borough and week). This approach allows for more in-depth insights compared to purely descriptive methods.

Several studies in other urban contexts offer relevant comparisons. Billings, Leland & Swindell (2016) found no increase in crime near new light rail transit stations in North Carolina, USA, a finding that contrasts with the potential identification of high-risk areas in this study. Conversely, Erikson Irvin & La Vigne (2015) conducted a spatio-temporal analysis of crime at Washington, DC Metro Rail, identifying station characteristics that attract or generate crime, which aligns with the goals of this research to understand local risk factors.

Stec & Klabjan (2018) represent a significant contribution to the field by utilizing recurrent and convolutional neural networks for crime prediction in specific geospatial areas and days in Chicago and Portland, achieving an accuracy of 75.6% and 65.3%, respectively. While their results demonstrate high predictive power at a finer spatiotemporal granularity, the different urban contexts and datasets necessitate a tailored approach for Mexico City. This study explores traditional machine learning models as a baseline before potentially considering more advanced neural network architectures in future work.

The existing literature underscores the complexity of crime in public transportation and the need for data-driven approaches to effectively analyze and predict these events.

This research builds upon these foundations by focusing specifically on low-impact crimes and robberies in the unique context of the Mexico City Metro and Metrobús, leveraging a robust dataset and developing a practical tool for stakeholders.

3 Methodology

The project's methodology for data analysis is structured based on an adapted version of the CRISP-DM (Cross-Industry Standard Process for Data Mining) methodology. This framework provides a flexible approach, allowing for movement back and forth between phases as needed. The data analysis process in this project encompasses several key stages: (1) Data Integration Process (2) exploratory data analysis (EDA), (3) data architecture definition, (4) multidimensional data analysis, (5) designing predictive models.

3.1 Data Integration Process

The data used in this analysis project primarily consists of publicly available datasets from the Fiscalía General de Justicia (FGJ) of Mexico City and the Sistema de Transporte Colectivo (STC) Metro and Metrobús. The technical report details several key datasets:

Carpetas de Investigación (Crime Investigation Files) from the FGJ: These are official reports of crimes that contain consolidated data from 2019 to 2022. This dataset includes information on the crime committed (category and type), the date and time of the report opening, the date and time of the crime, and the approximate geographic coordinates (latitude and longitude) of the incident. While the raw dataset initially contained 1,248,791 records, after filtering for relevance to the project's scope (low-impact crimes and robberies in and around Metro and Metrobús stations) and removing records with null values in critical fields, the dataset was reduced to a sample of 655,800 records for analysis.

Víctimas en Carpetas de Investigación (Information about Victims in Investigation Files) from the FGJ: This is a complementary database that contains the same information as the investigation folders but also includes additional characteristics of the victims, such as age and sex. While this dataset initially spanned from 2019 to 2023, the data used for this project was limited to 2022 due to potential updates or modifications by the authorities for more recent data.

Geoespacial Data (Shapefiles) of the STC Metro and Metrobús Networks: These files provide the location, name, type, and line of each station within both transportation systems. This data was obtained from the Open Data Portal of Mexico City.

Afluencia (Ridership) Data of the Metro: This dataset includes the daily number of people entering each Metro station since 2010, broken down by date, year, month, line, and station.

Afluencia (Ridership) Data of the Metrobús: Initially, the publicly available Metrobús ridership data spanned from 2005 but was only available at the line level, lacking station-specific information. However, historical ridership data for Metrobús disaggregated by station was obtained through contact with relevant authorities in Mexico City by Alvarado (2023) and subsequently provided to the project authors.

Administratively, Mexico City is divided into alcaldías or boroughs, which replaced the former delegaciones in 2016. These boroughs are the primary political-administrative divisions of the capital.

It is important to note that these datasets underwent significant data integration processes, including extraction, cleaning, and transformation (ETL):

- Filtering the investigation folders to focus on low-impact crimes and robberies occurring within a defined radius of Metro and Metrobús stations. For practical purposes, a radius of 540 m for Metro stations and 270 m for Metrobús stations was determined based on the analysis of crime-station distances.Supplementing the filtered crime data with a manually created catalog that maps the FGJ's crime classifications to their equivalents in the National Classification of Crimes for Statistical Purposes (CNDFE), adding fields for category, variable, and class of crime according to this standardized classification.
- Imputing missing values for characteristics like age and sex of victims using statistical measures (mean or mode) calculated within specific groupings of data based on time, space, and crime type.Handling outliers in the age variable.
- Geospatial processing using QGIS to map crime locations, station locations, and urban equipment, and to determine the nearest station and urban equipment to each reported crime.
- Homogenizing data, particularly station names and station types, across different datasets to enable proper merging and analysis.
- Transforming the ridership data to a consistent format for both Metro and Metrobús.

The resulting integrated and preprocessed data formed the basis for exploratory data analysis, the development of a multidimensional data architecture, and the generation of predictive models for crime risk levels.

3.2 Exploratory Data Analysis (EDA)

This allowed to observe initial trends and findings related to the crime phenomenon within and around the Metro and Metrobús stations from various perspectives.

During these earlier stages, constant exploration of the data was performed to understand patterns, missing values, and distributions.

However, a more formal EDA was conducted using the resulting dataset from the data transformation process. The primary technique used during this stage was data visualization through Tableau.

Specifically, the EDA phase involved the creation of several visualizations:

Distribution of crimes by the original FGJ crime categories was visualized to understand the initial composition of the crime data, as shown in Fig. 1. It provides a visual representation of the initial distribution of crime categories as recorded in the investigation files of the Fiscalía General de Justicia (FGJ). This figure shows how the 1,248,791 records in the raw dataset were divided among various types of crimes before any filtering was performed for the project's specific focus. It illustrates the original proportions of different crime categories reported to the FGJ.

The crime categories included are: Delitos de bajo impacto (low-impact crimes), Robo a transeúnte en vía pública con y sin violencia (robbery of passersby in public roads with and without violence), Robo de vehículo con y sin violencia (vehicle theft with and without violence), Robo a negocio con violencia (business robbery with violence), Hecho no delictivo (non-criminal act), Robo a repartidor con y sin violencia (delivery person robbery with and without violence), Violación (rape), Robo a pasajero a bordo del metro con y sin violencia (robbery of subway passengers with and without violence), Homicidio doloso (intentional homicide), Lesiones dolosas por disparo de arma de fuego (intentional injuries by firearm), Robo a pasajero a bordo de microbús con y sin violencia (robbery of minibus passengers with and without violence), Robo a casa habitación con violencia (residential robbery with violence), Robo a cuentahabiente saliendo del cajero con violencia (robbery of bank clients leaving ATMs with violence), Robo a pasajero a bordo de taxi con violencia (robbery of taxi passengers with violence), Robo a transportista con y sin violencia (carrier robbery with and without violence), and Secuestro (kidnapping).

The category with the highest number of records in the original distribution is Delitos de bajo impacto (low-impact crimes). Figure 1 presents a baseline understanding of the types of crimes initially documented by the FGJ, setting the stage for the subsequent data filtering and analysis that focused on specific crime categories relevant to the study of security in the Metro and Metrobús systems.

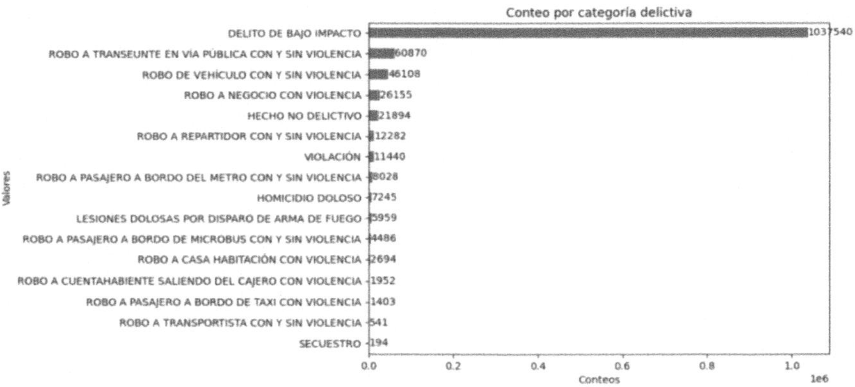

Fig. 1. Distribution of FGJ Crime Categories

After filtering and data integration, the distribution of the filtered crime data by FGJ crime category was again visualized in Fig. 2. It demonstrates the composition of the dataset after the initial steps of data cleaning and filtering, highlighting the crime categories that were considered relevant for further analysis in the study of crime around Metro and Metrobús stations.

The relationship between violence in crimes and the sex of the victims was explored after categorizing crimes based on the presence, absence, or lack of specification of violence according to the CNDFE. The dataset was reduced to a sample of 655,800 records, and Fig. 2 shows the distribution of these remaining records by the FGJ's crime categories. The list includes: Delitos de bajo impacto (Low-impact crimes), robo a cuentahabiente saliendo del cajero con violencia (Robbery of bank clients leaving

ATMs with violence), robo a pasajero a bordo de microbús con y sin violencia (Robbery of minibus passengers with and without violence), robo a pasajero a bordo de taxi con violencia (Robbery of taxi passengers with violence), robo a pasajero a bordo del metro con y sin violencia (Robbery of subway passengers with and without violence), robo a transeúnte a bordo de taxi público y privado con violencia (Robbery of passersby on board public and private taxis with violence), secuestro (Kidnapping).

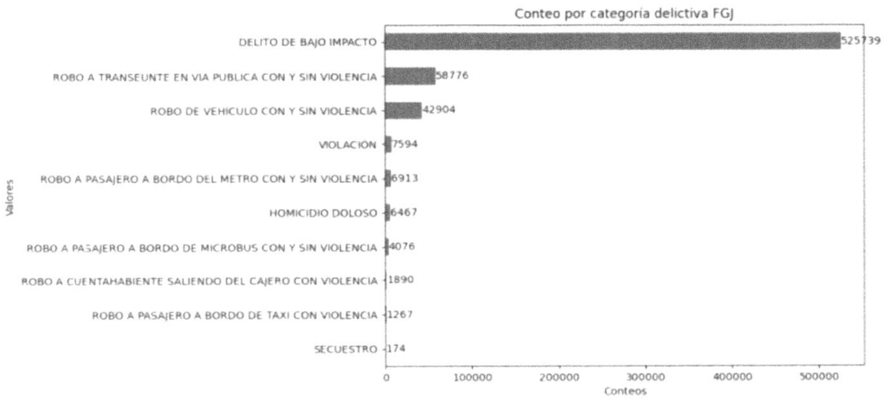

Fig. 2. Distribution of the filtered crime data by FGJ crime category

Figure 3 is a visual representation of the geographic locations where the criminal events recorded in the FGJ investigation files occurred throughout Mexico City. It takes the raw location information from the FGJ investigation files and transforms it into a visual map, allowing to see where crimes are happening across Mexico City and to prepare for subsequent analyses involving the proximity of these events to the public transportation systems and other urban elements.

From 2019 to 2023, criminal activity intensified in the urban boroughs of Mexico City with flat terrain, highlighting the widespread geographic presence of crime. In contrast, southern boroughs such as La Magdalena Contreras, Tlalpan, and Milpa Alta recorded lower crime incidents compared to their more densely urban counterparts. After spatial overlay operations and measuring the distance to the nearest center at the point level, the investigation records were enriched with better geographic context, creating a spatial association among the investigation files, transport stations, transport stations (Metro and Metrobús), and urban infrastructure. Figure 4 show the spatial association between crime Incident, nearest Station, and nearest urban amenity. It highlights the spatial aspect and specifies that it likely refers to the nearest station and urban equipment, which is implied in the subsequent text.

Figure 5 visually clarifies how the nearest neighbor algorithm creates a direct association between every crime report and a specific Metro station based solely on geographical proximity, which leads to the city being conceptually divided into zones of influence around each station.

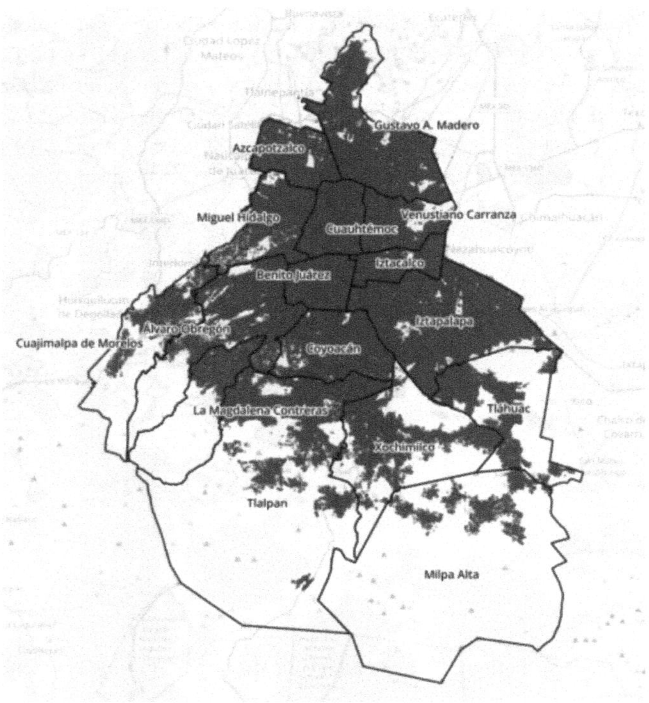

Fig. 3. Spatial Distribution of Recorded Crimes in Mexico City

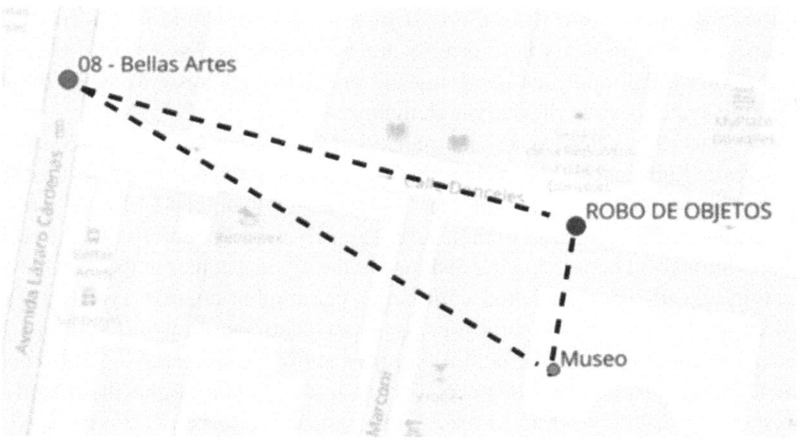

Fig. 4. Visualizing Proximity: Crime Scene, Public Transport, and Urban Infrastructure

This is an important step in the project's methodology for analyzing crime patterns in relation to public transportation. Visually demonstrates the refined spatial association between crime incidents and Metro stations after applying a distance-based filter. This step narrows down the dataset to include only those crimes that occurred within a defined proximity of the stations, allowing for a more focused analysis of the relationship between crime and public transportation infrastructure. It is important to note that different radii are used for the STC Metro (540 m) and the Metrobús (270 m). The rationale for these specific distances likely stems from an analysis of the typical distances between stations of each transportation systems.

Fig. 5. Crime reports associated with the nearest subway station (buffers of 540 m)

3.3 Data Architecture Definition

This stage focuses on designing how the data will be organized and structured to facilitate analysis. The project opted for an online analytical processing (OLAP) system architecture due to its ability to store data in multiple dimensions or categories, forming data cubes that allow for analysis from various perspectives.

This implicitly involves using a multidimensional data model for the database, which differs from the entity-relationship model by not prioritizing normalization and supporting complex queries for historical data analysis. The specific model implemented was a constellation schema, a hybrid of star and snowflake models, allowing for multiple fact tables and interconnected dimensions.

This model comprises 8-dimension tables (time, day phase, space, stations, urban amenities, crime, victim sex, victim age, and 2 fact tables investigation files and ridership. Incident Facts Table (tabla de hechos de carpetas de investigación) contains records of reported incidents (carpetas de investigación) and includes foreign keys that link each incident to various dimensions, such as when and where it occurred, the type of crime, and characteristics of the victim. Ridership Facts (tabla de hechos de afluencia de las estaciones) is the second fact table, focusing on the ridership (afluencia) data for the Metro and Metrobús stations. It also uses foreign keys to connect to relevant dimensions. The dimension tables contain hierarchical attributes that describe the different aspects of the data, while the fact tables store the measures: crime counts, ridership statistics, and foreign keys linking them to the dimensions.

This model is designed to facilitate the analysis and prediction of crime categories within and around the STC Metro and Metrobús systems. The resulting tables were then exported to a Microsoft SQL Server database (Fig. 6).

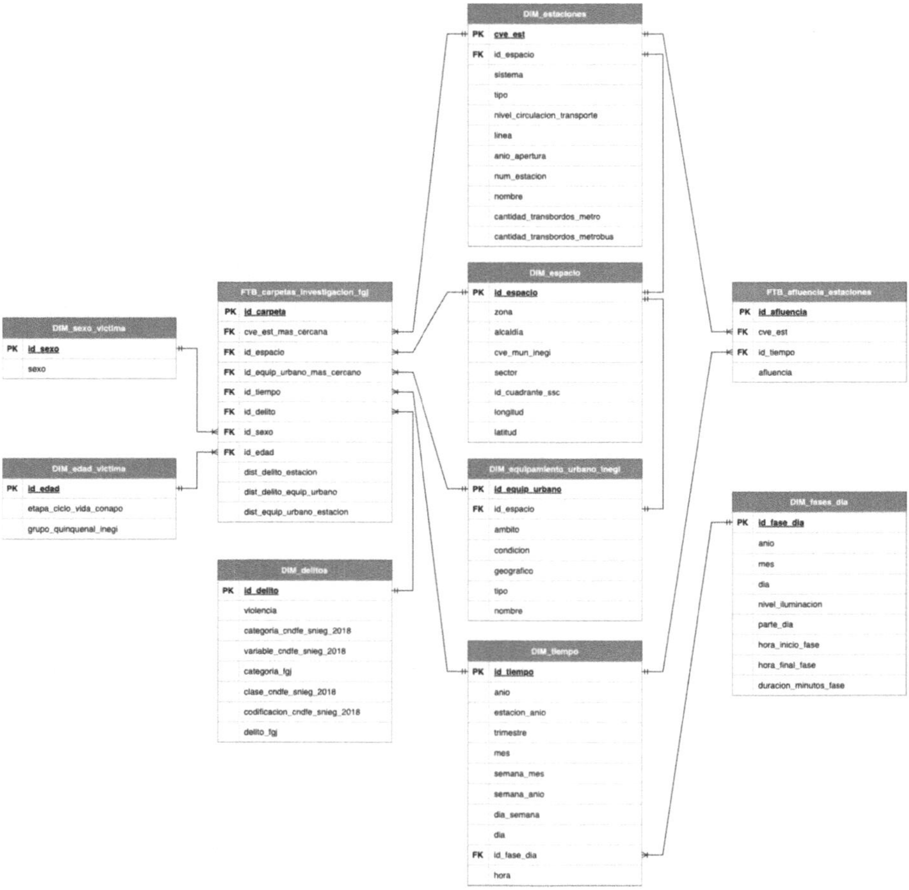

Fig. 6. Multidimensional Data Model for Time, Space, and Urban Topics

3.4 Multidimensional Data Analysis

This stage centers on analyzing the structured data through the lens of multiple dimensions. The use of data cubes allows for a richer and more accessible representation of information, improving query efficiency. Key operations in multidimensional analysis, such as roll-up (aggregating data to a higher level) and drill-down (exploring data at a more detailed level), were used to navigate different granularities of data based on the hierarchies within each dimension. These operations facilitated the exploration of the data to discern trends and patterns, such as identifying space-time conditions most prone to certain crimes, which informs the development of prevention strategies.

3.5 Predictive Models

Based on ridership and other relevant features, the predictive modeling phase focused on developing a classifier to predict the level of crime risk (moderate or high) at a given time and location. This model development inherently involves data analysis to identify features and patterns relevant for forecasting crime risk levels. This involved creating a categorical variable representing crime risk (moderate and elevated) based on percentiles of aggregated crime counts. Different datasets were created by grouping data by week of the year, municipality or police sector, adapted crime category, and inclusion/exclusion of victim gender. Classification models were then tested using these datasets. The process involved:

Feature Engineering: Features were derived from the dimension tables, including temporal features (year, week of the year), spatial features (municipality, police sector), and ridership data (total weekly ridership). This stage also involved generating the categorical target variable, which classifies weekly crime counts into risk levels using the 50th percentile as the threshold on the grouped dataset.

Data Preprocessing and Balancing: Min-Max normalization was applied to scale continuous features. To address class imbalance across different crime categories, a 2:1 ratio criterion was used: random undersampling was applied when the majority class exceeded this threshold; otherwise, oversampling was used, which was the case for most instances, to balance the training data between moderate and high-risk classes.

Model Selection and Training: Several classification algorithms were evaluated, including **logistic regression, K-nearest neighbors (KNN), support vector machines (SVM), decision trees, and random forests**. The models were trained using the preprocessed crime data associated with STC Metro and Metrobús stations, grouped at a weekly level and by different spatial aggregations (borough and police sector). An 80/20 train-test split was applied, where the training set was used for model development and hyperparameter tuning through cross-validation.

Hyperparameter Tuning and Evaluation: A **GridSearch** approach with 5-fold cross-validation was employed to find the optimal hyperparameters for each model. The performance of the models was evaluated using metrics such as **accuracy, precision, recall, and F1-score**. The model exhibiting the best balance of these metrics on the validation set was selected for final evaluation on the held-out test set.

Ridership Prediction: SARIMA (Seasonal Autoregressive Integrated Moving Average) models were implemented to forecast weekly ridership for different regions (municipalities) and transportation systems. These predictions were later integrated into the crime risk prediction framework.

3.6 Analysis and Temporal Predictions

This final data analysis stage involves developing dashboards to present the findings on crime patterns over time. These dashboards, built using Streamlit and Plotly, allow users to explore trends and predictions based on filtered queries to the multidimensional database. The trend analysis shows crime hotspots, while the exploration section provides detailed information about crime classes, victim demographics, and the distance of crime incidents from stations for specific locations and timeframes.

4 Results

Figure 7 visually maps the entire data journey in the project, from initial data sources through various processing and modeling stages, culminating in the interactive dashboard and its predictive crime risk map. It highlights the interrelation between different components and the overall flow of information required to achieve the project's objectives.

- Data Sources: The architecture would illustrate the sources of data used in the project.
- Intermediate Processing Steps and Tools: The diagram would show the various stages of data processing and the tools employed at each step
- Predictive Model Development: The architecture would illustrate the development of the "Propuesta híbrida del modelo clasificador del nivel de riesgo delictivo" (hybrid proposal of the crime risk level classifier model)
- The interactive dashboard with the "Mapa del nivel de riesgo delictivo" (Crime Risk Level Map), which is powered by the predictive models and "secciones de tendencias y exploración" (trends and exploration sections) of the dashboard, which are based on filtered queries to the multidimensional database.

For data transformation and spatial analysis, the software QGIS is used. Throughout the data handling process (including exploration, analysis, and model development), Jupyter notebooks are used, primarily working with CSV format files. The libraries NumPy and Pandas are the main tools for data manipulation. The developing predictive models (as part of the hybrid model), Scikit-learn is used. Models are saved using pickle files. Development of the interactive dashboards, the libraries Streamlit and Plotly are used. The platform is hosted on a VPS running a Docker container.

The multidimensional analysis allowed for the examination of crime patterns from various perspectives, such as the distribution of incidents by municipality, police sector, time of day, and day of the week, for both the STC Metro and Metrobús systems. This analysis identified key trends and high-risk areas within the transportation networks. For example, certain lines and stations exhibited a higher concentration of reported crimes.

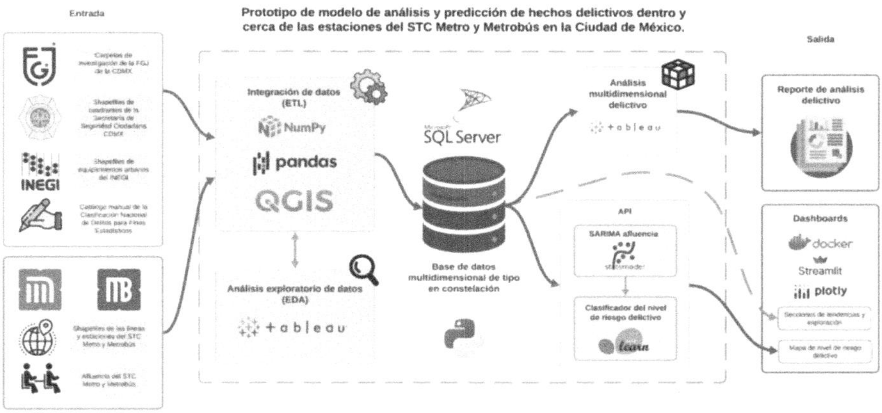

Fig. 7. Spatial data science architecture

Temporal patterns, such as an increase in crime on Fridays followed by a decrease over the weekend, were also observed.

The Fig. 8 provides a baseline view of the crime trends and ridership in the STC Metro system as a whole, without any specific geographic or line-based filtering applied. This allows users to get a general overview before narrowing down their analysis by selecting specific zones, boroughs, or lines using the available filters, showing a map of Mexico City with the geographical locations of the STC Metro stations. These stations would be categorized and colored based on their average historical crime incidence, likely using a traffic light scale (green for lower, amber for medium, and red for higher average crime counts) and varying point sizes to further emphasize the hotspots. Since no specific region is selected by default, the map would likely display all STC Metro stations across the entire city. The bar chart display the top 10 STC Metro stations with the highest average number of crime incidents for the current day of the week, based on the historical data from 2019 to 2023. Finally the information about STC Metro stations with the highest average ridership is included.

Predictive Model Performance focuses on the outcomes and effectiveness of the predictive models developed in the study. It highlights several key aspects regarding the performance of both the crime risk classification models and the ridership prediction models. Decision tree-based algorithms generally demonstrated promising results across the different experimental setups.

The models demonstrated the ability to predict crime risk levels (categorized as moderate or high) with reasonable accuracy. The top-performing classifier achieved 77% accuracy on the test set, taking into account that predictions were made at a meaningful temporal aggregation level of weekly data, which underscores the effectiveness of the proposed modeling approach.

Training used preprocessed crime data from STC Metro and Metrobús stations, aggregated weekly and by borough and police sector. A crucial aspect of this approach is the incorporation of ridership forecasts generated by SARIMA models into the crime risk prediction framework.

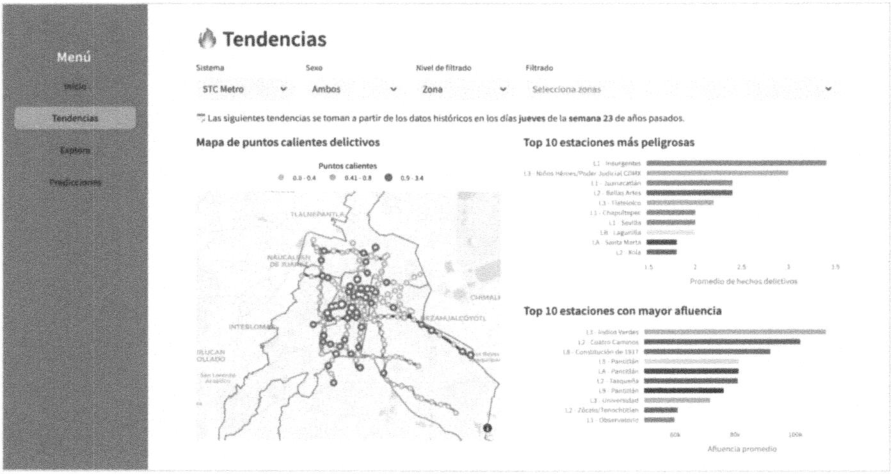

Fig. 8. Displaying crime hotspots and trends: most dangerous stations, and stations with the highest traffic for the STC Metro.

Incorporating ridership forecasts added valuable contextual information to the crime risk predictions, leveraging the observed correlation between passenger flow and criminal activity. By estimating the expected number of people in specific areas at given times, the models could enhance their sensitivity and accuracy in predicting crime risk.

The SARIMA models used for ridership prediction effectively captured temporal patterns in passenger volumes, as confirmed by diagnostic tests showing a strong fit to historical data. This good fit is essential because the reliability of the ridership predictions directly impacts the effectiveness of the integrated crime risk prediction. A significant contribution to this predictive capability was the integration of ridership forecasts generated by SARIMA models, which effectively captured temporal trends in passenger numbers and leveraged the relationship between ridership and crime.

The predictive model that was developed to power the interactive dashboard's crime risk level map providing predictions of the crime risk level (moderate or high) for specific boroughs and weeks in the future. Input Parameters:

- Specifies the transportation system, either "STC Metro" or "Metrobús".
- Indicates the year for the prediction, currently set to "2024" but can be extended for future predictions.
- The specific week of the year (ranging from 1 to 53) for which the prediction is requested.
- The category of crime to consider. The valid options are "Robo a transeúnte y pasajero en transporte público", "Robo de vehículo y autopartes", "Delitos sexuales", "Lesiones", "Amenazas", or "Fraude".
- Allows filtering predictions by the sex of the user, with options being "Female", "Male", or omitting the parameter for a general prediction

Figure 9 demonstrates how the prediction model is visualized on the interactive dashboard, allowing users to quickly identify boroughs with a higher or moderate predicted risk of specific crimes in the STC Metro for a chosen future week. The boroughs are colored based on a binary risk level scale: red indicates a high level of risk, and a muted yellow indicates a moderate level of risk

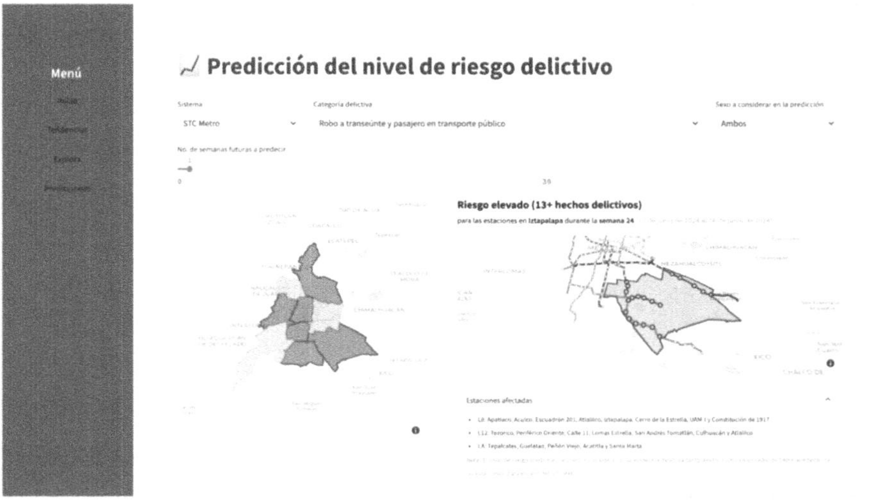

Fig. 9. Visualization of weekly predictions for the STC Metro

5 Conclusions

The project successfully developed a model for analyzing and predicting low-impact crimes and robberies in the Mexico City Metro and Metrobús systems between 2019 and 2022. The integration of diverse public data sources enabled the identification of specific crime patterns in both transport systems and facilitated the prediction of crime risk levels based on ridership. The findings highlight precise spatio-temporal patterns for different crime types and express crime incidence in relation to ridership for prediction purposes. The project underscores the necessity of understanding spatial patterns, urban infrastructure, and user dynamics, along with utilizing advanced technologies for crime analysis and prediction. The adopted CRISP-DM methodology and Kanban for task management were effective. The data integration process involved significant data cleaning and transformation. Exploratory data analysis was crucial for initial findings and defining the data architecture. The development of predictive models involved testing various algorithms, with decision tree-based models showing superior performance, particularly when grouped by borough. The interactive dashboard effectively integrates the project's key results. The study contributes to a precise understanding of crime dynamics in major public transport systems in a densely populated city.

Acknowledgments. The authors would like to thank IPN, SECIHTI, Project CF-2023-G-1170, SIP-20250112, SIP-20242869, COFAA, UPIITA-IPN, ESCOM-IPN, and UAEMEX for their invaluable support.

References

Alvarado, V.: Afluencia diaria del metrobús de la línea 1 desglosada por estación. Twitter (2023). https://twitter.com/Ar7ois/status/1706

Newton, A.D.: Crime on public transport. In: Encyclopedia of Criminology and Criminal Justice, pp. 709–720 (2014). https://core.ac.uk/reader/19453760

Smith, M.J., Clarke, R.V.: Crime and public transport. Crime Justice **27**, 169–233 (2000). https://www.jstor.org/stable/pdf/1147664.pdf

Smith, M.J., Cornish, D.B.: Secure and tranquil travel: preventing crime and disorderon public transport. Jill Dando Institute of Crime Science, University College London (2006). https://doi.org/10.1007/s10610-008-9084-5

Billings, S.B., Leland, S., Swindell, D.: The effects of the announcement and opening of light rail transit stations on neighborhood crime. J. Urban Affairs **33**(5), 549–566 (2016). https://doi.org/10.1111/j.1467-9906.2011.00564.x

Irvin-Erickson, Y., La Vigne, N.: A spatio-temporal analysis of crime at Washington, DC metro rail: stations' crime-generating and crime-attracting characteristics as transportation nodes and places. Crime Sci. **4**(1), 1–13 (2015). https://doi.org/10.1186/s40163-015-0026-5

Stec, A. Klabjan, D. (2018). Forecasting crime with deep learning. arXiv preprint arXiv:1806.01486

Clarke, R.V.: Situational crime prevention: theory and practice. British J. Criminol. **20**(2), 136–147 (1980)

Newman, O.: Defensible Space: Crime Prevention Through Urban Design. Macmillan (1972)

Pantazis, C.: Fear of crime, vulnerability and poverty. British J. Criminology **40**(3), 414–436 (2000)

Shaw, C.R., McKay, H.D.: Juvenile Delinquency and Urban Areas. University of Chicago Press (1942)

Von Hirsch, A., Garland, D., Wakefield, A. (eds.).: Understanding Crime: Data, Theory and Policy, pp. 207–265. Cambridge University Press (2003). (Bissler, G. (2003). Fear of crime at railway stations)

Location Intelligence for Urban Resources, Mobility, and Commerce

Analyzing Water Consumption Patterns in Mexico City: A GIS and Data Science Approach

Israel Hernández-Vázquez[1], Antonio Jonathan Luna-Sánchez[1], Arturo Benjamin Hurtado-Perez[2](✉), Christophe Claramunt[3], Roberto Zagal-Flores[1], and Felix Mata[2]

[1] Escuela Superior de Cómputo ESCOM-IPN, México City, México
[2] UPIITA-IPN, México City, México
ahurtadop1500@alumno.ipn.mx
[3] Naval Academy Research Institute, 29240 Lanvéoc, France

Abstract. Water scarcity in Mexico City has become an increasingly urgent issue, exacerbated by inefficient and unequal consumption patterns across its urban fabric. This study advances Geographic Information Systems (GIS) research by developing and applying an integrative spatial analysis framework specifically tailored to the complexities of urban water management. Beyond its application to Mexico City, the research demonstrates how GIS can be used to fuse heterogeneous datasets, including those from SACMEX (Mexico City's Water System), INEGI (National Institute of Statistics and Geography), and DENUE (National Directory of Economic Units), into a unified analytical environment. Through a combination of exploratory data analysis (EDA), spatial data mining, and clustering techniques, the study identifies critical disparities in water consumption at multiple spatial scales, from boroughs to neighborhoods. A key contribution is the implementation of a layered system architecture for managing historic spatiotemporal data, enabling dynamic visualization of consumption patterns. The findings reveal that socio-economic and demographic variables play a decisive role in shaping spatial water demand, with marginalized communities facing disproportionate challenges. While previous spatiotemporal analyses of water consumption in Mexico City have primarily focused on aggregated borough-level data or isolated socio-demographic correlations, they have often lacked multiscale integration, high-resolution neighborhood-level analysis, or interactive visualization tools to support policy development. This research addresses these limitations by providing a fine-grained, multilayered analytical approach that enhances the scientific understanding of urban water use. Beyond offering immediate policy-relevant insights for Mexico City, the methodological framework proposed here contributes to GIS research by providing a scalable, transferable approach for analyzing urban resource consumption patterns. Future work will focus on incorporating real-time data streams, expanding sector-specific analysis, and integrating additional variables and domains required for a comprehensive understanding of water dynamics. This study represents a first step toward building an adaptive, equitable, and efficient urban water management strategy.

Keywords: Water Consumption · GIS · Data mining · Mexico City

M. F. Mata-Rivera et al. (Eds.): W2GIS 2025, LNCS 15946, pp. 123–137, 2026.
https://doi.org/10.1007/978-3-032-01723-9_9

1 Introduction

Water scarcity in Mexico City is an increasingly urgent issue, aggravated by inefficient consumption habits, particularly in urban settings. According to the Secretariat of the Environment in Mexico (SEDEMA acronym in spanish), these consumption patterns significantly contribute to the city's ongoing water crisis. The situation has become even more dire following the COVID-19 pandemic, which began in February 2020, exacerbating existing inequalities, especially in access to potable water. At least five boroughs in Mexico City experienced severe water shortages, which complicated efforts to maintain hygiene, crucial for combating the virus (Castillo, 2021).

This research emphasizes the importance of water conservation, particularly among marginalized communities, where water exclusion has become a critical challenge. Effective water management strategies are essential to understanding and improving consumption behaviors (UNESCO, 2020). The integration of data from multiple sources—namely SACMEX (Mexico City's Water System), INEGI (National Institute of Statistics and Geography), and DENUE (National Directory of Economic Units)—forms the foundation of this study. Our objective is to create a methodology to analyze water consumption in Mexico City, identify inefficiencies and inequities, and propose actionable solutions for better resource distribution.

Understanding water availability and consumption patterns is crucial, particularly in urban areas like Mexico City, which face growing socio-economic and environmental challenges. The global population, which grew from 2.6 billion in 1950 to 8 billion in 2022, is projected to reach 10 billion by 2050, further straining water resources. In Mexico, water availability has been significantly decreasing, with per capita water availability falling from 10,000 m3 in 1960 to 3,200 m3 today. Projections suggest that by 2030, it will fall below 3,000 m3 per capita annually, placing immense pressure on the country's water resources, particularly in large metropolitan areas like Mexico City, Monterrey, and Guadalajara (Perló, 2005). Figure 1 highlights the population distribution of these primary metropolitan areas, showing the concentration of inhabitants in regions facing water scarcity.

In 2020, the agricultural sector accounted for 76% of total water usage, primarily for crop irrigation and livestock production. The public water supply accounted for 15%, serving households, industries, and other connected users. Self-supplied industries, which extract water directly from natural sources such as rivers, lakes, and aquifers, consumed 5%. Additionally, water used for electricity generation in thermoelectric plants represented 4%, though this often results in thermal pollution and water contamination from chemicals used in cooling processes. Notably, there is limited data on water usage in the livestock sector, which relies on substantial amounts of water for animal consumption, cleaning production units, and waste disposal. The lack of comprehensive monitoring in this sector remains a critical gap in understanding total water consumption. Moreover, the impact of thermoelectric plants on water quality due to pollutants like chlorine further exacerbates the challenges surrounding water resource management (Garcia, 2013). This paper seeks to address these challenges by utilizing GIS and data science methodologies to model water consumption patterns across Mexico City, identify areas of inefficiency, and propose actionable solutions to improve water management at the municipal and regional levels. By leveraging integrated data from SACMEX, INEGI, and DENUE, we

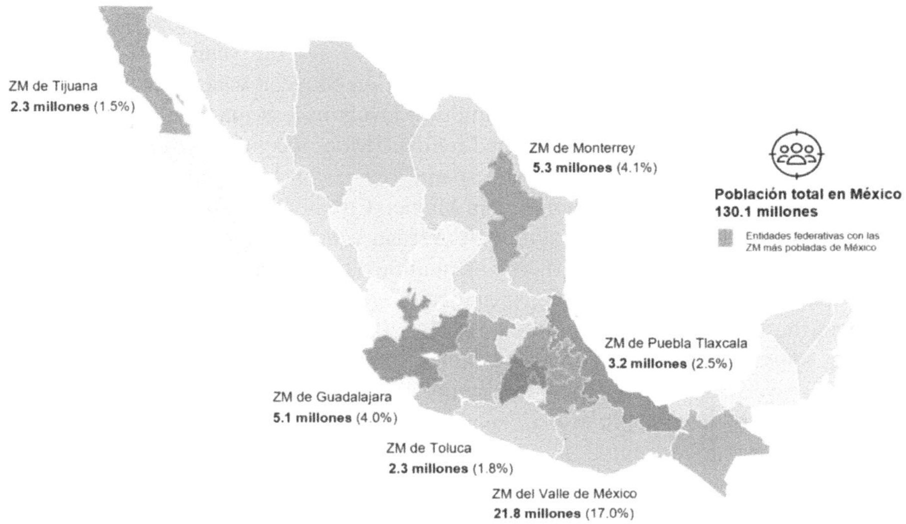

Fig. 1. Population of the Main Metropolitan Areas in Mexico (millions of inhabitants) prepared by IMCO 2020.

aim to provide a detailed spatial analysis of water usage that can inform future policy and management strategies.

2 State of the Art

Time series analysis has become a widely used technique for studying water consumption patterns. For instance, Wang et al. (2024) combined time series clustering, seasonal analysis, and entropy analysis to identify residential water consumption patterns and their main drivers. Similarly, Waraga et al. (2021) applied time series clustering to assess water consumption in Dubai, one of the most water-stressed cities globally. These studies highlight the importance of addressing water consumption as a spatio-temporal phenomenon. However, in the case of Mexico, spatio-temporal analyses of water consumption at the national level are still lacking. To date, no comprehensive national-level analysis of water consumption has been conducted, as most available studies are limited to local or municipal scales.

In contrast, there are studies that focus solely on spatial analysis. For example, Hernández-Mena et al. (2021) employed multivariate statistical techniques to assess the quality of water supply from wells, springs, and surface water bodies in Michoacán. Likewise, Fullerton et al. (2006) analyzed monthly water consumption in Ciudad Juárez using a linear transfer function (LTF) procedure. Both studies emphasized the lack of sufficient temporal data as a significant limitation for obtaining more robust results.

Research on water consumption in Mexico City dates back to 2000, when an initial estimate was made for the city and its metropolitan area. Since then, more recent spatial analyses of water consumption in the city have been conducted, including studies by Ramos-Bueno et al. (2021) and Medina-Rivas et al. (2022), who examined residential water consumption at the neighborhood level for the years 2010 and 2019, respectively. Both studies found an inverse correlation between water consumption and socioeconomic status, with higher consumption levels in less marginalized areas and lower consumption in more disadvantaged regions. More recently, Medina-Rivas et al. (2025) employed statistical analysis and spatial regression to explore spatiotemporal changes in per capita water consumption in Mexico City households between 2010 and 2019. Their findings indicate that although average water consumption has decreased over time, this decrease reflects growing inequalities in water access, mainly driven by intermittent supply, localized shortages, and geographic factors such as altitude.

Along the same lines, Ramos-Bueno et al. (2024) developed a spatial panel data modeling approach that incorporates variables such as water users, meter coverage, groundwater wells, and water supply to conduct spatiotemporal analyses of these factors and estimate average per capita water consumption between 2004 and 2022. This study concluded that water consumption in Mexico City has slowed over time; however, this reduction is associated with a decline in meter coverage, suggesting that smaller volumes of water are actually being delivered. Moreover, the study highlights that this reduction is uneven, being particularly noticeable in the peripheral areas of the city.

Collectively, these studies demonstrate significant progress in the spatial and temporal analysis of water consumption. Nonetheless, there remains a clear absence of comprehensive national-level studies that integrate both spatial and temporal dimensions of the phenomenon.

3 Methodology

This section outlines the methodological framework followed in this research, consisting of four main phases: (1) Data Sources and Structure, (2) Data Structure Diagnosis and Hierarchical Organization, (3) Layered System Architecture, and (4) Exploratory Data Analysis (EDA) to analyze water consumption patterns in Mexico City. The methodology integrates data from multiple sources, employing a structured, systematic, and scalable approach to ensure that data is effectively organized, integrated, analyzed, and visualized to generate actionable insights.

3.1 Data Sources and Structure

The dataset used in this study spans from 2017 to 2021 and is organized with the following variables: year, bimonthly period, type of consumption, land use type, region, block, borough, neighborhood, socioeconomic level, ticket, water consumption, and a description of data sources. This study draws on data from three key sources:

- SACMEX (Sistema de Aguas de la Ciudad de México): Provides bimonthly water supply data at the block level, including both metered and estimated consumption values.
- DENUE (Directorio Estadístico Nacional de Unidades Económicas): Supplies economic data on registered business units across Mexico, classified by sector, location, and other relevant attributes.

- INEGI (Instituto Nacional de Estadística y Geografía): Offers demographic, economic, and geographic data derived from national censuses, surveys, and other official records.

Each of these datasets has its own structure and attributes, requiring careful preprocessing to enable their integration into a unified analytical environment.

3.2 Data Structure Diagnosis and Hierarchical Organization

After analyzing the datasets, we identified key differences in structure, temporal resolution, and spatial granularity. To address these challenges, we developed four hierarchical data models to systematically organize and align the datasets:

- DENUE Hierarchical Model: Structured from national to local levels (federal entity → municipality → locality → business unit), this model organizes economic units by geographic and sectoral hierarchies.
- INEGI Hierarchical Model: Derived from official census structures, this model spans national to neighborhood levels (federal entity → municipality → AGEB → block → household), integrating demographic and geographic data.
- Colonias_CDMX Hierarchical Model: Specifically focuses on Mexico City's internal divisions (borough → neighborhood → block), facilitating localized spatial analysis.
- SACMEX Hierarchical Model: Structured by borough → neighborhood → block → service identifier, aligning water consumption data to geographic and administrative units (see Fig. 2).

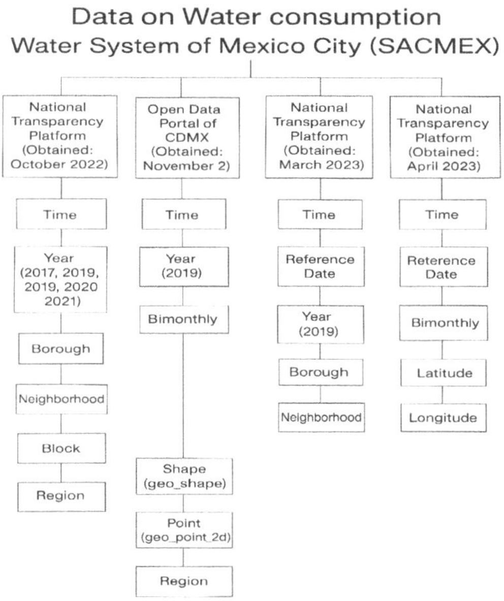

Fig. 2. Hierarchical Structure of SACMEX Data

3.3 Data Integration Process

Integration across these hierarchical models was achieved by establishing common spatial identifiers (borough codes, neighborhood names, block IDs) and temporal keys (year, bimonthly period). Cross-referencing these keys enables seamless merging of heterogeneous datasets, allowing multiscale analysis of water consumption patterns.

3.4 Layered System Architecture

To support the integration and analysis of the datasets, we designed a customized layered system architecture inspired by the classical three-tier model commonly used in software engineering to promote modularity, scalability, and maintainability (see Fig. 3). While the system retains the fundamental logic of presentation, persistence, and data storage layers, it extends the classical model by incorporating specialized modules for geospatial data processing and dynamic visualization generation, tailored specifically for urban water management applications.

This architectural enhancement represents a key novelty of the system. Unlike traditional three-tier models focused solely on transactional or static data applications, our architecture integrates geospatial analytical capabilities as a native component of its design, allowing for real-time spatial querying and dynamic generation of thematic maps related to water consumption patterns.

The architecture comprises the following layers:

- Presentation Layer: Provides an interactive web interface for data visualization, enabling users to explore spatial and temporal water consumption patterns intuitively. This layer supports the on-demand generation of dynamic maps based on user queries, enhancing flexibility for exploration.
- Persistence Layer: Manages data access logic, acting as an intermediary between the presentation and database layers, ensuring seamless, efficient retrieval of both attribute and spatial data.
- Database Layer: Houses the integrated datasets from SACMEX, DENUE, and INEGI within a multidimensional database schema. The database is designed for optimized spatial querying through SQL and Python, supporting advanced GIS functions.

Additionally, the system is designed to support the automatic insertion of new data through configurable pipelines. As new datasets or updates from SACMEX, DENUE, or INEGI become available, they can be incorporated into the system with minimal manual intervention, ensuring that analyses remain up to date. This functionality is critical for maintaining relevance in evolving urban water management contexts.

The system's organized architecture, featuring separated and interoperable layers, ensures robust performance and maintainability. Its scalable design allows for integration of additional datasets, expansion to other geographic regions, and adaptation to broader urban resource monitoring tasks.

This structured approach ensures that subsequent analyses are both systematic and scalable, providing a comprehensive and adaptable framework for understanding and managing water consumption patterns in Mexico City.

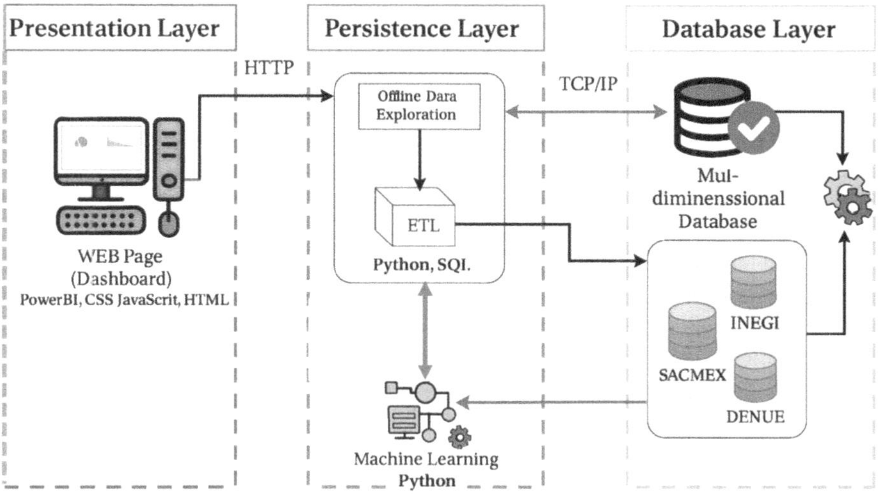

Fig. 3. Architecture of the Urban Data Water Monitor System

3.5 Exploratory Data Analysis (EDA)

With the integrated dataset, we conducted Exploratory Data Analysis (EDA) to uncover patterns, trends, and potential anomalies. EDA serves as the foundation for advanced modeling by providing initial insights into relationships between variables such as water consumption, land use, demographic factors, and economic activity. Techniques Used: Graphical Visualizations: Histograms, scatter plots, and box plots to illustrate variable distributions and relationships.

Descriptive Statistics: Central tendency measures (mean, median) and variability metrics (standard deviation) to summarize the dataset. Findings from the EDA are summarized in the Experiments and Results section, where we highlight actionable insights such as spatial inequalities in water consumption and their correlation with socioeconomic indicators. Findings from the EDA are summarized in the Experiments and Results section, where we highlight actionable insights such as spatial inequalities in water consumption and their correlation with socioeconomic indicators.

3.6 Data Science and GIS Techniques

In addition to Exploratory Data Analysis (EDA), this study incorporates several data science and GIS techniques to provide a more comprehensive understanding of spatial and temporal water consumption patterns in Mexico City. These methods allow for both descriptive and predictive insights, offering actionable findings for water resource management.

To uncover spatial patterns in consumption behaviors, we applied clustering algorithms, specifically K-Means clustering, to the integrated dataset. This unsupervised learning technique partitions neighborhoods into distinct groups based on shared characteristics such as average water consumption, socioeconomic level, and predominant land use. The resulting clusters reveal underlying structures in the data that are not immediately apparent through simple visualizations or descriptive statistics. These groupings help decision-makers prioritize areas for targeted interventions or further investigation.

Data mining techniques were also used to extract meaningful relationships between consumption patterns and socio-economic or geographic variables. We employed correlation analysis and association rule mining to detect patterns linking high or anomalous consumption with specific demographic or land use conditions. These analyses provide evidence-based foundations for understanding the drivers of water demand across different parts of the city. In terms of GIS techniques, spatial joins were used to relate water consumption data to geographic features such as administrative boundaries or nearby economic infrastructure. Buffer analyses were employed to explore how proximity to specific facilities or urban features might influence consumption behavior.

Together, these data science and GIS techniques form an integrated analytical framework that is systematic and spatially explicit.

4 Experiments and Results

This section presents a detailed spatial analysis of water consumption patterns across the boroughs of Mexico City, based on historical records and supported by choropleth map visualizations. This analysis facilitates the identification of areas exhibiting disproportionately high water consumption, thereby informing targeted strategies for more efficient and equitable water resource management.

Figure 4 specifically addresses the question: How much water does an individual consume on average every two months in Mexico City? The answer varies significantly depending on the place of residence, revealing pronounced spatial disparities in water use. The map displays the average bimonthly per capita water consumption for each neighborhood, considering only those areas with reliable consumption data.

The data used for this analysis were obtained from the Open Data Portal of Mexico City (https://datos.cdmx.gob.mx/dataset/consumo-agua), encompassing total, domestic, and mixed water consumption records.

These findings highlight the uneven distribution of water consumption throughout the city, underscoring the need for localized water management policies. The following sections further examine the relationship between water consumption patterns and socio-demographic variables to provide deeper insights into the underlying drivers of these disparities.

While Fig. 5 highlights the boroughs with the highest water consumption, the data also reveals marked spatial disparities across Mexico City's administrative divisions. This heterogeneity underscores the need for differentiated strategies in urban water management. According to the spatial analysis, Gustavo A. Madero stands out as the borough with the highest recorded consumption, totaling 962,290 cubic meters (962.29 million liters), which represents 19.5% of the city's total water usage. Close behind is Cuauhtémoc, with 718,333 cubic meters (718.33 million liters), accounting for 14.55% of the total. These pronounced differences highlight the strategic relevance of these boroughs for targeted interventions. Elevated consumption levels in these areas indicate the urgent need for focused conservation policies, hydraulic infrastructure optimization, and localized demand management strategies tailored to their specific urban dynamics.

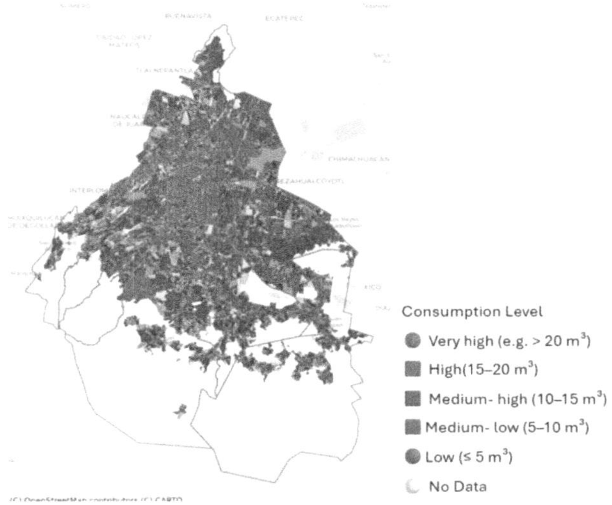

Fig. 4. Spatial distribution of average bimonthly per capita water consumption by neighborhood in Mexico City.

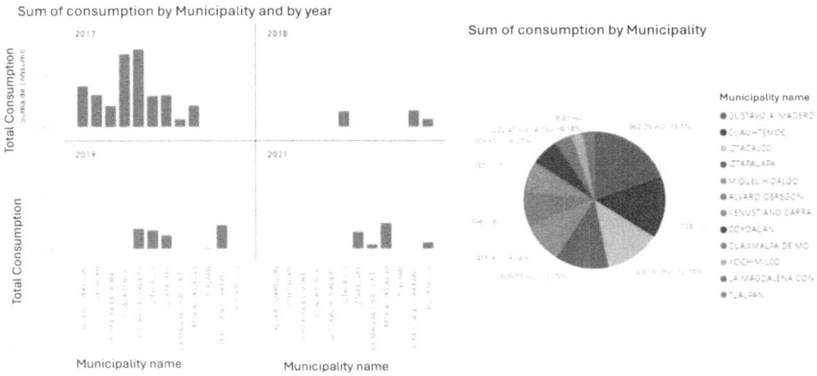

Fig. 5. Historical Water Consumption by Boroughs in Mexico City: Top Consumers

As a result, Gustavo A. Madero and Cuauhtémoc emerge as priority areas for the design of evidence-based reduction strategies and geospatially informed infrastructure improvement programs, essential for enhancing the efficiency and sustainability of the city's water management system.

To support more detailed spatial analysis, Fig. 6 introduces an interactive geovisualization of water consumption patterns across Mexico City's boroughs. This visualization integrates multiple filtering capabilities, including temporal segmentation by year and bimonthly periods, consumption typologies, development indices, and land use classifications. These features enable users to conduct granular spatiotemporal analyses, providing a more nuanced understanding of urban water consumption dynamics and supporting data-driven decision-making processes.

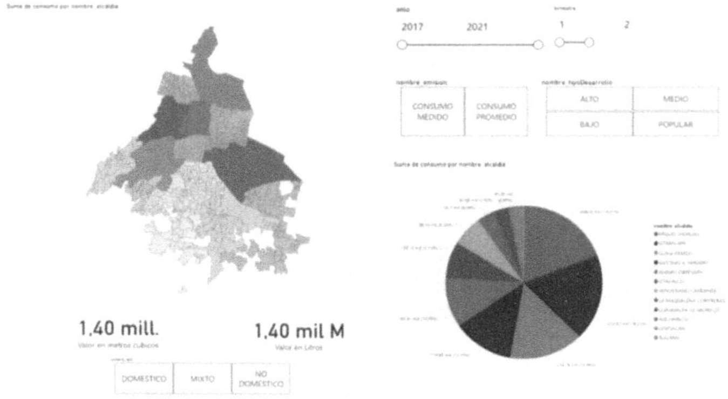

Fig. 6. Interactive Visualization of Water Consumption Patterns Across Boroughs

The enhanced functionality of Fig. 6 allows users to navigate between graphical and territorial representations of the data, with filtering options that facilitate detailed exploration of consumption dynamics. This level of detail strengthens the analytical connection between water consumption patterns and demographic and socio-economic factors, offering deeper insights into how these variables shape urban water demand.

As can be seen, demographic and socio-economic variables play a significant role that is revealed in water consumption patterns. Understanding these correlations is crucial to uncovering water consumption behaviors in certain population groups and geographic areas.

Further enriching the analysis, Fig. 7 presents a historical overview of water consumption by neighborhoods over the years. Notably, 2017 recorded the highest total consumption, with 3,282,217 cubic meters, corresponding to 66.5% of the total usage for that year. The fifth bimonthly period of 2017 also exhibited peak consumption, a pattern consistently repeated in 2018. Additionally, the Gustavo A. Madero borough consistently ranked among the highest consumers of water, both annually and across each bimonthly period.

Complementary to these historical patterns, Fig. 8 explores water consumption in relation to development indices. It reveals that populations with lower development indices exhibited the highest levels of consumption, followed by populations categorized under the popular development index. In contrast, populations with higher development indices recorded lower consumption levels, with the medium development index segment exhibiting the lowest overall usage.

Regarding usage categories, Fig. 9 shows that domestic use accounts for the largest share of total water consumption, followed by non-domestic usage, while mixed-use consumption represents the smallest proportion of demand.

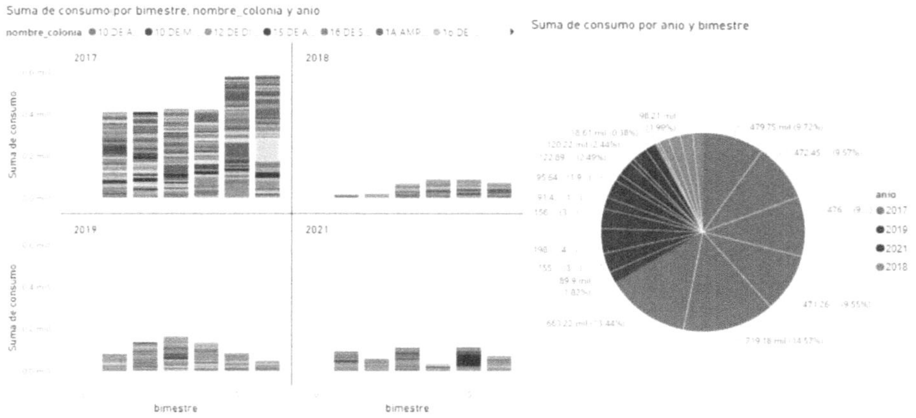

Fig. 7. Water Consumption by Neighborhoods Over the Years

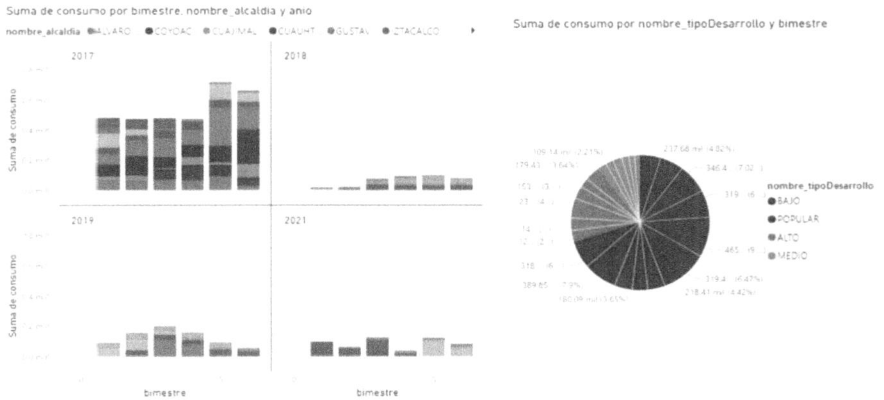

Fig. 8. Water Consumption by Development Index

A more detailed view of sector-specific patterns is provided in Fig. 10, revealing that cafeterias, soda fountains, ice cream parlors, soft drink vendors, and related establishments consistently rank as the highest-consuming economic entities across all boroughs. The second-largest consumers are multiple banking institutions, indicating a correlation between commercial activity types and water demand intensity.

Finally Fig. 11 presents a highly detailed interactive visualization of neighborhood-level water consumption in Mexico City. While structurally similar to the borough-level visualization described previously, this figure distinguishes itself by offering a micro-scale analytical perspective. Users can engage with the data through multiple filters—year (2017–2021), bimonthly period, type of consumption, type of development, and land use—allowing for the precise examination of localized consumption trends. A critical feature of this visualization is its inclusion of per capita water consumption metrics (in cubic meters per quarter), providing nuanced insights into how water usage varies not

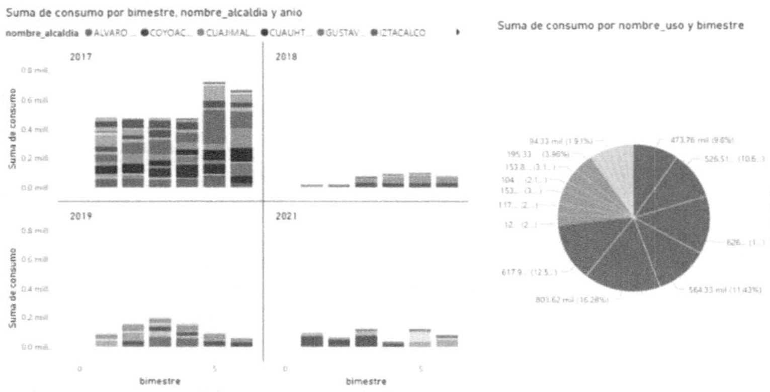

Fig. 9. Water Consumption by Usage Type

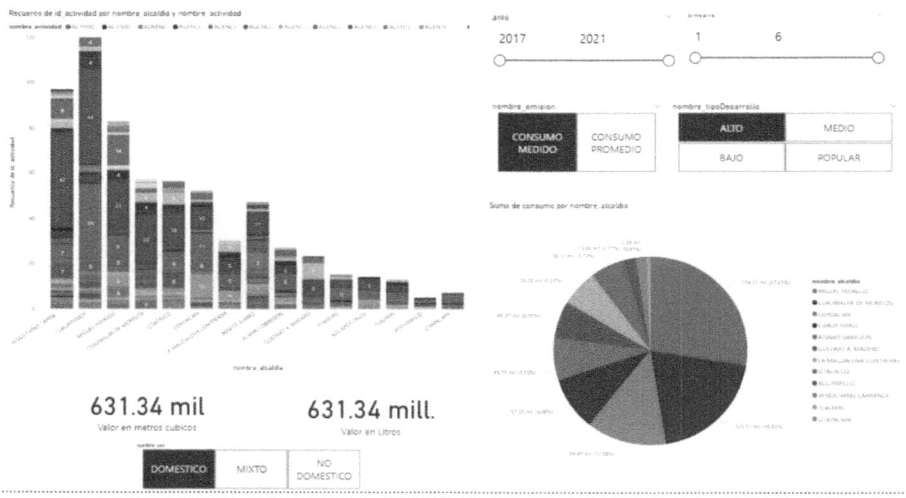

Fig. 10. Sector-Specific Water Consumption

only by geographic location but also according to demographic and urban characteristics. This level of detail is particularly valuable for identifying specific neighborhoods with disproportionately high or low consumption, which can then be analyzed in relation to land use patterns, socio-economic profiles, or infrastructure conditions. Key Insight: The neighborhood-level focus of Fig. 11 enables the micro-diagnosis of consumption trends and inefficiencies, offering key inputs for targeted interventions, such as localized infrastructure upgrades or neighborhood-specific conservation strategies. In contrast to broader aggregated views, this detailed perspective reinforces evidence-based policy-making aimed at achieving greater equity and efficiency in urban water management.

These spatial and sectoral analyses collectively provide a robust foundation for understanding the multifaceted nature of water consumption in Mexico City. By integrating

Fig. 11. Demographic data visualization by neighborhoods SACMEX.

spatial patterns, socio-economic indicators, and sector-specific demand, this study highlights not only where water consumption is highest but also why these patterns emerge. The clear influence of demographic, infrastructural, and economic variables underscores the importance of localized, evidence-based water management strategies. Future efforts should focus on leveraging these insights for the design of targeted interventions, particularly in high-demand neighborhoods and sectors, to promote sustainable consumption practices, improve hydraulic infrastructure, and ensure a more equitable distribution of water resources across the city.

5 Conclusions and Future Work

The spatial integration and multidimensional analysis of water consumption data presented in this study provide critical evidence of the spatial inequalities in water usage across Mexico City. By applying GIS and data science methodologies, this work contributes actionable knowledge to support the development of evidence-based policies aimed at achieving more sustainable and equitable water distribution. A key result of this research is the identification of Gustavo A. Madero and Cuauhtémoc as the boroughs with the highest recorded water consumption, together accounting for over 34% of the city's total. This highlights the strategic importance of these areas for targeted reduction strategies and infrastructure optimization, essential steps toward improving urban water management.

Moreover, the interactive visualizations and demographic breakdowns developed here demonstrate how socio-economic conditions significantly influence water consumption patterns, reinforcing the need for integrated approaches that consider both physical and social dimensions of urban water use. The neighborhood-level diagnostics offered by this framework enable precisely targeted interventions, strengthening the analytical basis for localized infrastructure improvements and conservation strategies.

6 Future Work

While the analyses and visualizations presented establish a solid foundation, further research is necessary to advance this line of inquiry. Future work should focus on:

a) Sector-Specific Water Consumption, Incorporating data from sectors such as agriculture and industry would provide a more comprehensive picture of total urban water demand, enabling a better understanding of non-residential consumption dynamics. b) Real-Time Data Integration, Leveraging real-time consumption data would enhance the capacity for dynamic and adaptive resource management, improving the responsiveness of water governance systems. c) Inclusion of Additional Variables and Domains: To achieve a truly comprehensive understanding of water consumption dynamics, future studies should integrate broader environmental, infrastructural, and socio-political variables, offering a more holistic view of the factors shaping water demand.

This study represents a critical first step toward building that comprehensive framework, providing foundational insights that can inform more sophisticated and targeted interventions in the ongoing effort to ensure sustainable and equitable urban water management for Mexico City.

Acknowledgments. The authors gratefully acknowledge the support provided by the Secretaría de Investigación y Posgrado of the Instituto Politécnico Nacional (SIP-IPN) through the research projects 20253692, 20254771, and 20250343. We also express our gratitude to the Comisión de Operación y Fomento de Actividades Académicas (COFAA), as well as to the Secretaría de Ciencia, Humanidades, Tecnología e Innovación (SECIHTI) for their valuable financial and institutional support. This research would not have been possible without their contribution.

References

1. Castillo, N.O., Valderrama Santibáñez, A.L., Chiatchoua, C.: (2021). Factores determinantes del consumo productivo de agua y sus efectos en la actividad económica de México. Economía, Sociedad y Territorio **21**(66), 505–537. https://doi.org/10.22136/est20211659
2. García Lirios, C., Carreón Guillén, J., Hernández Valdés, J., López Lena, M. M., Bustos Aguayo, J. M. (2013). Actitudes, consumo de agua y sistema de tarifas del servicio de abastecimiento de agua potable. POLIS, Revista Latinoamericana **12**(34). https://www.redalyc.org/articulo.oa?id=30528135019
3. Perló, M., González, E. (2005). Guerra por el agua en el Valle de México? En La Huaracha, creadores visuales (eds.) Guerra por el agua en el Valle de México, p. 37
4. UNESCO: Informe mundial de las Naciones Unidas sobre el desarrollo de los recursos hídricos 2020: Agua y cambio climático (2020). https://es.unesco.org/themes/water-security/wwap/wwdr/2020
5. Fullerton, T.M., Tinajero, R., Barraza de Anda, M.P.: Short-term water consumption patterns in Ciudad Juárez, Mexico. Atlantic Econ. J. **34**(4), 467–479 (2006). https://doi.org/10.1007/s11293-006-9031-0
6. Hernández-Mena, L., et al.: GIS, multivariate statistics analysis and health risk assessment of water supply quality for human use in Central Mexico. Water **13**(16), 2196 (2021). https://doi.org/10.3390/w13162196

7. Medina-Rivas, C.M., Morales-Novelo, J.A., Rodríguez-Tapia, L., Revollo-Fernández, D.A.: Mexico City's decline in per capita domestic water use: A comprehensive spatial-temporal study. Urban Water J. **22**(1), 1–15 (2025). https://doi.org/10.1080/1573062X.2024.2423400
8. Medina-Rivas, C.M., Rodríguez-Tapia, L., Morales-Novelo, J.A., Revollo-Fernández, D.A.: Spatial inequality of domestic water consumption in Mexico City. Water Resour. Econ. **40**, 100210 (2022). https://doi.org/10.1016/j.wre.2022.100210
9. Ramos-Bueno, A., Perevochtchikova, M., Chang, H.: Socio-spatial analysis of residential water demand in Mexico City. Tecnología y Ciencias del Agua **12**(2), 59–110 (2021). https://doi.org/10.24850/j-tyca-2021-02-02
10. Ramos-Bueno, A., Galeana-Pizaña, J.M., Perevochtchikova, M.: Urban water consumption analysis through a spatial panel modeling approach: a case study of Mexico City, 2004–2022. Water Supply **24**(9), 3179–3195 (2024). https://doi.org/10.2166/ws.2024.191
11. Wang, R., Zhao, X., Qiu, H., Cheng, X., Liu, X.: Uncovering urban water consumption patterns through time series clustering and entropy analysis. Water Res. **262**, 122085 (2024). https://doi.org/10.1016/j.watres.2024.122085
12. Waraga, O.A., Abdeljaber, A., Abu Talib, M., Abdallah, M.: Investigating water consumption patterns through time series clustering. In: 2021 14th International Conference on Developments in eSystems Engineering (DeSE), pp. 44–49 (2021). https://doi.org/10.1109/DeSE54285.2021.9719367

Geospatially-Informed Recommendations for Automobile Purchases: Integrating Spatial Analysis for Enhanced Decision-Making

Fabian Ramirez[1(✉)], Maryam Lotfian[2], and Felix Mata[1]

[1] UPIITA-IPN, México City, Mexico
framirezl1900@alumno.ipn.mx, dos@ipn.mx
[2] University of Applied Sciences and Arts Western Switzerland, Delémont, Switzerland
maryam.lotfian@heig-vd.ch

Abstract. This research proposes an integrated recommendation framework to support automobile purchase decisions by aligning consumer preferences with spatial and technical factors. In response to the challenges faced by car buyers, particularly those with limited automotive expertise and overwhelmed by excessive information, the model leverages sentiment analysis from social media and combines it with spatial variables, including dealership density, vehicle availability, circulation restrictions, environmental suitability, and pricing. These factors are then matched with technical specifications to generate personalized and context-aware vehicle suggestions. Using Mexico City as a case study, the empirical analysis reveals that regional differences in infrastructure, regulatory policies, economic conditions, and environmental constraints strongly shape vehicle preferences. The findings show that consumers in areas with stricter vehicle regulations and better service infrastructure tend to prefer vehicles with higher initial costs but lower long-term maintenance demands. While the system is built around the socio-economic and infrastructural peculiarities of Mexico City, it has been designed with modular and configurable components, allowing it to be adapted to international contexts with similar data availability. Nevertheless, the dependence on locally specific variables should be explicitly acknowledged when considering its broader applicability. This raises the question of scalability and transferability, inviting further research into how the framework can be generalized across diverse urban and regulatory environments.

Keywords: Recommender System · Spatial Data Analysis · Machine Learning

1 Introduction

The process of purchasing a vehicle has become increasingly complex, especially in large urban environments where consumers are faced with an overwhelming variety of options, technical specifications, and promotional content. Despite the growing availability of online resources, buyers—particularly those without deep automotive knowledge—often struggle to navigate conflicting reviews, dense specifications, and biased marketing. The result is decision fatigue and uncertainty, even after prolonged research [2, 13].

M. F. Mata-Rivera et al. (Eds.): W2GIS 2025, LNCS 15946, pp. 138–154, 2026.
https://doi.org/10.1007/978-3-032-01723-9_10

This complexity is further compounded by external influences such as subjective opinions, brand appeal, and aggressive advertising, which often overshadow critical factors like fuel efficiency, safety features, and long-term maintenance costs [7, 20]. In parallel, users must manually gather and compare data from multiple sources—review websites, technical spec sheets, and multimedia content—making the selection process time-consuming and inconsistent [14, 18].

These challenges are especially pronounced in dense metropolitan areas like Mexico City, where spatial constraints (e.g., dealership distribution, traffic congestion), environmental policies, and regulatory restrictions vary greatly by region [10, 11]. Consumers in such contexts must account not only for personal preferences but also for local realities—such as emission zones, service center accessibility, and road infrastructure—when choosing a vehicle [13].

To address these multifaceted challenges, this paper proposes a geospatially informed vehicle recommendation system that integrates machine learning, sentiment analysis, and spatial data analysis. The goal is to provide context-aware suggestions that align not only with user preferences but also with geographic, regulatory, and service accessibility constraints [12, 14, 21].

We investigate the following core research question: Can a recommendation system accurately interpret individual preferences and regional constraints to generate tailored, practical vehicle suggestions?

Using Mexico City as a case study, the system is evaluated in terms of its ability to match user profiles with vehicle specifications, local dealership availability, regulatory constraints, and social sentiment data. While the proposed framework is rooted in the specific socio-spatial characteristics of Mexico City, it is designed with modular components to support adaptation to other urban environments with comparable data availability [13, 16].

2 State of the Art

The increasing reliance on digital platforms for automotive purchasing has highlighted the limitations of current recommendation systems, particularly those that overlook contextual variables such as geography and sentiment. This section reviews relevant literature and systems across three domains: vehicle recommendation systems, cross-domain recommender approaches, and comparative system architectures.

2.1 Related Automotive Recommendation Systems

Digital behavior studies indicate that 95% of car buyers use online sources to inform their decisions, with 60% of searches coming from mobile devices [1]. Cox Automotive's "Car Buyer Journey" report [2] found that buyers spend nearly 14 h researching across multiple third-party websites. By the time they reach a dealership, most consumers have completed 90% of their decision-making process [2, 13]. However, the overwhelming information volume often leads to decision fatigue, especially among users with limited technical knowledge.

Recent vehicle recommendation systems attempt to address this complexity using various machine learning techniques. The model proposed by Thomas and Vaidhehi [20] utilizes a hybrid recommender system combining user-to-user and item-to-item collaborative filtering. It relies on a synthetic dataset of 300 users and 224 car models. While effective, this system lacks integration with real-time or unstructured data sources. Similarly, the ontology-based recommender by Le, Abel, and Gouspillou [21] emphasizes semantic alignment between user profiles and vehicle attributes but does not incorporate spatial, social, or environmental context, limiting its adaptability in dynamic markets.

Additional contributions, such as those by González-Delgado [7] and Babu & Vaidhehi [18], employ unsupervised learning and hybrid filtering to enhance automotive decision-making. González-Delgado's system scrapes user opinions and classifies preferences based on fuel efficiency, brand perception, and technical performance, demonstrating that hybrid models can effectively combine subjective and objective indicators.

2.2 Cross-Domain Recommender Approaches

Insights from other application domains support the evolution of recommender systems beyond static attribute matching. In the **literature domain**, the LEEme system [15] employs collaborative filtering to group users by interest and recommend high-rated books. Its success in increasing user engagement demonstrates the relevance of preference clustering in personalization strategies.

Job recommendation platforms also benefit from machine learning and text mining. Apaza Alanoca [3] applied TF-IDF to extract structured data from resumes and job postings, which improved the matching process. Espinosa et al. [6] applied a hybrid of classification models and content-based filtering to align academic pathways with market needs, increasing recommendation precision.

In **tourism**, Valenzuela-Sabogal et al. [4] designed a semantic web-based system that clusters traveler data for more relevant suggestions. Badouch and Boutaounte [5] further demonstrated that hybrid models combining collaborative, content-based, and machine learning approaches yield better accuracy and context-awareness in tourism recommendations.

Additional examples, such as Campigotto et al.'s FAVOUR algorithm [16], introduce situation-aware routing systems for transportation that integrate personal preferences and multimodal data. Similarly, Boodaghians et al. [17] explore the influence of word-of-mouth recommendations in automobile markets, highlighting the growing role of social factors in decision-making.

2.3 Comparison with Existing Models

While several existing systems achieve strong accuracy, they typically rely on structured datasets and fixed user-item matrices. Our approach diverges in several ways:

- **Data sources**: Instead of relying solely on synthetic or structured datasets [20, 21], our system uses real-time, unstructured inputs from social media (e.g., X), review portals, and manufacturer websites. It processes this data through web scraping and

NLP, particularly using the VADER algorithm [14], to extract sentiment and user motivations.

- **Spatial integration**: Unlike prior work, our model incorporates Geographic Information Systems (GIS) to contextualize recommendations. Drawing from Tobler's First Law of Geography [13], we recognize that geographic proximity and service infrastructure significantly affect user behavior.
- **Dynamic filtering**: Existing systems like Thomas & Vaidhehi [20] or Calman [19] focus on pre-defined item-user mappings. In contrast, our system applies clustering (k-Modes [12]) to build profiles based on both preferences and sentiment, then filters them through spatial constraints and regulatory zones.
- **Evaluation metrics**: Many systems focus on accuracy (e.g., [20] claims 83% user satisfaction). Our evaluation expands to include **coverage, novelty, and diversity**, as discussed in Cruz Guerrero et al. [9] and Báez et al. [2], which are vital for assessing user-centric performance in real-world deployments.

In comparison to ontology-driven models like Le et al. [21], our design allows for contextual adaptability and real-time updates. This is particularly important for dynamic markets such as Mexico City, where vehicle circulation restrictions, environmental zones, and infrastructure constraints must be accounted for [10, 11].

3 Methodology

This methodology is structured into five stages: Data Collection, Data Preprocessing and Transformation, User Profiling via Unsupervised Clustering, Spatial Integration through GIS Analysis, and Generation of Final Recommendations. The overall architecture is illustrated in Fig. 1, which depicts the integration of machine learning, spatial data, and user-centric modeling within the recommendation framework.

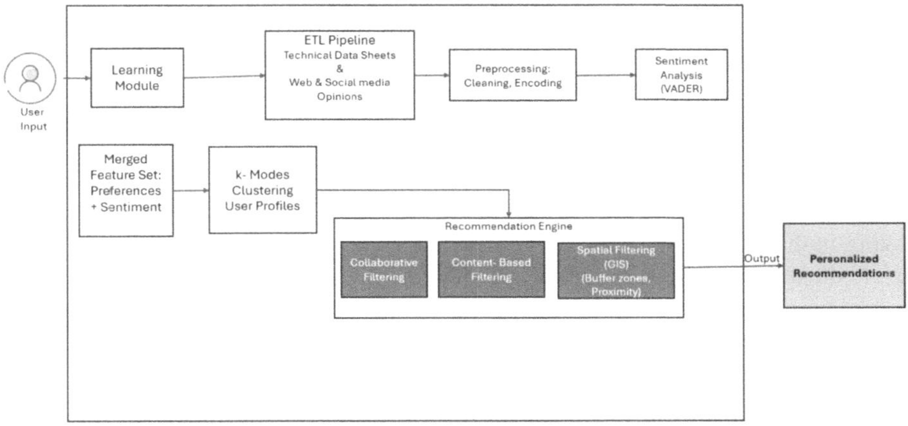

Fig. 1. Framework of Recommendation Process

The methodology for developing the automobile recommendation framework integrates a machine learning algorithm, K-modes [12], with GIS and spatial analysis to generate personalized and geographically aware vehicle recommendations. The process begins with the systematic collection of user requirements and preferences, alongside vehicle specifications. These inputs inform the selection of a hybrid recommendation model that integrates collaborative filtering and content-based filtering, allowing the system to leverage both user behavior and technical attributes.

Data collection follows an ETL (Extract, Transform, Load) process. Data is extracted from external repositories, including automotive review websites using web scraping technique, social media mainly X, vehicle specifications, and open datasets, such as dealership locations. During the transformation phase, preprocessing techniques such as data cleaning, normalization, encoding categorical variables, and feature engineering are applied to prepare the data for machine learning analysis. In the final loading phase, the transformed data is structured for efficient querying and model training.

The framework constructs personalized user profiles using the unsupervised machine learning k-Modes, it is an extension of the k-Means clustering algorithm. The k-Means algorithm is the most commonly used centroid-based partitioning clustering algorithm [12] to cluster categorical data. These models segment users based on their preferences and behaviors and opinions, identifying patterns such as vehicle type preferences and sentiment derived from online reviews. This profiling ensures that recommendations are tailored to each user's unique needs. The core recommendation model combines collaborative filtering, which utilizes data from similar users' preferences, and content-based filtering, which refines recommendations based on detailed vehicle specifications.

A crucial component of the framework is the integration of spatial analysis. Geographic data, such as proximity to local dealerships, service centers, and other points of interest, is incorporated into the recommendation process. Proximity analysis ensures that recommendations are personalized and contextually relevant based on the user's location. Factors like dealership density, traffic conditions, and local market dynamics are considered, ensuring that recommendations are both geographically optimized and accessible. This spatial integration enhances the practicality of recommendations by ensuring that vehicle options are aligned with user preferences and accessible within the user's region. The framework generates personalized recommendations that aim to reduce cognitive overload by providing clear, actionable insights. By incorporating both user preferences and geographic context, the framework helps users make informed decisions more efficiently. The proximity analysis ensures that the most relevant vehicle options are highlighted, improving the overall user experience and facilitating decision-making in the car-buying process. The recommendation framework is depicted in the Fig. 1, illustrating the integration of machine learning, spatial data, and user-centric modeling.

3.1 User Input and Profiling

The user data extraction process, crucial for characterizing user preferences and generating personalized recommendations, was carried out in two phases. The first phase focused on identifying the motivations, needs, or key drivers behind car purchases, alongside pinpointing the specific vehicle features associated with satisfying these needs. In the second phase, a method was developed to extract user insights from web forums, news articles, and social media platforms like X. The objective was to capture user motivations while ensuring ease of extraction and analysis. As a result, eight general motivations commonly associated with car purchases were identified, as summarized in Table 1.

Table 1. General motivations for car purchases.

Name	Description
Comfort	Refers to all elements that contribute to maximizing comfort inside the vehicle
Safety	Encompasses all features that enhance vehicle safety, including both active and passive safety measures
Performance	Covers all aspects that enable the vehicle to handle demanding tasks efficiently, particularly heavy-duty work
Technology	Includes all technological elements, whether related to driving systems or infotainment features
Economy	Refers to cost-related factors, ranging from manufacturing materials to the overall purchase price
Efficiency	Covers all aspects aimed at optimizing fuel consumption or achieving high performance
Sportiness	Encompasses features that provide a sporty experience, such as body design, lightweight materials, fast acceleration, and high-speed capabilities
Luxury/Prestige	Includes elements that convey luxury and high status

Aesthetic preferences and brand loyalty were excluded from the list, as these are considered more superficial reasons for purchase.

3.2 Data Extraction and Integration (ETL Pipeline)

Following the second phase, a data extraction method was developed for gathering motivations, user preferences, and vehicle evaluations from multiple web-based sources. To create a framework for generating vehicle recommendations, a comprehensive ETL (Extract, Transform, Load) process was developed. This process begins with the extraction of vehicle technical specifications and user preference data. Sources include manufacturers' official websites, review portals, and social media. The extracted data, initially unstructured, is transformed through data cleaning, encoding, and normalization to make it suitable for analysis.

A dataset was compiled, including over 64 vehicle attributes categorized into five main groups: powertrain, exterior features, interior features, comfort and technology, and safety. The collection encompasses over 400 vehicle records from 18 brands and 150 models, with 116 columns representing specific vehicle characteristics. To link vehicle specifications with user motivations, a semantic mapping matrix was created using logical domain analysis. This matrix aligns motivations (e.g., comfort, safety) with specific vehicle attributes, forming the basis of user profiles. Unstructured opinions from forums, reviews, and social platforms like X are processed using Natural Language Processing (NLP) techniques. Specifically, VADER (Valence Aware Dictionary and sEntiment Reasoner) is applied to quantify the sentiment polarity and strength of user feedback. These sentiment scores are then combined with technical features to enrich the input space for clustering. User profiling is performed using the k-Modes algorithm, which is designed to handle categorical data. This clustering technique identifies groups of users with similar preferences and sentiment-derived attitudes, enabling the system to generate meaningful and customized recommendation profiles. All cleaned and enriched data is then loaded into a PostGIS-enabled relational database, ensuring efficient querying during the recommendation process.

3.3 Sentiment and Feature Enrichment

To further enhance the recommendation system, web scraping techniques are employed to collect additional user feedback from automotive websites, news articles, and social media platforms. This data includes user reviews, star ratings, and narrative evaluations. The enrichment process includes: a) Website Selection: Identifying reputable sources. b) HTML Analysis and Web Scraping: Parsing website structures and deploying spiders to extract data. c) Data Cleaning and Structuring: Removing noise, duplicates, and inconsistencies to convert unstructured content into a format compatible with the rest of the system.

Sentiment analysis using VADER is also applied here, transforming qualitative text into structured sentiment indicators that reflect public perception. VADER is particularly suitable for this type of informal, short-form text, providing polarity scores (positive, negative, neutral, and compound) for each review. The sentiment scores are then integrated into the dataset as additional features, capturing the emotional tone of user experiences. These enriched sentiment indicators are later used in the recommendation engine to refine vehicle rankings, ensuring they reflect evolving public opinion and nuanced user feedback. Additionally, sentiment scores are geotagged based on the source location or mentioned region, enabling the generation of spatial sentiment heatmaps. These maps are used in Sect. 3.5 to visually represent satisfaction levels across geographic zones, helping users quickly interpret service quality by area. This sentiment layer ensures the recommendation engine remains aligned with dynamic user experiences and social trends.

3.4 Spatial Proximity Analysis and Integration

Proximity analysis plays a pivotal role in the vehicle recommendation system by incorporating geographic and environmental data to deliver suggestions that are not only personalized but also contextually grounded in the user's location. This spatial component ensures that recommended vehicles align with practical and logistical considerations, such as service accessibility, maintenance feasibility, and local availability. The system considers a range of contextual criteria, including affordability, average service response times, historical reports of spare part shortages, and service coverage density. These factors—derived from user reviews and dealership data—are integrated with technical attributes to generate recommendations that reflect both user preferences and the realities of their geographic context. To operationalize this, buffer zones (e.g., 5 km radius) are generated around vehicle dealerships and service centers, serving as spatial filters that constrain the recommendation output to nearby and serviceable vehicles. However, the spatial analysis goes beyond basic buffering. The system also examines spatial autocorrelation patterns, such as clusters of high user satisfaction or service efficiency, identified through the spatial distribution of sentiment scores and service feedback. The underlying assumption is that user experiences and vehicle satisfaction levels are not randomly distributed across space. For example, regions with dense concentrations of positive sentiment or frequent recommendations for certain vehicle types may indicate localized preferences or service advantages. These patterns are detected using spatial statistical techniques, such as hot spot analysis and service density gradients, enabling the system to adjust recommendation weights dynamically. To enrich this layer, sentiment analysis is integrated using (NLP) and the VADER algorithm, which classifies user opinions by polarity and intensity. These sentiment scores are geotagged based on the review source location or mentioned geographic areas, allowing the system to spatially interpolate or aggregate satisfaction levels. This enables the generation of sentiment heatmaps that reflect how perception varies by region, guiding the engine to favor vehicles with both technical relevance and positive local perception. This process reflects Tobler's First Law of Geography, "everything is related to everything else, but near things are more related than distant things", by detecting spatial dependencies in consumer sentiment, service quality, and brand performance. Rather than merely filtering by proximity, the system uses these insights to improve contextual sensitivity and ensure that recommendations are both physically accessible and spatially validated through user experience. Figure 2 illustrates the application of buffer zones around vehicle dealerships and service centers in Mexico City, using a uniform 5-km radius. This geospatial visualization, generated using GIS tools, maps the distribution of automotive services across the urban area. These buffer zones act as spatial constraints, ensuring that only vehicles within a practical commuting distance are included in the recommendation set.

This methodological approach reflects real-world accessibility constraints while facilitating efficient access to both vehicle purchasing options and after-sale service infrastructure. To further refine the spatial analysis, the model incorporates a semantic layer of user sentiment, extracted from automotive review platforms and social media using NLP techniques. The VADER algorithm is applied to derive polarity scores, which are linked to geographic coordinates. By combining spatial proximity with sentiment-based reputation, the system ranks nearby vehicles not only by location and technical compatibility but also by public perception and satisfaction. This dual-filtering mechanism enhances the contextual relevance and credibility of the recommendations, ensuring alignment with both logistical constraints and social trust. This integrated approach ensures that recommendations are not only viable in geographic terms but also socially validated and experience-driven, delivering a more robust and context-aware user experience. Figure 2 visually reinforces how proximity and sentiment are jointly considered within this geospatial framework.

Fig. 2. Buffer Zone Implementation for Localized Vehicle Recommendations

3.5 Recommendation Engine and Output Visualization

The recommendation engine synthesizes user profiles, sentiment-enriched data, and spatial constraints to generate vehicle suggestions that are displayed through an interactive geospatial map. Rather than presenting a static ranked list, the system delivers a dynamic, map-based interface where recommended vehicles are visualized as geolocated markers linked to the nearest dealerships or points of sale. Around each dealership and service center, buffer zones with defined radii are rendered to represent the spatial filtering applied to the recommendation set. Superimposed on these zones are color-coded sentiment heatmaps, in which areas of high satisfaction are displayed in green and those of low satisfaction in red, based on sentiment scores derived from VADER analysis of geotagged user reviews and social media content.

This dual-layer visualization, combining spatial proximity (via buffers) and perceptual insight (via sentiment), enables users to quickly evaluate both service accessibility and regional satisfaction trends. Interactive filtering options further enhance personalization by allowing users to refine results based on specific motivations such as safety, fuel economy, or driving comfort. Through this integrated visual interface, users are empowered to understand not only which vehicle options are recommended but also why they are contextually relevant, grounded in geographic proximity, infrastructure availability, and collective user opinion.

Ultimately, the map-based output functions as a geospatial decision-support tool that reduces cognitive effort while enhancing transparency, trust, and usability in the recommendation process.

4 Recommendation Process and Vehicle Evaluation

The recommendation process was designed to leverage both technical vehicle specifications and user preferences, utilizing a hybrid model that integrates content-based and profile-based filtering techniques. By incorporating spatial data and external evaluations (such as ratings and reviews), the system aims to provide more personalized, accurate, and contextually relevant vehicle suggestions. The process is structured in multiple phases, including data extraction, clustering, similarity analysis, and testing, to ensure the effectiveness of the recommendation engine.The key data elements considered in this process include:

- A list of vehicles described by their technical specifications.
- A weighted list representing user preferences (user profile).
- Vehicle rating sheets sourced externally.

Since user interaction involves providing a set of preferences (rather than direct interaction with items like ratings), collaborative filtering was excluded. This technique requires direct user ratings of items, differing from the current system's reliance on external data sources for ratings. Content-based filtering, which evaluates item attributes (in this case, vehicle specifications), was initially considered. However, adjustments were necessary, as user profiles are generated based on predefined preferences, not direct item interaction. Vehicle ratings, categorized and available, further influenced the system's design.

Ultimately, a hybrid recommendation system was implemented, utilizing a cascading model where the output of one recommender serves as the input for the next, integrating both content-based and profile-based approaches.

4.1 Data Collection and Extraction

The first step in the recommendation process is the extraction of detailed vehicle specifications from reliable sources, including manufacturers' websites, as is detailed in Sect. 3.2. These preferences are mapped to specific vehicle attributes through logical domain analysis, linking user interests to particular features. This mapping creates a detailed user profile that serves as the basis for the profile-based filtering in the recommendation system.

To further refine recommendations, external sources such as user reviews, ratings, and vehicle evaluations from websites like Motorpasión México, ¿Qué coche me compro?, and Auto Test are included. These sources provide valuable user-generated content that is used to assess the popularity and quality of various vehicles based on real-world experiences. Data such as ratings, pros/cons, and textual reviews are extracted and structured into a format suitable for analysis and comparison. The websites provide structured automotive data, including textual reviews, numerical ratings, and evaluations. Vehicles are categorized by brand and model, allowing for easy extraction and comparison. Table 2 provides a summary of the selected websites and the type of data each contributed to the system.

4.2 Clustering and Similarity Analysis

The k-modes clustering algorithm is applied to the dataset to uncover patterns and group users based on shared vehicle preferences. This allows the system to segment users into clusters that exhibit similar behavior and preferences, ensuring that the recommendation

Table 2. Summary of automotive websites providing vehicle reviews, ratings, and comparison tools.

Website	Description	Relevant Information
Motorpasión México	News and articles on the automotive industry, including electric vehicles and vehicle reviews	Attribute-based vehicle ratings (numerical/graphical format), Pros and cons (text format)
¿Qué coche me compro?	Tool for vehicle comparison and selection, including reviews and ratings	Overall rating (numerical and star-based), Section-specific ratings (numerical/graphical), User opinions (text format)
Auto Test	Vehicle evaluations, including detailed ratings and comparisons	Attribute-based ratings (numerical/graphical format), Pros and cons (text format)

engine prioritizes suggestions that resonate with specific user groups. **Optimal K Determination:** The elbow method is used to identify the ideal number of clusters, with $K = 6$ being determined as the optimal value. Additional methods, such as silhouette plots, confirm that this choice provides the best separation of clusters, offering distinct and meaningful groupings based on user preferences. **Cluster Interpretation:** After clustering, each group's defining features are identified, helping to interpret which vehicle attributes are most valued by each cluster. This allows the recommendation system to tailor suggestions to the needs of each user segment.

4.3 Vehicle Similarity Calculation and Vectorization

To calculate the similarity between vehicle models, the dataset's "overview" column, containing vehicle attributes, is vectorized into a sparse matrix. Using cosine similarity, the system compares vehicles to determine which models are most similar based on their specifications. This enables the recommendation engine to suggest vehicles that closely match the user's profile, based on the attributes they prefer.

4.4 Recommender System Testing

The recommender system was tested for its ability to generate accurate and relevant recommendations using both profile-based and content-based filtering techniques.

- **Profile-Based Filtering Testing:** The profile-based system prioritizes vehicle recommendations based on user preferences as extracted from the clustering process. The system was tested to ensure that the recommendations align with the users' most valued vehicle attributes, confirming that the system correctly ranks vehicles according to user interests.
- **Content-Based Filtering Testing:** The content-based filtering method was tested using various similarity metrics, such as Manhattan distance and cosine similarity,

with and without TF-IDF weighting. Results indicated that cosine similarity, particularly when combined with TF-IDF weighting, provided the most accurate and consistent results for vehicle comparisons.

4.5 Incorporating Proximity and Location-Based Analysis

These spatial and sentiment-based insights are ultimately projected onto the interactive recommendation map (see Sect. 3.5), reinforcing the system's location-awareness. The heatmaps, derived from VADER, analyzed sentiment scores linked to geolocated user reviews (see Sect. 3.3), help contextualize vehicle satisfaction by region. In addition to the standard filtering techniques, proximity analysis is integrated into the recommendation process to refine suggestions based on geographic and environmental factors. This involves analyzing the user's location to provide recommendations that account for regional availability, local market conditions, and proximity to dealerships or service centers.

By including spatial data, the system ensures that the vehicle suggestions are not only relevant to the user's preferences but also contextually appropriate for their location.

5 Results and Experiments

This section presents the results of spatial analyses focused on the geographic distribution of car dealerships, user preferences, and traffic-related constraints that influence vehicle recommendations. By integrating geospatial data with social media feedback, we analyze how factors such as dealership density, traffic congestion, vehicle circulation restrictions, and urban accessibility shape both vehicle availability and consumer decision-making. The insights derived from this analysis inform the refinement of recommendation algorithms and support strategic planning for dealerships. Each subsection details specific findings, supported by maps and figures, that highlight spatial patterns and their implications for inventory management, service accessibility, and personalized vehicle suggestions. In doing so, we establish clear links between spatial dynamics and user-centered automotive strategies.

5.1 Urban Preferences and Cost-Sensitivity Clusters

Figure 3 illustrates spatial variations in vehicle preferences across four urban zones of Mexico City: Center, South, North, and West. These patterns emerge from the integration of sentiment analysis and dealership service data, and are visualized through a heatmap, where color intensity reflects the level of consumer vehicle preference based on location. The color legend for the heatmap is as follows: Red areas represent high preference intensity, typically associated with strong consumer demand, positive sentiment, and high service infrastructure availability. Yellow areas indicate moderate preference levels, often linked to balanced sentiment and moderate service access. Blue areas denote lower preference, correlating with limited dealership presence, economic constraints, or concerns about long-term maintenance. From a regional perspective, in the West and Northwest zones, users tend to prefer vehicles with higher initial costs but lower maintenance demands, reflecting strong post-sale service networks and efficient parts logistics. In the Central and Eastern zones, affordability is the main driver of consumer choice, though limited access to spare parts raises concerns about long-term ownership costs. The North shows a moderate preference pattern, where users prioritize reasonable purchase prices and the availability of local repair services, as evidenced by blue and yellow zones indicating balanced sentiment and service conditions. In the South and Southwest, the lower preference intensity suggests reduced dealership presence and possible economic or infrastructure limitations, contributing to more cautious consumer behavior. This spatial representation highlights how vehicle preferences are not only shaped by technical attributes or user profiles, but also by local infrastructure, economic conditions, and geospatial service accessibility.

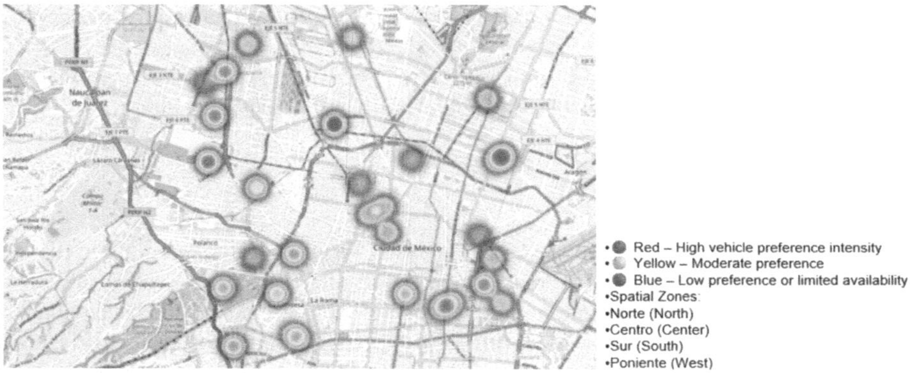

Fig. 3. Geographic Distribution of Vehicle Preferences in Mexico City Based on Initial Costs, Maintenance, and Spare Parts Availability

A portion of the map (South, South-West, and South-East) presents mixed patterns due to varying population densities and limited access to dealership networks. This geographical analysis underscores the role of economic factors and proximity to services in shaping vehicle preferences in Mexico City. By integrating these factors into a heatmap, we can observe clear spatial patterns that highlight the differences in consumer needs across urban zones, providing valuable insights for manufacturers and service providers to tailor their offerings to local preferences.

5.2 Regulatory Zones and Fuel-Efficient Vehicle Availability

Figure 4 illustrates a proximity analysis of vehicle circulation restriction zones in Mexico City, highlighting their influence on dealership accessibility and vehicle recommendation patterns. The map presents a heatmap overlay, where red indicates areas with high proximity to environmentally regulated zones (e.g., low-emission areas), and blue denotes areas with little restriction impact. Blue location pins represent individual dealership positions. These tend to cluster near or within regulated zones, reflecting a higher concentration of dealerships offering electric, hybrid, or fuel-efficient vehicles, aligning with the compliance requirements. In contrast, peripheral areas that are farther from circulation-restricted zones (shown in cooler tones) show a broader variety of available vehicle types, including less fuel-efficient or larger models.

Fig. 4. Map of Proximity Analysis to Vehicle Circulation Restrictions Zones

Dealerships in environmentally regulated zones should prioritize maintaining inventories of compliant vehicle models. Recommender systems must integrate local policy data to enhance relevance and avoid suggesting non-compliant vehicles to users in these areas.

5.3 Socioeconomic Patterns in Vehicle Selection

This section shows the spatial distribution of user preferences for Executive car vehicles across Mexico City in Fig. 5. The heatmap employs a circular symbol-based color gradient to indicate intensity of preference: The spatial pattern reveals that central and high-income corridors exhibit the strongest preference for executive cars, as evidenced by the concentration of red and yellow zones. These areas align with dense commercial and residential infrastructure, greater purchasing power, and stronger dealership networks. In contrast, southern and peripheral regions display predominantly blue zones, indicating lower demand, likely due to economic constraints or lesser alignment with Executive car vehicle profiles. This spatial visualization supports a more nuanced understanding of consumer behavior by geography. It confirms that vehicle preferences are not uniformly distributed but are shaped by a combination of economic status, spatial accessibility, and environmental considerations. As such, automotive dealerships can use these insights to adapt inventory management, location strategy, and targeted marketing to local demand clusters.

The observed correlations validate the importance of segmenting vehicle recommendations not only demographically, but also geographically, in response to spatial trends in consumer preferences. These experimental results confirm that integrating spatial,

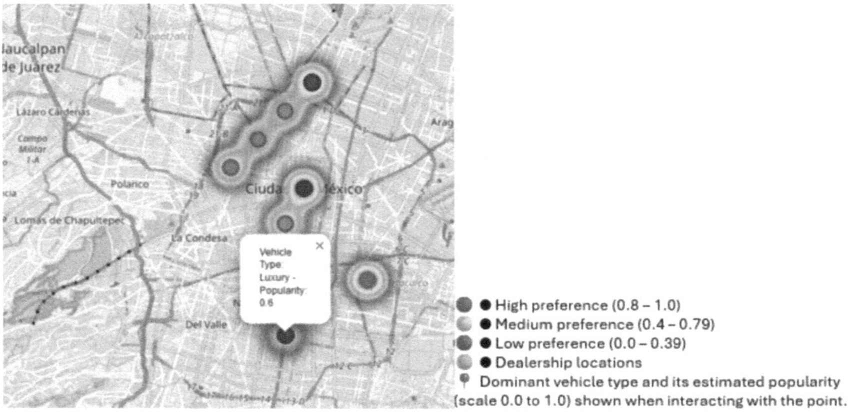

Fig. 5. Spatial Distribution of Vehicle Preferences in Mexico City

regulatory, and inferred socioeconomic factors enhances the precision and contextual relevance of vehicle recommendations. By leveraging these geographically embedded insights, both the recommendation system and stakeholders—such as manufacturers, dealers, and urban planners—can better align their strategies with localized user needs and infrastructural realities.

6 Discussion and Future Work

This spatial integration represents a significant advancement over traditional recommender systems that rely solely on technical attributes or collaborative filtering. While past research has explored hybrid models and content-based approaches, few systems have operationalized geospatial filtering as a dynamic component of the recommendation engine. Furthermore, aligning user sentiment extracted from social media and automotive forums with objective vehicle data allows the system to incorporate perceived value and user frustration factors, such as spare part delays or maintenance costs. This results in recommendations that are not only precise but reflect real-world ownership experience, increasing their practical utility. However, the study also identifies some limitations. The use of publicly available datasets restricts the granularity of real-time inventory data from dealerships. Additionally, the sentiment analysis, while robust, may benefit from more advanced natural language understanding models to capture nuance and sarcasm. The integration of regulatory data (e.g., emissions rules) is currently limited to static zone mapping and could evolve toward more dynamic compliance verification.

The proposed system distinguishes itself by incorporating dynamic, unstructured data sources such as social media and real-time geospatial data, enabling a higher level of adaptability to user context. Unlike existing methods, which rely on static datasets and lack environmental awareness, the proposed framework leverages regulatory and geographic variables to improve recommendation feasibility. Moreover, its evaluation approach extends beyond accuracy to include novelty and diversity, offering a more robust assessment of recommendation quality.

Several extensions of this research are planned:

1. Dynamic Inventory Integration Future versions of the system will incorporate real-time dealership inventory APIs, enabling recommendations to reflect actual stock and delivery times.
2. Multi-Criteria Decision Algorithms The recommendation engine will be extended with multi-criteria decision-making techniques such as AHP or TOPSIS, allowing users to explicitly prioritize trade-offs.
3. Deep Sentiment and NLP Enhancement Implementation of transformer-based language models will enhance the extraction of nuanced user opinions from textual reviews.
4. User Interface and Usability Testing A front-end web platform is currently under development to present recommendations to users. Future work will evaluate the system's usability through human-centered design and user testing protocols.

7 Conclusion

This study presents a novel vehicle recommendation system that integrates technical specifications with geospatial and sentiment data to deliver context-aware, personalized suggestions. By incorporating dealership locations, environmental regulations, and service accessibility into the recommendation process, the system addresses practical constraints often overlooked in traditional models.

The results confirm that geographic factors such as dealership density, traffic congestion, and emission control zones significantly influence vehicle availability and consumer preferences. In particular, urban areas with better service infrastructure show a tendency toward higher-cost, lower-maintenance vehicles, while peripheral zones emphasize affordability and accessibility.

By aligning user sentiment—extracted from social media and automotive forums—with spatial data, the system provides a richer understanding of consumer behavior and vehicle satisfaction at a regional level. This dual integration enhances both the accuracy and practicality of recommendations.

Overall, the framework demonstrates the value of combining spatial intelligence and machine learning in decision-support systems. Its modular architecture allows for adaptation to other urban environments, offering a scalable solution for improving vehicle selection in diverse markets.

References

1. Alamilla Medina, G.A., Andrade Ojeda, F.I., Barrera López, E.: Intelligent recommendation system with augmented reality. Undergraduate thesis, Instituto Politécnico Nacional, Mexico (2016) https://tesis.ipn.mx/jspui/bitstream/123456789/21953/3/Sistema%20de%20Recomendaciones%20Inteligente%20con%20Realidad.pdf
2. Báez, L.C., Orozco, R.P., Ledesma, E.F.R.: Recommendation systems in decision-making. J. Systemics Cybern. Inform. **11**(5), 47–53 (2013). https://www.iiisci.org/Journal/CV$/risci/pdfs/CA044PI13.pdf

3. Apaza Alanoca, H.: Text mining to build a data mining model for job offer recommendation. Undergraduate thesis, Universidad Nacional Amazónica de Madre de Dios, Peru (2019). https://repositorio.unam.edu.pe/bitstream/handle/UNAM/84/T095_70490843_T.pdf?sequence=1&isAllowed=y
4. Valenzuela-Sabogal, G.M., Sosa-Cortes, J.S., Torres-Rojas, J.D.: Tourist recommendation system using data mining in Gualivá, Cundinamarca. Revista Ontare **8**, 71–87 (2020)
5. Badouch, M., Boutaounte, M.: Personalized travel recommendation systems: a study of machine learning approaches in tourism. J. Artif. Intell. Mach. Learn. Neural Netw. **3**(3), 35–45 (2023)
6. Espinosa, A., Leyva, R.A., Medina, K.A.: Recommendation system for vocational guidance applied to the systems engineering degree. Presented at the Third Week of Science, Technology, and Innovation, Facatativá, Colombia (2018)
7. González-Delgado, B.A.: Design of a recommendation system using machine learning algorithms. Master's thesis, ITESO, Mexico (2018)
8. Pantano, E., Priporas, C.V., Stylos, N.: "You will like it!" using open data to predict tourists' response to a tourist attraction. Tour. Manage. **60**, 430–438 (2017)
9. Cruz Guerrero, R., de los Á. Alonso Lavernia, M., Franco Árcega, A.: Predictive hybrid model and recommendations using data mining and artificial intelligence techniques. Programación Matemática y Software **9**(3), 18–24 (2017)
10. Bermúdez Martínez, R.: Study of attractive attributes in car purchasing in the city of San Luis Potosí. Master's thesis, Autonomous University of San Luis Potosí, Mexico (2020). https://repositorioinstitucional.uaslp.mx/xmlui/handle/i/7108
11. Gastell Piloto, A., Espinoza Parada, J.: Analysis of factors influencing productivity in the Mexican automotive sector (n.d.). https://www.web.facpya.uanl.mx/vinculategica/vinculategica_5_2/A.53.pdf
12. Huang, Z.: Extensions to the k-means algorithm for clustering large data sets with categorical values. Data Min. Knowl. Dis. **2**, 283–304 (1998). https://doi.org/10.1023/A:1009769707641
13. Tobler, W.R.: A computer movie simulating urban growth in the Detroit region. Econ. Geogr. **46**(sup1), 234–240 (1970). https://doi.org/10.2307/143141
14. Thomas, L.B., Vaidhehi, V.: The design of a web-based car recommendation system using a hybrid recommender algorithm. International J. Eng. Technol. **7**(3.4), 192–196 (2018)
15. Masodiqov, Q.: Recommendations for handling old car tires and ways to remove them. Int. J. Adv. Sci. Res. **2**(12), 175–182 (2022)
16. Campigotto, P., Rudloff, C., Leodolter, M., Bauer, D.: Personalized and situation-aware multimodal route recommendations: The FAVOUR algorithm (2016). arXiv preprint arXiv:1602.09076. Retrieved from https://arxiv.org/abs/1602.09076
17. Boodaghians, A., Russo, N., Hoffenson, S.: Word-of-mouth recommendations in an automobile market system. In: Proceedings of the ASME 2019 International Design Engineering Technical Conferences and Computers and Information in Engineering Conference (2019)
18. Babu, L.T., Vaidhehi, V.: Vehicle recommendation system using hybrid recommender algorithm and natural language processing approach. Int. J. Eng. Technol. **7**(3.4), 197–201 (2018)
19. Calman, M.A.: Payment vehicle recommendations based on payment rules. US Patent No. 8,655,705. U.S. Patent and Trademark Office, Washington, DC (2014)
20. Thomas, L., Vaidhehi, V.: The design of web based car recommendation system using hybrid recommender algorithm. Int. J. Eng. Technol. **7**(3.4), 192 (2018). https://doi.org/10.14419/ijet.v7i3.4.16772
21. Le, N.L., Abel, M.H., Gouspillou, P.: Towards an ontology-based recommender system for the vehicle sales area. In: Troiano, L., Vaccaro, A., Kesswani, N., Díaz Rodríguez, I., Brigui, I. (eds.) Progresses in Artificial Intelligence & Robotics: Algorithms & Applications. ICDLAIR 2021, vol. 441, pp. 157–170. Springer (2022). https://doi.org/10.1007/978-3-030-98531-8_13

Predicting the Spatial Longevity of Small and Medium-Sized Enterprises in Mexico City: A Location Intelligence Analysis of Veterinary Clinics

Diego Andrey Ruibi Zuñiga[1], Iván Antonio Verduzco Lozano[1](✉), Jesús Giovanni Perea Samaniego[1], Uriel Corona Bermúdez[2], Miriam Pescador Rojas[1], Roberto Zagal-Flores[1], Violeta Shaid Benitez Valerio[3], and Marcela Virginia Santana-Juarez[3]

[1] Escuela Superior de Cómputo (ESCOM), Centro de Investigación en Cómputo (CIC), Instituto Politécnico Nacional. UPALM-Zacatenco, 07320 Mexico City, Mexico
{druibiz1700,iverduzcol1700,jpereas1900}@alumno.ipn.mx, {mpescadorr,rzagalf}@ipn.mx

[2] Centro de Investigación en Cómputo (CIC), Instituto Politécnico Nacional. UPALM-Zacatenco, 07320 Mexico City, Mexico
ucoronab2020@cic.ipn.mx

[3] Facultad de Geografía, Universidad Autónoma del Estado de México, Estado de Mexico, 50110 Toluca de Lerdo, Mexico
vbenitezv165@alumno.uaemex.mx, mvsantanaj@uaemex.mx

Abstract. Small and medium-sized enterprises (SMEs) are the backbone of Mexico's economy; however, they frequently face high failure rates due to suboptimal location choices and limited access to market information. In this study, we introduce a geospatial framework for predicting the longevity of entrepreneurial SMEs in Mexico City, using veterinary clinics as a representative case. Our approach integrates multiple datasets—including socioeconomic, geographical, and criminal activity records—to construct an extensive feature set capturing neighborhood demographics, commercial surroundings, and urban infrastructure. We then apply supervised learning methods, including multilayer perceptrons, random forests, and gradient boosting classifiers, to classify the expected lifespan of each business establishment into three survival groups (1–2, 3–4, and 5–6 years). Experiments with cross-validation reveal that an optimized XGBoost model achieves a balanced accuracy of 88.68% on a held-out test set, outperforming other evaluated methods. A cluster analysis of nearby business types further identifies pivotal commercial co-locations—such as grocery stores, dining establishments, and complementary retail—that foster longer SME survival. This finding underscores the importance of geographic context, socioeconomic status, and consumer traffic patterns in determining SME viability. While our study focuses on veterinary clinics, the proposed methodology generalizes to other commercial sectors and can aid policymakers and entrepreneurs in mitigating failure risks through data-driven site selection. Overall, this work provides a robust framework for combining geospatial analysis and machine learning to enhance the strategic decision-making process for SMEs in metropolitan settings.

M. F. Mata-Rivera et al. (Eds.): W2GIS 2025, LNCS 15946, pp. 155–170, 2026.
https://doi.org/10.1007/978-3-032-01723-9_11

Keywords: Location Intelligence · GIS · Machine Learning · Veterinary Clinics

1 Introduction

Mexico City, composed of 16 boroughs (formerly alcaldías), is a major metropolitan area characterized by high population density, notable socioeconomic disparities, and a constantly evolving commercial dynamic. In this context, small and medium-sized enterprises (SMEs) account for 99.8% of businesses in the country, making them a pillar of the national economy [7]. However, these ventures face multiple challenges that hinder their consolidation; according to BBVA, 33% of SMEs close during their first year, and only 35% survive beyond five years of operation [2]. Among the main obstacles is the lack of integrated, easily analyzable data on competition, demographic profiles, and urban conditions, which impedes informed decision-making when selecting the optimal location.

This scenario becomes particularly complex for veterinary clinics, whose success relies on factors such as demographic composition, consumption patterns, and the socioeconomic profile of each urban area. To address these challenges, we propose a workflow that integrates data on socioeconomic conditions, crime rates, traffic patterns, urban marginalization, and demographics to develop a data-driven geomarketing tool. This tool aims to assist entrepreneurs in identifying the most suitable areas for establishing pet care businesses in Mexico City. The core objectives of this study are: (1) to characterize the socioeconomic, demographic, and crime-related contexts of veterinary clinics in Mexico City that have been operating for more than five years; (2) to develop a predictive model capable of estimating the potential lifespan of a veterinary business based on its location; and (3) to implement a spatial data visualization tool that facilitates a comprehensive understanding of the results and supports decision-making.

Preliminary results indicate that household composition in Mexico City has evolved, leading to increased demand for veterinary services in residential areas. A pilot analysis included 2,021 veterinary clinics registered in 2020, from which 733 features were extracted. These data reveal a significant concentration of clinics in the city's central zone, particularly in Iztapalapa (311 establishments) and Gustavo A. Madero (277). In Iztapalapa, most clinics are located in neighborhoods with medium-low marginalization levels, whereas in Coyoacán, clinics tend to be found in areas with low or very low marginalization. These differences underscore the importance of adopting a multidimensional approach—encompassing socioeconomic, commercial, and demographic factors—to optimize site selection for new veterinary clinics. Furthermore, the study observes a growing demand for pet-related services, driven by shifts in family structure and evolving urban consumption trends.

The proposed methodology is multidisciplinary and oriented toward geomarketing applications, thereby facilitating informed decision-making and the design of commercial expansion strategies in the veterinary sector. It highlights the importance of integrating geospatial data aligned with Mexico City's socioeconomic dynamics to effectively determine the location of new veterinary clinics.

2 Related Work

In [16], a geomarketing methodology based on large-scale spatial data and machine learning techniques is proposed. The study focuses on identifying location patterns and customer segmentation to optimize marketing decisions in urban environments. It employs retail sales data at the point-of-sale level, client distribution, rent rates, public transportation accessibility, and socioeconomic indicators. The key contribution lies in combining machine learning techniques (regression and classification) with spatial data to detect "hot spots" of commercial activity, thereby highlighting the importance of integrating spatial and demographic variables in geomarketing decisions to achieve more effective market segmentation.

In [17] the authors introduce a GeoAI (Geospatial Artificial Intelligence) approach that merges location-based data and AI methods to enhance urban planning and site-selection strategies within the business domain. Their data sources include urban sensors and social networks (e.g., Twitter, Foursquare), GPS and vehicular traffic records to evaluate mobility patterns, as well as cadastral and planimetric data for delineating construction areas and land use. Their main contribution demonstrates the utility of GeoAI (combining AI and GIS) to predict fluctuations in foot traffic around commercial areas. The study also underscores the relevance of integrating multiple data sources (governmental, private, and sensor-based) for more robust location intelligence.

The literature review in [19] examines research on geospatial data visualization, decision support systems, geo-business intelligence, and geomarketing, highlighting trends and research gaps in the field. The authors conclude that interactive spatial data visualization and the integration of heterogeneous spatial data (e.g., socioeconomic, traffic, climatic) are vital to strengthening both market analysis and urban planning.

In [12], Rohani and Chua used Google Maps data to analyze businesses in a Malaysian city. Their primary goal was to develop a classification model capable of predicting the type of business most likely to establish itself within a 200-m radius. To this end, they drew upon various sources, including business databases and reviews from Google Maps, local demographic and economic statistics (income levels, population density, commercial activity), and geographic information on roads, public transportation, and points of interest. Key findings include identifying optimal retail locations—maximizing visibility and accessibility—and noting that "close competition" plays a dual role: while areas with a high concentration of similar businesses may attract more customers, they also create fiercer competition. Additionally, the authors put forth a systematic method for evaluating different locations, incorporating relevant metrics such as travel times and customer flow.

At the regional level, some studies address the analysis of establishment location in central Mexico. In [15], the spatial distribution of pharmacies in the Gustavo A. Madero borough of Mexico City was examined without using data science or machine learning methods, aiming to determine the likelihood of success for a business based on socioeconomic characteristics and local commercial competition. Another study, titled *Geomarketing para la ubicación de nuevos sitios de farmacias en la zona metropolitana de Toluca* [14], concentrated on positioning new pharmacies in Toluca through quantitative and correlational methods [20–22]. In [3], a system based on Central Place Theory was developed to identify the geospatial characteristics of different types of businesses in Mexico City. Most of these works highlight the integration of multiple georeferenced data sources to address questions related to optimizing commercial sites, innovating business models, implementing geospatial visualization, and predicting consumption patterns. They further emphasize the importance of machine learning, spatial analysis, and advanced data visualization as key elements for guiding strategic marketing and business expansion decisions in complex urban settings. However, most of these studies do not incorporate data sources pertaining to specific urban challenges—such as the spatial distribution of crime in the study region—to identify potential locations. Nor do they employ predictive models that integrate social and economic data for estimating the operational lifespan of commercial establishments. Moreover, they generally do not perform an initial cluster analysis that informs their subsequent predictive modeling.

3 Methodology

The process for characterizing veterinary clinics, identifying potential locations, and predicting their operational lifespan is based on the CRISP-DM methodology, which comprises six sequential phases.

First, a business understanding phase was conducted to delineate the objectives and requirements of the project within the context of veterinary businesses in Mexico City. This was followed by the data understanding phase, where required data were collected from multiple sources, focusing on both business and socio-demographic characteristics. The subsequent data preparation phase involved integrating, cleaning, and transforming the datasets, including feature selection, handling missing values, and encoding categorical variables to ensure consistency and suitability for modeling. In the modeling phase, machine learning algorithms—such as multilayer perceptrons, random forests, and XGBoost—were trained, selected and optimized to predict the estimated lifespan of veterinary establishments based on the curated features. The evaluation phase entailed validation of model performance using cross-validation techniques and metrics to ensure robustness and generalizability. Finally, the deployment phase consisted of implementing the selected model within an interactive dashboard, thereby enabling entrepreneurs to access actionable insights regarding the viability and expected longevity of new veterinary businesses in specific neighborhoods of Mexico City, these phases can be summarized on three main phases: (1) data processing, (2) socio-spatial characterization, and (3) lifespan estimation.

3.1 Data Processing

Four primary sources were used to gather information on veterinary clinics and their surrounding geographic context: (1) the City of Mexico's Open Data Portal [4], which provided crime records; (2) the National Institute of Statistics and Geography (INEGI) [7], offering socioeconomic data, an Urban Marginalization Index, and characteristics of businesses and commerce at a regional scale [8]; (3) the National Statistical Directory of Economic Units (DENUE) [9], from which records pertaining to Mexico City for the period 2015–2020 were extracted to determine the distribution and features of businesses located near each veterinary clinic; and (4) the Google Maps API [1], used to identify unregistered veterinary clinics, as well as average traffic and vehicle flow data from TomTom [13].

The data sources were integrated using geographic attributes such as borough and neighborhood, and, when necessary, additional spatial identifiers like the Basic Geostatistical Area (AGEB)—a subdivision defined by INEGI—and city blocks (manzanas). After merging the datasets, a total of 733 features per record were obtained, from which 77 were ultimately selected for analysis. Missing values were imputed based on the nature of each feature; for instance, when street information was absent, the city's road network layer was used to calculate the Euclidean distance to the nearest street. For time series data associated with each veterinary clinic, linear interpolation was applied using available data from other years, and when a feature was entirely missing, central tendency measures were estimated using information from adjacent neighborhoods. Categorical variables were encoded using the one-hot encoding technique, which creates a binary column (presence or absence) for each category. To ensure all features were standardized at the neighborhood scale, city blocks and AGEBs belonging to each neighborhood were identified, and aggregation operations such as sums or averages were applied according to the specific feature.

Commercial Distribution Selection. To incorporate the layer of businesses surrounding each veterinary clinic, Python scripts in QGIS [11] were used to define 150-m "buffers" around each establishment. The businesses located within these areas of interest were selected, as illustrated in Fig. 1. This procedure allowed for identifying 648 types of businesses whose analysis is essential for understanding the geographic context of each clinic and determining whether a specific commercial category influences clinic performance.

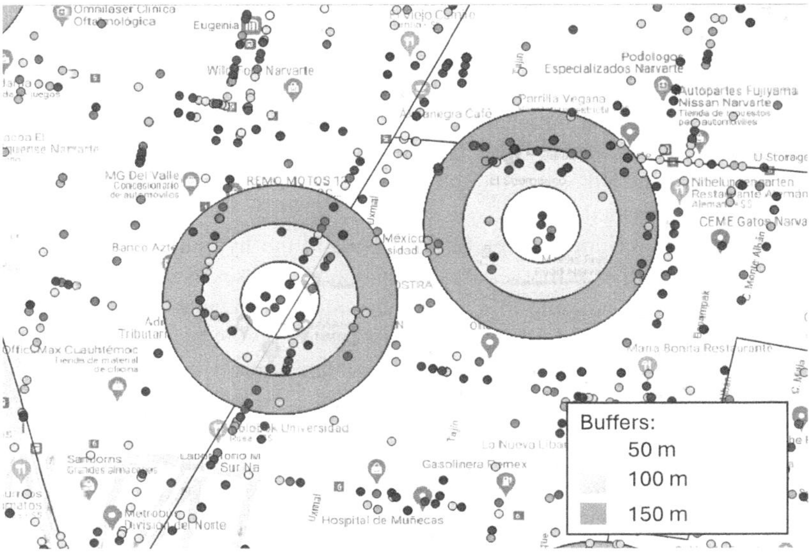

Fig. 1. Geographical context of each veterinary clinic using 150-m buffers.

3.2 Characterization of Veterinary Clinic Establishments

Based on each clinic's establishment date—recorded between 2015 and 2020 in Mexico City—its age in years was determined. This timeframe is suitable for identifying successful clinics that have been in continuous operation for six years (considering both 2015 and 2020 as completed years). Specifically, a clinic was considered to have a six-year lifespan if it opened in 2015 or earlier and remained operational through 2020. To support this, each clinic's opening date and the year it ceased operations were collected. Subsequently, three groups were created to label the operational lifespan: Group 1 spans 1–2 years, Group 2 spans 3–4 years, and Group 3 spans 5–6 years, the latter considered the most successful category.

To analyze the nearby businesses around each clinic, the types and frequencies of these businesses were identified in the different alcaldías (boroughs) of Mexico City. This geographic context reflects the socioeconomic, cultural, and lifestyle characteristics of local residents. These attributes were compiled into a dataset of up to 648 columns describing the types of businesses surrounding each clinic. To select the most significant columns and reduce dimensionality, Principal Component Analysis (PCA) was applied to the collected business data, reducing the 648 business-type columns to 50 principal components that capture over 90% of the variance.

Principal Component Analysis (PCA) was applied due to the dispersed and relatively high-dimensional nature of the surrounding business space, which could pose challenges for clustering algorithms and the interpretation of distances between points (i.e., the curse of dimensionality). It is worth noting that PCA was used exclusively for the clustering process, while the original set of characteristics were preserved and used in the other phases of the project.

Next, a cluster analysis was performed to determine which types of businesses characterize clinics that have been operating for more than five years at the colonia (neighborhood) scale (a colonia refers to a specific neighborhood or district within a municipality or city) clustering groups data records based on similarity measures from their attributes, characteristics, or metadata. The K-means algorithm was used with five clusters, determined using the elbow method. Each data point (in this case, each clinic) is assigned to the closest cluster centroid according to Euclidean distance. At the end of this process, the clinics were distributed into five clusters.

The K-Means algorithm was preferred based on the hypothesis that surrounding businesses may form clusters that reflect socioeconomic classes. By using a fixed number of clusters, it becomes possible to analyze and interpret them within this context. In contrast, algorithms such as DBSCAN classify certain points as outliers, which could imply that a clinic does not belong to any socioeconomic group. Additionally, DBSCAN relies on neighborhood density parameters, which may be less meaningful or harder to calibrate in the PCA-transformed space and in the context of surrounding businesses.

Figure 2 shows the distribution of businesses located near clinics in Mexico City. The groups with the highest number of veterinary clinics sharing common characteristics are Cluster 0 and Cluster 3. These clusters are predominantly surrounded by corner stores, beauty salons, and small-scale food retailers selling raw meat and prepared foods. This pattern suggests that most veterinary clinics are found in residential areas.

More specifically, Cluster 0 comprises clinics that are often located near stationery shops, restaurants serving prepared meals, laundries, dry cleaners, private dental offices, and cafés. These types of businesses are not as abundant in neighborhoods with lower socioeconomic status, implying that many clinics in this cluster may be situated in medium-to-high socioeconomic areas featuring more developed commercial zones.

By contrast, Cluster 3 consists solely of basic goods and personal services, such as corner stores, beauty salons, and local fast-food stalls (tacos and antojitos). The presence of food-related businesses guarantees a moderate, steady influx of people, potentially benefiting an animal-care establishment with a consistent local clientele.

Cluster 2 mirrors Cluster 3 but includes one distinct type of business not found in other clusters—retailers specializing in dairy and deli products—suggesting a location with a significant number of children or older adults.

Clusters 4 and 1 encompass fewer types of businesses surrounding veterinary clinics, yet they offer insights into alternative contexts that can favor animal-care services. Cluster 4 includes, for the first time, footwear and gift stores, baby clothing shops, leather or fur apparel, and candy retailers, in addition to beauty salons—commercial activities commonly associated with medium-high socioeconomic areas. Such shopping centers can be cost-prohibitive for new entrepreneurs, explaining the relatively small number of veterinary clinics in this cluster. Meanwhile, Cluster 1 features retailers of seeds, spices, dried chilies, and natural plants and flowers, suggesting veterinary clinics located near traditional markets or more rural zones.

Ultimately, the specific business types that distinguish each cluster shed light on key conditions that contribute to veterinary clinic survival.

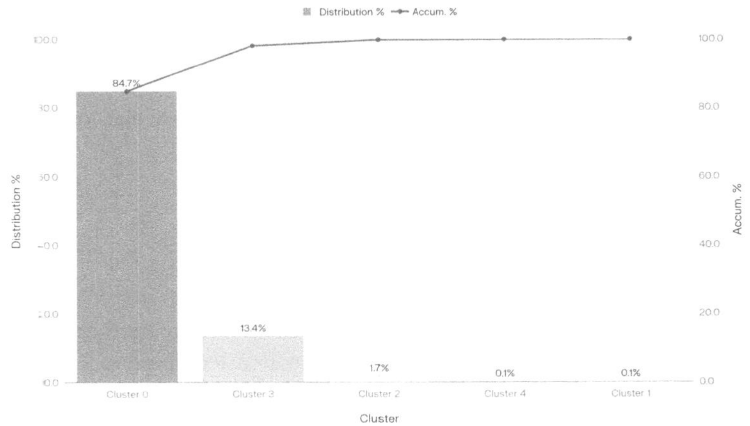

Fig. 2. Distribution of Nearby Businesses by Cluster

3.3 Predictive Model and Interactive Dashboard

The full dataset was divided into two subsets for separate tasks: one for training and one for model testing, using a 70%–30% split. Three classification models were considered to predict the lifespan of a pet-care business—categorized into three ranges (1–2, 3–4, and 5–6 years)—based on local crime data, population marginalization indices, and nearby commercial activities. In this case, no class balancing technique was applied, as the primary objective is to allow the model to learn from and reflect the natural distribution of the data. By preserving the original class proportions, we aim to ensure that the predictions remain faithful to the real-world phenomenon represented in the dataset, rather than artificially altering the data distribution.

The experiments conducted to identify the most relevant features for addressing the problem are presented here. Specifically, three classification algorithms were considered for predicting the operational lifespan of veterinary clinics: a Multilayer Perceptron (MLP) [6], a Random Forest (RF) [10], and XGBoost (XGBC) [5]. The hyperparameters in cross-validation for each model are shown in Table 1. Once the models described were trained, we evaluated them using the balanced performance metric, the results of the cross-validation are summarized in Tables 2, 3 and 4.

Table 1. Hyperparameters used by each model in the cross-validation process.

Model	Hyperparameters
MLP 1 MLP 2 MLP 3	Six-Layer MLP (500, 250, 100, 50, 10, and 3) Five-Layer MLP (712, 300, 100, 10, and 3) Four-Layer MLP (500, 250, 100, and 3)
RF 1 RF 2 RF 3	Number of Decision Trees (n_estimators): 50, Maximum Tree Depth (max_depth): 900 Number of Decision Trees (n_estimators): 100, Maximum Tree Depth (max_depth): 150 Number of Decision Trees (n_estimators): 200, Maximum Tree Depth (max_depth): 2000
XGBC 1 XGBC 2 XGBC 3	Number of Trees (n_estimators): 50, Maximum Depth (max_depth): 900 Number of Trees (n_estimators): 100, Maximum Depth (max_depth): 1500 Number of Trees (n_estimators): 200, Maximum Depth (max_depth): 2000

Subsequently, the training set was partitioned into five folds to perform K-fold cross-validation for each model variant. Cross-validation is a technique used to train and evaluate the performance of one or more models [23]. Essentially, it involves splitting the entire dataset into separate subsets for training and testing—as was done previously with a 70/30 split. The K-fold method divides the data into k folds, enabling the comparison of different models' performance to select the best one, or to fine-tune model parameters in order to prevent overfitting while enhancing prediction generalization. A stratified splitting technique was employed to ensure that the K-folds generated from the data maintain the same class proportions as the original dataset.

The K-Fold cross-validation was preferred over a single train-test split, given the limited size of the dataset and the presence of imbalanced classes. This approach aimed to ensure that the model was tested on records from the various categories of veterinary clinics, thereby improving the reliability of its predictive performance in a real-world setting. A single partition may not provide a reliable estimate of model performance and can lead to overfitting or underfitting depending on how representative the split is [24].

Additionally, the early stopping regularization technique was applied to the XGBoost and perceptron models, early stopping is a regularization technique used to prevent overfitting by stopping training when a model's performance on a validation set stops improving. It helps the model generalize better by avoiding unnecessary training that could lead to overfitting [25].

This approach ensures that the model is exposed to as much data as possible. For each model variant, a new model is generated for every fold during both training and prediction, thereby preventing repeated training on the same data and reducing the risk of learning from previous folds.

The performance report for each model includes balanced accuracy and categorical cross-entropy loss. Specifically, balanced accuracy is used when dealing with imbalanced classes—as is the case in this study—and is defined as the average of specificity and sensitivity [26].

After comparing the metrics across different numbers of epochs for the Multilayer Perceptron, Random Forest and XGBoost Classifier models, we obtained the results shown in Table 2, Table 3 and Table 4.

Table 2. Balanced performance achieved by each model in cross-validation

Model	Fold 0	Fold 1	Fold 2	Fold 3	Fold 4
MLP 1	0.7972	0.8107	0.7195	0.7266	0.8125
MLP 2	0.8040	0.8116	0.7629	0.7962	0.7968
MLP 3	0.8101	0.8058	0.7984	0.8020	0.8215
RF 1	0.7030	0.7084	0.6921	0.7001	0.6880
RF 2	0.7166	0.7249	0.6978	0.7039	0.6943
RF 3	0.7206	0.7207	0.7101	0.7198	0.7026
XGBC 1	0.8599	0.8456	0.8370	0.8664	0.8532
XGBC 2	0.8599	0.8456	0.8370	0.8664	0.8532
XGBC 3	0.8599	0.8456	0.8370	0.8664	0.8532

After training, the models were assessed for balanced performance with the results presented in Table 5. Therefore, the best-performing models are the XGBoost classifiers, regardless of the variant, as they consistently achieve higher accuracy than the other models in both balanced and unbalanced scenarios. We then selected the best model based on its results—XGBC 1—since it features the smallest hyperparameters, namely, 50 boosting rounds and a maximum depth of 900. When the model was retrieved, retrained with the training set, and subsequently tested, it achieved a balanced performance of 0.8868 on the test set.

The model can predict a veterinary clinic's lifespan with a balanced accuracy of approximately 88%, corresponding to an error margin of around 12%. Additionally, an area under the curve (AUC) of approximately 0.96 is obtained. Using this trained model,

Table 3. Logarithmic loss achieved by each model in cross-validation

Model	Fold 0	Fold 1	Fold 2	Fold 3	Fold 4
MLP 1	0.6713	0.6858	0.7967	0.7874	0.6280
MLP 2	0.6203	0.6516	0.7553	0.6017	0.5710
MLP 3	0.5450	0.5591	0.6372	0.5861	0.5597
RF 1	0.5375	0.5306	0.5194	0.5397	0.5466
RF 2	0.5246	0.5166	0.5134	0.5263	0.5321
RF 3	0.5119	0.5134	0.5135	0.5155	0.5225
XGBC 1	0.2989	0.3137	0.3248	0.3009	0.2871
XGBC 2	0.2989	0.3137	0.3248	0.3009	0.2871
XGBC 3	0.2989	0.3137	0.3248	0.3009	0.2871

Table 4. Epochs by each model in cross-validation

Model	Fold 0	Fold 1	Fold 2	Fold 3	Fold 4
MLP 1	8	5	5	5	5
MLP 2	5	5	5	5	5
MLP 3	5	5	5	5	5
XGBC 1	31	35	31	46	49
XGBC 2	31	35	31	46	49
XGBC 3	31	35	31	46	49

Table 5. Mean Balanced Performance in Cross-Validation for Each Model

Model	Balanced Performance
MLP 1	0.7733
MLP 2	0.7943
MLP 3	0.8076
RF 1	0.6983
RF 2	0.7075
RF 3	0.7147
XGBC 1	0.8524
XGBC 2	0.8524
XGBC 3	0.8524

we then derive the percentage likelihood that a new business—established in any given *colonia or* neighborhood —would fall into each of the predefined lifespan categories. In other words, the entrepreneur would be informed of the probability that their clinic would operate for 0–2 years (range 1), 2–4 years (range 2), or more than 4 years (range 3) in the targeted neighborhood. These results are shown in Fig. 3.

This outcome indicates that, despite the imbalanced nature of the classes in this study, the predictive model has attained a satisfactory level of generalization.

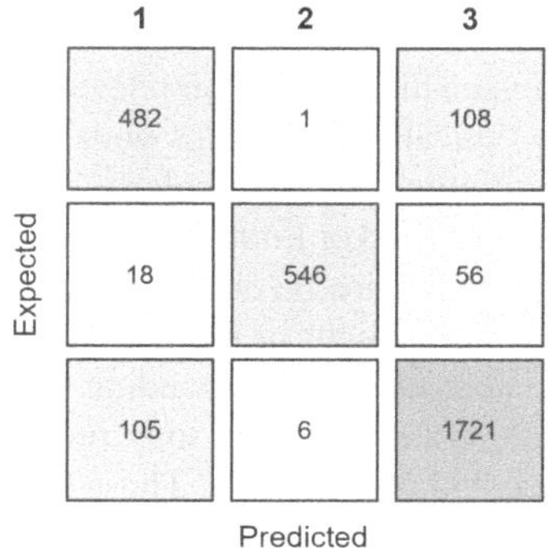

Fig. 3. Confusion Matrix of the selected Model

4 Results

Figure 4 shows a web deployment of the predictive model where entrepreneurs choose a potential location, and the system then predicts the operational lifespan of a veterinary clinic in that location. By selecting a borough of interest in the interactive map, the user can pinpoint a specific location. Internally, the system identifies the corresponding colonia (neighborhood) based on that point, retrieves the relevant socioeconomic data from the database, and creates a 200-m area of influence to gather information on local businesses. With this data, the pretrained model then estimates how long a pet-care business could potentially operate at that location.

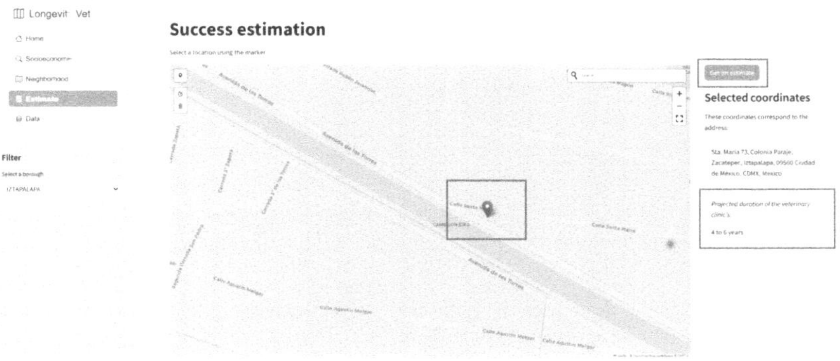

Fig. 4. Estimated lifespan of a veterinary clinic's based on user-provided location.

According to the results of the spatial and clustering analysis, two potential location strategies emerge. The first strategy considers areas with a high proportion of non-single individuals—either separated or married—and the presence of corner stores. Alternatively, areas with organic product shops located near shopping centers or that offer premium products are also promising. The second approach is supported by the strong positive correlation between higher education levels and the presence of à la carte restaurants. Generally, higher education correlates with higher income, which enables individuals to spend more on dining out—particularly at à la carte restaurants, which tend to be more expensive than fast food or limited-service establishments. Overall, both shopping centers and public markets are favorable for veterinary clinics, highlighting a trend where pet care services are sought in proximity to other businesses that allow owners to accomplish parallel activities while attending to their pets.

Individuals who are separated or live alone may prefer shopping at local grocery stores due to their convenience and accessibility. These stores typically offer a quicker and easier shopping experience for those who do not require large quantities of products, making them more appealing compared to large supermarkets. Separated individuals often face different economic realities than families or couples, such as lower incomes or tighter budgets. Grocery stores frequently offer products at more affordable prices or in smaller packages, which may be better suited to their financial needs. This may suggest a change in the trend of family composition in Mexico City.

According to Fig. 5, there is a strong positive correlation between the presence of corner stores, stationery shops, and "tortilla sellers" (popular Mexican product) in areas where residents have limited access to basic education (SBASC, percentage of population aged 15 and over without basic education according to DENUE), low social security coverage (PSDSS, percentage of population without entitlement to health services), and higher levels of overcrowding (OVHAC,percentage of overcrowded homes). In such densely populated urban settings, where housing space is limited and incomes are lower, essential goods offered at affordable prices become crucial. These findings suggest that in neighborhoods with lower education levels and higher informal employment, basic necessities remain a priority for consumers.

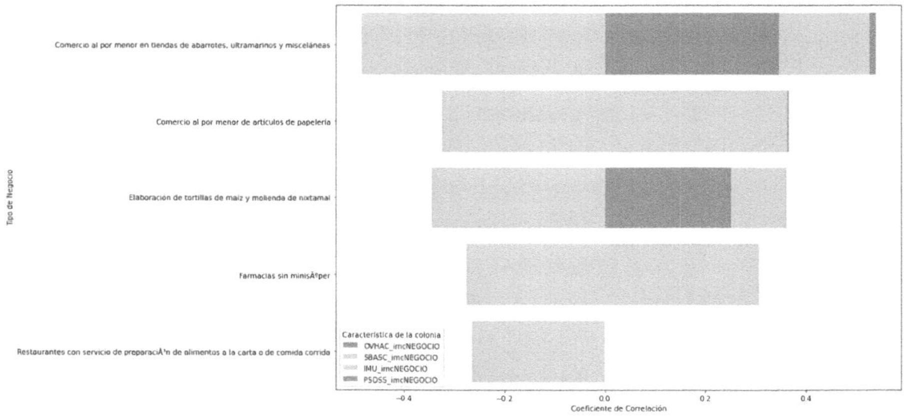

Fig. 5. Correlation between the presence of key businesses around veterinary clinics and the economic characteristics of the population

Consequently, businesses such as corner stores often thrive under these conditions, even though residents may lack access to formal jobs and social security. By extension, veterinary clinics can also succeed in these areas, as Mexican families tend to allocate part of their income to pet care regardless of their educational or economic constraints. A lack of formal employment, a college degree, or spacious housing does not prevent many Mexican households from investing in their pets' well-being. Therefore, entrepreneurs in the pet-care sector need not be deterred by such socioeconomic indicators, as evidence shows that veterinary clinics can remain viable for more than four years in neighborhoods facing these challenges.

Figure 6 shows the dashboard with aggregated data for the "Ramos Millan" neighborhood in the Iztacalco borough, highlighting its potential as a location for a veterinary clinic. The dashboard displays the accumulated number of business robberies, indicating that this neighborhood has a higher crime rate compared to others in the same borough, as well as demographic details such as the proportion of married and separated individuals. The "Nearby Businesses" panel lists the closest establishments, including retail stationery shops and communal dining/snack bars, among others. Additionally, it presents various statistical indicators: Number of veterinary clinics: 4, Average rating: 4.1, Marginalization level: Low, Business-related crimes targeting physical establishments: 4, Economically Active Population: 4873, Population with Internet access: 1670, Total population: 3291, and Vehicle traffic flow: 87.

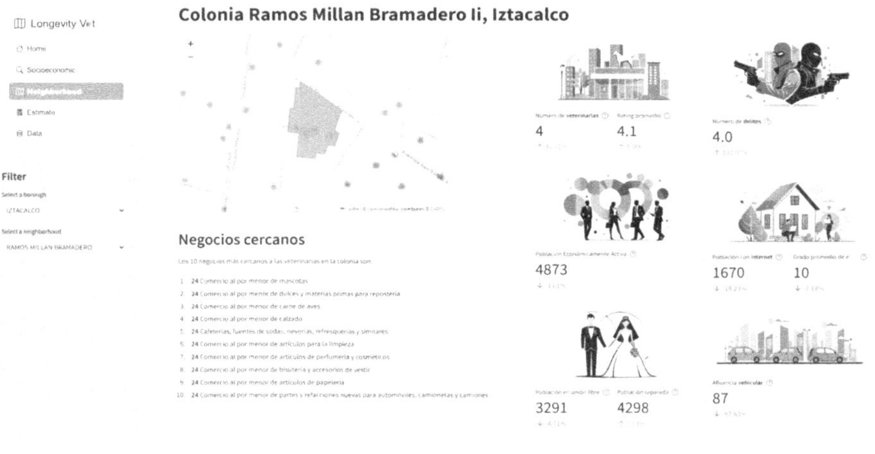

Fig. 6. Relevant Neighborhood Trends

5 Conclusions

This work underscores the significant influence of socioeconomic context, demographic characteristics, and the presence of specific businesses on the potential longevity of newly established veterinary clinics in Mexico City. By integrating both public and private data sources and applying advanced Location Intelligence, GIS, and Machine Learning methods, it emerges that XGBoost classifiers outperform alternative models, even under class-imbalanced conditions, thereby demonstrating robust generalization capabilities.

Additionally, the findings highlight how factors such as nearby businesses, vehicle traffic, robbery rates, and socioeconomic and demographic profiles can enable clinics to operate beyond the average five-year mark. The tendency for individuals who live alone or are separated to favor local grocery stores also suggests possible shifts in the city's family-economic composition, emphasizing convenience and accessibility.

Overall, the proposed methodology—combining spatial analysis, data science, and predictive modeling—offers a multidisciplinary framework for identifying optimal locations and informing strategic decisions within the veterinary sector. The resulting dashboard and predictive model equip entrepreneurs with valuable tools to pinpoint high-potential areas based on socioeconomic, demographic, and commercial factors, laying the groundwork for further research and broader applications of Location Intelligence, GIS, and Machine Learning in diverse urban contexts.

Despite these contributions, there are some limitations that should be acknowledged. First, the study relies on data sources that, while diverse, are not fully exhaustive; for instance, the integration of private databases such as rental prices or cost per square meter was not possible due to access restrictions, potentially limiting the granularity of the analysis. Second, the temporal scope of the data is restricted to information available up to 2020, which may not fully capture recent changes in urban dynamics, business closures, or new openings.

Future improvements could include incorporating more granular private databases, such as rental prices and cost per square meter, as well as integrating more recent data—beyond 2020—to enhance model accuracy and adapt to evolving urban dynamics. In addition, analyzing competitors' pricing and services would further segment potential locations and strengthen strategies for establishing new businesses in Mexico City.

Acknowledgments. The authors would like to thank IPN, SECIHTI, Project CF-2023-G-1170, SIP-20250112, SIP-20242869, COFAA, UPIITA-IPN and ESCOM-IPN.

References

1. Google Cloud: Google Cloud APIs library (2023). https://console.cloud.google.com/apis/library. Accessed 23 Sep 2023
2. BBVA México: Por qué fracasan los negocios pequeños? (2023). https://www.bbva.mx/educacion-financiera/blog/por-que-fracasan-los-negocios-pequenos.html. Accessed 28 May 2023
3. Carrillo García, N.: Diseño de un sistema inteligente de mercadotecnia geoespacial aplicando aprendizaje automático. Master's thesis, Centro de Investigación en Computación, Ciudad de México, México (2022). https://tesis.ipn.mx/handle/123456789/31714
4. Gobierno de la Ciudad de México: Portal de datos abiertos de la Ciudad de México
5. Guestin, C.: XGBoost: A Scalable Tree Boosting System (2016). https://www.kdd.org/kdd2016/papers/files/rfp0697-chenAemb.pdf

6. Hagan, M.T., Demuth, H.B., Beale, M.H.: Neural Network Design (2nd edn.). Martin Hagan (2014)
7. Instituto Nacional de Estadística y Geografía: Demografía de los establecimientos mipyme en el contexto de la pandemia por COVID-19 (335/22) (2022). https://www.inegi.org.mx/contenidos/saladeprensa/aproposito/2022/EAP_Demog_MIPYME22.pdf. Accessed 28 May 2023
8. Instituto Nacional de Estadística y Geografía (INEGI): AGEB urbana del censo de población y vivienda 2020 (2020). https://www.inegi.org.mx/contenidos/programas/ccpv/2020/datosabiertos/ageb_manzana/ageb_mza_urbana_09_cpv2020_csv.zip. Accessed 14 Sep 2023
9. Instituto Nacional de Estadística y Geografía (INEGI): Directorio estadístico nacional de unidades económicas 11/2022 (2022). https://www.inegi.org.mx/contenidos/masiva/denue/denue_09_csv.zip. Accessed 14 Sep 2023
10. Jesús, E.Z.J.: Aplicación de algoritmos random forest y xgboost en una base de solicitudes de tarjetas de crédito. Ingeniería Investigación y Tecnología, **21**(3) (2020). ISSN 2594-0732, https://doi.org/10.22201/fi.25940732e.2020.21.3.022
11. QGIS: Sistema de información geográfica libre y de código abierto. https://www.qgis.org/es/site/
12. Rohani, A.M.B.M., Chua, F.-F.: Location Analytics for Optimal Business Retail Site Selection. In: Murgante, B., et al. (eds.) Computational Science and Its Applications – ICCSA 2018. LNCS, vol. 10961, pp. 392–405. Springer, Cham (2018). https://doi.org/10.1007/978-3-319-95162-1_27
13. TomTom: TomTom products (2023). https://www.tomtom.com/products/
14. Valerio, V.S.B.: Geomarketing para la ubicación de nuevos sitios de farmacias en la zona metropolitana de Toluca. Licenciatura thesis, Universidad Autónoma del Estado de México, Estado de México, México (2020). https://ri.uaemex.mx/bitstream/handle/20.500.11799/109707/Tesis%20Violeta%20Shaid2.pdf?sequence=1&isAllowed=y
15. Zendejas Rodríguez, G.: Aplicaciones de Geomarketing en la Industria Farmacéutica: Delegación Gustavo A. Madero. UNAM, Ciudad de México, México (2013)
16. Kim, Y., Jang, E.: A machine learning approach to geomarketing: spatial big data analysis of retail patterns in urban environments. Comput. Environ. Urban Syst. **84**, 101505 (2020)
17. Chang, Y.S., Tsou, M.H.: Integrating GeoAI with location-based data for advanced location intelligence in business and urban planning. GeoInformatica **26**(4), 593–611 (2021)
18. Breukelman, B., de Reuver, M.: Location-based data analytics for business model innovation: a framework and case example in the retail sector. Technol. Forecast. Soc. Chang. **177**, 121513 (2022)
19. Weinzerl, T., Thöne, T., Malaka, R.: Geo-data visualization and spatial decision support: a systematic literature review. ISPRS Int. J. Geo Inf. **8**(8), 346 (2019)
20. Velasquez, L. and Palacios, R.: Geomarketing para la localización de una sucursal de Almacenes Rayco en el departamento de Nariño, San Juan de Pasto. Bachelor's thesis, Universidad de Nariño (2015)
21. Romero, L.P.: Geomarketing en salud para ubicar oferta de servicios médicos de valor. Caso: proyecto de investigación para ubicar una nueva oferta hospitalaria. Salud Uninorte **24**(2), 319–340 (2008)
22. Chasco, C.: El geomarketing y la distribución comercial. Investigación y Market. **79**, 6–13 (2003). http://www.cartografia.cl/download/geomar%20comercial.pdf
23. DataScientest. Cross-validation: definition and importance in machine learning. data scientest (2024). https://datascientest.com/es/cross-validation-definicion-e-importancia. Accessed 12 Apr 2024
24. Abu-Mostafa,Y.S., Magdon-Ismail, M., Lin, H.-T.: Learning From Data: A Short Course (2012)

25. Goodfellow, I., Bengio, Y., Courville, A.: Deep Learning. MIT Press. Chapter 7, Section 7.8: Early Stopping (2016): https://www.deeplearningbook.org/
26. Olugbenga, M.: Balanced accuracy: when should you use it? Neptune.ai. (2023). https://neptune.ai/blog/balanced-accuracy#:~:text=Balanced%20Accuracy%20is%20used%20in,lot%20more%20than%20the%20other. Accessed 12 Apr 2024

Author Index

M. F. Mata-Rivera et al. (Eds.): W2GIS 2025, LNCS 15946, pp. 171–172, 2026.
https://doi.org/10.1007/978-3-032-01723-9

The manufacturer's authorised representative in the EU is Springer Nature Customer Service Centre GmbH, Europaplatz 3, 69115 Heidelberg, Germany. If you have any concerns regarding our products, please contact ProductSafety@springernature.com

Printed and bound by CPI Group (UK) Ltd, Croydon, CR0 4YY
01/10/2026
02225952-0005